365 Winter Warmer
SLOW COOKER RECIPES

SUZANNE BONET • CAROL HILDEBRAND • ROBERT HILDEBRAND

365 Winter Warmer
SLOW COOKER RECIPES

SIMPLY SAVORY AND DELICIOUS 3-INGREDIENT MEALS

FAIR WINDS
PRESS
BEVERLY, MASSACHUSETTS

© 2012 Fair Winds Press

Text © 2005 Suzanne Bonet and 2006 Carol and Robert Hildebrand

First published in the USA in 2012 by

Fair Winds Press, a member of

Quayside Publishing Group

100 Cummings Center

Suite 406-L

Beverly, MA 01915-6101

www.fairwindspress.com

16 15 14 13 12   1 2 3 4 5

ISBN: 978-1-59233-541-1

Digital edition published in 2012
eISBN: 978-1-61058-612-2

This book is a compilation of two previously published books: *3-Ingredient Slow Cooker Recipes*, by Suzanne Bonet, and *3-Ingredient Slow Cooker Comfort Foods* by Carol and Robert Hildebrand. Library of Congress Cataloging-in-Publication Data available

Printed and bound in the U.S.A.

CONTENTS

INTRODUCTION

"Chic" is a term wholly dissociated from the slow cooker, yet the popularity of the lowly slow cooker is on the upswing. A growing health-consciousness and desire to simplify are lifestyle reasons for the slow cooker's rediscovery.

But other reasons exist, too. What's nicer than coming home to the aroma of Rosemary-Lamb Stew (page 164) or Gingered Pineapple Chicken (page 178) after a long day away? Cheaper cuts of meat taste tender and moist after slow cooking, and this helps with the budgetary stresses felt by graduate students, young adults, and growing families. Time-stressed households want to eat in, but they don't want freezer food, pizza, and microwave-centered meals day after day. They yearn for the flavorful, home-prepared variety. Everyone today seems to be strapped for time and money and togetherness. Yes, everyone is on the lookout for flavorful yet simple foods whose preparation doesn't take time away from family, school, career, or hobbies.

So, it's time to scramble to the back of the pantry and retrieve the appliance you've been snubbing, being a person of high culinary goals. Don't look now, but cheaper cuts of meat are suddenly chic at the country's best restaurants. It seems everyone is discovering that lamb shanks, pot roast, and brisket are mighty tasty when cooked right, and we're here to help you figure out how to do that.

Why just three ingredients? Because the recipes in this collection were selected to ensure that the slow cooker is utilized as intended— as an appliance that makes your life easier, simpler, less costly, and more satisfying. The problem with most slow-cooker recipes is that they expect too much from you. They require lots of ingredients and steps before you "fix it and forget it." Not the recipes in this collection. These truly are simple recipes, featuring only three ingredients, not counting water, salt, and black pepper. Best of all, these recipes are memorable, not mushy!

CHAPTER 1

GETTING TO KNOW YOUR SLOW COOKER

Slow Cooker Types, Sizes, Features, and Safety

S low cookers were introduced in the 1970s, and to date, more than 100 million have been sold. The Crock-Pot was the original slow cooker, and it still makes up 85 percent of the market. The catchy brand name, belonging to the Rival Company, became synonymous with the slow cooker. Today, we may still forget and call slow cookers by the wrong name, but that doesn't change the facts: All Crock-Pots are slow cookers, but not all slow cookers are Crock-Pot brand. Cuisinart, Farberware, Hamilton Beach, West Bend, and many other companies manufacture slow cookers as well.

What exactly is a slow cooker? It's a small, stand-alone appliance that cooks food slowly in a ceramic pot. The slow cooker's heating element surrounds the food with heat, so that the food cooks evenly. This eliminates the need to stir the cooking food, making its preparation extremely convenient for the cook. Some slow cooker-type appliances have heat coils on the bottom only, as well as adjustable thermostats. These are not true slow cookers, however. If you have this type of cooker, refer to your product manual for advice on how to adapt the recipes in this cookbook.

When first introduced, slow cookers came with two settings, LOW and HIGH, which most slow cookers still have. The exact temperatures of these settings vary by manufacturer, but LOW is generally about 200°F (90°C) and HIGH is about 300°F (150°C). These temperatures, though low in comparison to those used in conventional cooking, exceed food-safety standards.

For most slow-cooker recipes, it's possible to set the slow cooker to LOW and leave it unattended for the length of the recommended cooking time. But while the cooking times are flexible, it is possible that unexpected delays—getting stuck in a major traffic jam, for instance—could result in overcooked food. Many of the newer slow cookers therefore are programmable and often come with a WARM temperature setting, which is approximately 140°F (60°C), to prevent overcooking and to keep food at a safe temperature for up to four hours. This feature is also convenient if you want to hold foods at serving temperature for late-arriving family members or at potluck gatherings.

Even if you have a basic slow cooker with only a LOW and a HIGH temperature setting, the Rival Company sells a remarkable device called the Smart-Part Module. This little item works like a timer. Just insert the plug of your slow cooker into the module and set the cooking time. The module will automatically switch your slow cooker to WARM when your meal is finished cooking. It works with any brand of slow cooker that has a ceramic pot and that is rated 400 watts (3.3 amps) or less.

SLOW COOKERS AND BACTERIA

The slow cooker's lengthy cooking time, its direct heat, and the steam locked inside the pot thanks to its tight-fitting lid all work in concert to destroy bacteria when commonsense food-handling procedures are followed. In the 1970s, when slow cookers were first introduced, some people unknowingly practiced unsafe food-handling procedures and promoted the growth of enough bacteria in their slow-cooked food to cause illness. These days, slow cookers operate at higher temperatures, killing bacteria faster and better.

Although most slow-cooker food-safety practices are common sense, you probably need to refresh your memory. So, take a peek at the food-safety tips on page 15. You'll be glad you did.

The Basic Slow Cooker

When shopping for a new slow cooker, it's easy to become over-whelmed by the many types of cookers and variety of features available. Therefore, it's useful to understand the components of a basic slow cooker.

A basic slow cooker consists of an electric cooking pot with two temperature settings, LOW and HIGH. The pot is usually made of stoneware and is inserted in a base that contains the heating element, although less-expensive slow cookers can be single units and may even have only one temperature setting. If the cooking pot is remov-able, it often can be washed in the dishwasher, although you should consult your manufacturer's instructions to be sure. Some stoneware pots have an unfinished, porous bottom, which is fine for cooking but not for washing in the dishwasher. A removable cooking pot can also double as a serving dish. Even the basic slow cooker generally has a tempered glass lid to allow easy viewing of the cooking food, and often has handles that stay cool and are designed for easy gripping.

Slow-Cooker Features and Sizes

Beyond the basics is a dizzying array of special features. Some slow cookers are fully programmable. One model has a divided pot to cook two recipes at the same time. Another model is entirely cool to the touch, even when cooking on HIGH. Many come with a feature that automatically switches the unit to a temperature that safely keeps food warm once the cooking time has elapsed. A designer-style slow cooker makes an especially pretty appearance at the dinner table, doubling as an elegant serving dish. With some, the cooking pot goes from the base to the stovetop, oven, refrigerator, or freezer. A few even have nonstick interiors, and some have blinking lights that sig-nal if the power went off during the cooking time. Even without all of these improvements, however, the basic slow cooker is more than adequate for preparing and serving a delightfully tasty and conve-nient meal.

Slow cookers come in a variety of sizes, from 1 quart, perfect for dips, to 6 1/2 quarts, great for large quantities, roasts, and large birds. Since slow cookers cook best and most safely when they're at least half full of food and no more than two-thirds full, the quantity that you typically cook should determine the size of slow cooker you purchase. Generally, a 3 1/2- to 5-quart slow cooker is the best option for the average household.

Checklist of Slow-Cooker Features

If you don't already have a slow cooker, or if you're in the market for a new one, here are a few things to think about before you make your purchase.

What size slow cooker would be best for your needs?

- 1 quart, if you'll primarily be making dips and sauces.
- 3 1/2 to 4 quarts, if you'll be cooking for 4 or fewer people.
- 5 to 6 1/2 quarts or larger, if you'll be cooking for 5 or more people or if you like leftovers.

What shape slow cooker would be better for you?

- Round, the standard shape, if you'll be making a variety of recipes.
- Oval, if you'll be cooking a lot of roasts and whole chickens.

What other basic design features would be beneficial?

- A removable insert, if you'd like to serve your food directly from the slow cooker or put the cooking container in the dishwasher.
- A nonstick pot, to make cleanup easier.
- A lightweight slow cooker or removable pot, to keep the unit light enough to safely handle. Stoneware pots are heavy to begin with and can become very heavy when filled with food. Some slow cookers are made of aluminum, which is much lighter than stoneware.

- A decorative unit, if your slow cooker will be doubling as a serving dish. Slow-cooker exteriors are now made of stainless steel and come in solid colors, but you can still get units decorated with ivy and other kitchen motifs.

Which bells and whistles are worth the added cost for you?

- A WARM setting, the most practical feature not included on basic slow cookers, is worthwhile if you tend to return home later than expected.

- The cool-to-the-touch feature is important if you have little fingers around the house that could get burned.

- An aluminum pot insert is helpful if you prefer to sear meat before cooking it and would like to do so in the slow cooker rather than on the stove. The aluminum insert can also double as a griddle.

- A programmable temperature control is useful if you need flexibility. According to the U.S. Department of Agriculture, slow cookers are safe when used exclusively on LOW, but some cooks prefer to cook on HIGH for an hour, then reduce the temperature to LOW, and finally switch it to WARM once the food is done. This shortens the time that food is between 40°F (4°C) and 140°F (60°C), the temperature range in which bacteria multiply most rapidly. This method also shortens the cooking time slightly without hurting the slow-cooked flavor.

- An electronic database of recipes is helpful if you like to experiment. Before purchasing a unit with this feature, make sure you can read the LED screen, which by necessity is small.

Some slow cookers also come with accessories such as a dust cover, travel case, and meat rack. Some of these items are universal and can be purchased separate from the slow cooker, but not all are.

Slow-Cooker Safety

Once you have chosen the appropriate slow cooker for your needs and preferences, you have to learn how to cook safely with it. Be certain to consult your manufacturer's instruction booklet and follow all the safety recommendations. Here are a few of the more frequently cited safety precautions.

- *Do not submerge the base of the slow cooker in water.* In addition, before putting the removable pot or insert in the microwave, on the stovetop, in the oven, or in the broiler, make sure it can be used that way. If the directions don't explicitly state that something can be done with the slow cooker, be safe and don't do it.

- *Do not preheat the slow cooker, and never turn it on unless it has food in it.* The temperature gap between a hot slow cooker and cold food may cause a crack or, at the very least, may cause food to stick to or burn in the pot.

- *Do not put cold water in a hot slow-cooker pot.* The pot may crack. Wait until the pot has cooled to wash it.

- *Do not use a chipped or cracked ceramic pot.* Not only is a damaged pot impossible to wash thoroughly, but it may also fall apart at the worst possible time—while you're cooking.

- *Think twice before filling an insert away from the base.* Most slow cookers have crockery inserts, which can be heavy even when empty. Adding food increases the weight, raising the risk of dropping the insert or spilling its contents while trying to insert it into the slow cooker.

- *Follow common sense when storing foods in the slow cooker.* Sometimes, of course, you'll want to prepare slow-cooker ingredients in advance, and that may mean storing a few of the ingredients in the crockery insert and stowing the insert in the refrigerator overnight. If you do this, keep any meat separate from the vegetables and other ingredients until it's time to cook them.

You should never allow meat juices to touch other ingredients except during cooking. In addition, if you fill the insert the night before, you may find that potatoes or fruit become discolored or pasta or rice absorb too much liquid.

- *Never store leftovers or reheat food in the slow cooker.* Bacteria multiply quickly under certain temperature conditions. Instead, divide large amounts of leftovers among several small, shallow containers, then stow the containers in the refrigerator. This will allow even the center of the food in each container to cool down quickly enough to prevent bacteria growth. The danger zone for food is between 40°F (4°C) and 140°F (60°C), the temperature range in which bacteria can multiply quickly in food, causing the potential for food-borne illness. Never allow food to be in the danger zone for more than two hours.

- *Learn how to use a kitchen thermometer.* It's one of the most useful kitchen gadgets you'll find. According to the Partnership for Food Safety Education (www.fightbac.org/pdf/cook.pdf), you can be sure that foods are thoroughly cooked when they reach the following temperatures:

      Beef roasts, 145°F (60°C) (medium rare) or
      160°F (70°C)(medium)
      Ground beef, 160°F (70°C)
      Raw sausages, 160°F (70°C)
      Ready-to-eat sausages, 165°F (75°C)
      Pork roasts, pork chops, ground pork, 160°F (70°C)
      (medium) or 170°F (80°C) (well done)
      Whole poultry, 180°F (85°C)
      Chicken breasts, 170°F (80°C)
      Leftovers, 165°F (75°C)

- *Do not serve food from a slow cooker that was accidentally shut off for a period of time during cooking.* If you come home and find your clocks blinking, throw out the food in your slow cooker even if it looks well cooked. You most likely will have no idea how long the electricity was out and whether or not the food temperature was in the danger zone for too long. If you are present when the electricity goes out, finish cooking the food on your gas stove or find a friend or relative with a working stove.

While slow-cooker safety is important, it's also important that your finished dishes look appealing and taste even better. In the next chapter, you'll find tips and techniques for individual foods and food groups.

CHAPTER 2

USING YOUR SLOW COOKER

Slow-Cooker Basics

This cookbook contains 365 easy and tasty recipes, but you can convert many of your favorite conventional recipes for use with the slow cooker if you follow a few basic rules. The following guidelines will also ensure your success with recipes specifically designed for the slow cooker.

Meat and Poultry

Unquestionably great in the slow cooker are roasts, ham, ground beef, sausage, and whole and cut-up chicken. Throw them in the pot and go, as long as you understand these guidelines.

- Buy roasts, hams, and birds that fit inside your slow cooker with some headroom to spare. Slow cookers should be at least half full for the contents to cook properly, yet should never have less than a generous inch of space at the top. Turkey bones poking at the lid is also a no-no, since the lid must close well to seal in the moisture and flavor. Overfilling the slow cooker with liquid is sure to produce a sloppy mishap when the food reaches the simmering point.

- Opt for inexpensive and lean cuts of meat. Buying a beautifully marbled roast is more than unnecessary for taste and tenderness when slow cooking—it's a waste of money. The moist, gentle heat of the slow cooker will transform even the leanest, toughest cuts into tender morsels.

- Trim all visible fat, even from lean meat. You don't need the extra fat calories, and the slow cooker doesn't need the help.

- Remove poultry skin only if you prefer. Some people prefer the skin left on, claiming that the meat is more tender and succulent when cooked that way. Others prefer the skin removed before cooking to reduce the fat and calories. As long as there is sufficient liquid to cover the meat, cooking it with the skin on is unnecessary. Whether to consume the cooked skin or not is a personal preference.
- Precook ground meat and sausage. This will render out the fat before the meat is added to the slow cooker. The only time you shouldn't precook ground meat or sausage is when you're making meatloaf or the like. For meatloaf, choose an extra-lean grade for the healthiest preparation.
- When filling the slow cooker, put the vegetables on the bottom and the meat on the top. This is because meat cooks faster than vegetables. Until you're familiar with how they cook in your pot, check meats and poultry for doneness after 6 or 7 hours on LOW, even if the recipe states a cooking range of 8 to 10 hours. Check sooner if the cooking range given is 4 or 5 hours.

Fish and Shellfish

This category of food is relatively new to the slow cooker, but with proper handling, you can enjoy tasty and healthful fish and shellfish dishes with no muss or fuss.

- Use firm fishes such as cod, catfish, haddock, salmon, and tuna in your dishes. Don't substitute more delicate fishes such as flounder, which won't hold up through extended periods of cooking.
- Add shellfish towards the end of cooking, according to the recipe instructions. Shrimp, scallops, and minced clams toughen if they're overcooked.

Vegetables

Vegetables pair well with meat to make one-pot meals, stews, and soups, but there are a few things you need to know.

- Add greens and less dense or strongly flavored vegetables during the last 20 to 60 minutes of cooking. Cruciferous vegetables, for instance, need to be cooked for the longest periods of time, whereas leafy vegetables, such as spinach and kale, will cook in the brief time it takes them to warm up to the temperature of the surrounding food. Depending on the quantity of vegetables added, the temperature of the pot will dip for a time. Take this into consideration when timing how long it will take for the food to finish cooking. The more vegetables you add, the longer it will be before your dinner is ready for the table.
- Chop vegetables into pieces or chunks of uniform size for even cooking. In most cases, vegetable pieces should be no more than an inch or so thick. The smaller the chunks, the faster they will cook. If you would prefer your slow cooker to cook for 10 hours, you can chop your vegetables a smidgeon larger than if you want to get dinner on the table in 8 hours sharp.

Rice, Barley, Pasta, and Beans

Rice, barley, pasta, and beans often accompany meat in the slow cooker, but each has its own special requirements for cooking.

- Use raw long-grain rice over quick-cooking rice, pearl barley over quick-cooking barley, and brown or wild rice over white rice. They require more time to cook, which makes them more convenient. The fact that they're more flavorful and nutritious is a bonus. Pearl barley and brown rice take approximately two to four times longer to cook than their more processed counterparts. Wild rice, which is really a variety of grass and not a rice at all, takes even longer to cook.
- Add uncooked pasta to the pot during the last 1 to 2 hours of cooking to avoid overcooking. Alternatively, cook the pasta on the stove, drain it, and add it during the last 5 to 15 minutes of cooking, although you lose convenience and flavor this way. Cook pasta until it's al dente and no softer, as it may continue to cook in the

pot. You can use this method for barley and rice, too, but again, you'll sacrifice some convenience and flavor.

- Use canned or precooked beans and legumes for convenience. Uncooked dried beans take much longer to cook. For maximum tenderness, do not add sweet or salty foods, or acidic foods such as tomatoes, until the other foods in the recipe are fully cooked or close to it.

Dairy Products

Dairy products contribute much to the taste of a slow-cooked dish, but they, too, have special requirements.

- Stir natural cheese, sour cream, yogurt, milk, cream, and soy products into the pot immediately before serving. The same goes for rice milk and nut milks. Continue cooking only until the cheese has melted or the sauce is thoroughly heated. Dairy products and the like may separate and appear to curdle if cooked for about an hour—and certainly when cooked longer.

- Use pasteurized processed cheese, canned evaporated skim milk, and nonfat dry milk in recipes that call for extended cooking times. These processed dairy products hold up to heat beautifully without separating.

- Opt for canned condensed cream soups over ready-to-eat soups. They're processed and very stable for slow cooking.

Flavorings, Herbs, Spices, and Garnishes

Properly flavoring and garnishing food will help your meals come out of the slow cooker tasting simply fabulous.

- Use sugar, brown sugar, maple syrup, and the like without reservation. They add flavor with no downside in slow cooking, other than the calories.

- Consider carefully when selecting a sugar substitute for your slow-cooker recipe. Splenda (sucralose) is heat-stable plus has no aftertaste. Even though Sweet'N Low (saccharine), Sweet One (acesulfame-k), and Stevia are heat-stable, they often leave a slight aftertaste. Aspartame formulations such as NutraSweet and Equal are not heat-stable, and although they have no aftertaste, they are not recommended because they lose sweetness after extended heating.

- Expect slow-cooked flavorings and spices to have different characteristics than you're used to. Slow cooking increases the flavor intensity of peppers and bay leaves, for instance. On the other hand, it tends to cause onion, ground cinnamon, and other ground spices to lose flavor. Many slow-cooker recipes, therefore, specify whole herbs and spices, which you can tie together in a piece of cheesecloth and add to the pot. In the absence of whole spices in your pantry, add ground herbs and spices near the end of cooking.

- Garnish your meals to offset the fading that slow-cooked foods may experience. Add visual appeal with some grated cheese, a dollop of sour cream, or a sprinkle of chopped fresh or dried parsley, cilantro, chives, tomatoes, or green peppers.

Baked Goods

You may be surprised that you can bake in your slow cooker, but it's true. Some slow cookers come with a covered baking unit and a rack. If yours didn't, improvise.

- If your slow cooker didn't come with a baking unit, use any oven-safe pan. Pyrex bakeware or a large coffee can will also work.

- For recipes that require a lid on the baking pan or unit, use any oven-safe lid. If you don't have an oven-safe lid, try 5 to 6 layers of paper toweling.

- Use the slow-cooker lid in addition to the baking-pan lid, unless the recipe specifically states otherwise.

- Always use a rack when the recipe calls for one. If your slow cooker didn't come with one, use any oven-safe rack. A rack elevates the pan off the floor of the slow cooker to provide circulation for even baking.

- When adapting recipes for the slow cooker, always remember that the baking times for baked goods must be doubled or quadrupled.

As you can see, the slow cooker is a versatile small appliance— just about everything can be prepared in it. Whether you're an expert or just starting to learn about slow cooking, you will prepare excellent food if you follow the simple guidelines in this chapter. Convert favorite family recipes or enjoy one of the quick-and-easy recipes in this cookbook. Either way you create wonderful dishes with minimal effort.

Even shopping to stock the pantry can require just minimal effort. In the next chapter, you'll see what foods to keep on hand so that you're always prepared to make a slow-cooker meal that's table-ready with very little work.

CHAPTER 3

STOCKING YOUR SLOW-COOKER PANTRY

The Foods That Help Your Slow Cooker Make Your Life Easier

A certain segment of society would have us believe that only from-scratch-and-all-natural constitutes genuine home cooking. That's all well and good, except that if we don't have the time to slave over the stove every night, we certainly don't have the time to make Worcestershire sauce from scratch. It makes sense, then, for the well-stocked slow-cooker pantry to contain a variety of prepared foods that enhance meat, poultry, beans, and other meal fixings. This makes it a cinch to fill your slow cooker and come home later to a fragrant, delicious meal that's table-ready—and isn't that our goal?

Note that your angst concerning the use of frozen and canned food can also be laid to rest. Frozen and canned vegetables and fruits are processed immediately after harvest, before they lose nutrients. Fresh produce, on the other hand, loses nutrients on the way to the grocery store. So, never feel guilty again about using frozen or canned foods. Because of the quick processing, they're often more nutritious than fresh fruits and veggies.

Prepared spice and herb mixes are not only convenient, but also economical. Spices have a shelf life of about six months, so buying individual spices can be an exercise in futility, since they are almost always used in scant quantity. When you buy mixed herbs and spices, you're more likely to use the entire bottle before the contents lose flavor. This holds true for other seasonings and flavorings as well. How many times have you purchased a special ingredient for one recipe, only to have it languish in the refrigerator or spice rack until it was past its prime? So, cooking with prepared foods saves you time and money, and in many cases it increases the nutritional content of your food. How can you argue with that?

We're fortunate that supermarkets stock more than the basics these days. Canned tomatoes, for instance, come in fifty-four varieties at one national grocery store. Anyone can find mushroom soup condensed, dried, flavored as golden mushroom soup, combined with chicken, and probably in other ways as well. Each of these products contributes a unique blend of seasonings and flavorings to your slow-cooker recipes without your having to stock the individual flavorings and take the time to measure them out.

The Slow-Cooker Pantry, Refrigerator, and Freezer

While it's difficult in a cookbook to take into account every reader's taste preferences, here is a general list of ingredients to consider keeping on hand. All the ingredients listed work well in the slow cooker, and many are available preseasoned, which saves time and money. Start by purchasing the nonperishables that you love, and add others to your pantry as your budget allows. Because there are so many varieties and flavors of many of these products available, it's impossible to list every one. As a rule of thumb, when you're shopping without a specific recipe in mind, grab the can of seasoned tomato sauce, for instance, that is the most appealing to your taste buds.

BAKING SUPPLIES

All-purpose baking mix

Baking chocolate, unsweetened

Cake mixes, variety

Cornstarch

Flour

DAIRY PRODUCTS

Butter, salted and/or unsalted

Cheese, cream

Cheese, Parmesan, grated

Cheeses, shredded, variety

Eggs

Milk, condensed

Milk, evaporated

DRESSINGS, SAUCES, SOUPS

Bouillon, beef, chicken, and vegetable

Broth, beef, chicken, and vegetable

Dressings, variety

Glazes, variety

Marinades, variety

Pasta sauce

Soups, condensed cream of mushroom, chicken, and celery

Teriyaki sauce

Tomato paste

Tomato sauce

FLAVORINGS, SEASONINGS

Bay leaves

Black peppercorns (and a grinder)

Chili mix, dry

Chili sauce

Corn syrup

Dressing mixes, dry, variety

Honey

Hot sauce

Italian seasoning (recipe on page 28)

Ketchup

Maple syrup, pure

Mustard, Dijon

Mustard, yellow, prepared

Salt, iodized or sea

Soup mixes, dry, variety

Soy sauce

Sugar, brown, light and/or dark

Sugar, cinnamon (recipe on page 27)

Sugar, vanilla (recipe on page 28)

Sugar, white

Tabasco sauce

Worcestershire sauce

FRUITS

Fruits, canned, variety

Fruits, dried, variety

Pie fillings, canned, variety

Jams and preserves, variety

LEGUMES, PASTA, RICE

Chick peas, canned

Kidney beans, canned

Pasta, dry, variety

Rice, converted, raw

White beans, canned

MEAT, POULTRY, FISH

Beef, ground

Beef brisket

Beef pot roast

Chicken, canned

Chicken, whole

Chicken breasts

Chicken legs

Chicken wings

Pork chops

Pork roast

Ribs

Salmon, fresh

Salmon, canned

Sausages

Stew meat

Tuna, canned

NUTS

Almond halves

Mixed nuts

Pecan halves

Peanuts, shelled

Walnut halves

OIL, VINEGAR

Cooking spray

Oil, olive

Vinegar, apple cider

Vinegar, balsamic

Vinegar, white

VEGETABLES

Carrots, baby and regular, fresh
or frozen

Celery, fresh or frozen

Chiles, canned

Corn, canned

Corn blends, canned

Mushrooms, fresh or dried

Onions, fresh or frozen

Potatoes, hash brown, frozen

Potatoes, white, fresh or frozen

Salsa, fresh or canned

Sweet potatoes, fresh or canned

Tomatoes, crushed, canned

Tomatoes, whole, canned or dried

Vegetables, mixed, frozen

Vegetables, seasoning-blend, frozen
(recipe on page 29)

Vegetables, stew, frozen

Slow-Cooker Seasoning and Flavoring Mixes

It's possible to create seasoning and flavoring mixes at home in addition to purchasing them at the store. You can find recipes for many mixes, but here are a few that are especially popular (and that you'll find in recipes throughout this book). Feel free to adjust the proportions of the ingredients according to your taste.

🧂 Cinnamon Sugar

1/2 cup (100 g) granulated sugar

2 tablespoons (14 g) ground cinnamon

Put the sugar and cinnamon in a small bowl and stir to combine. Store the mixture in an airtight container in a cool place.

Vanilla Sugar

2 cups (100 g, or 50 g) granulated or powdered sugar

1 vanilla bean

Put the sugar in an airtight container, then push the vanilla bean down into the sugar until it's completely submerged. Let the sugar with the vanilla bean sit undisturbed for 1 to 2 weeks, then remove the bean. Store the mixture in the airtight container in a cool place.

Italian Seasoning

1 teaspoon dried oregano

1 teaspoon dried basil

1 teaspoon dried rosemary

1 teaspoon dried thyme

1 teaspoon dried marjoram

1 teaspoon dried sage

1 teaspoon dried savory

Put the oregano, basil, rosemary, thyme, marjoram, sage, and savory in a small bowl and stir to combine. Store the mixture in an airtight container in a cool place.

⌗ Seasoning-Blend Vegetables

3 onions

2 stalks celery

1 green pepper

1 red pepper

Dice the onions, and cut the celery, green pepper, and red pepper into chunks of uniform size. Place the chopped vegetables in a plastic freezer bag, and store them in the freezer until you need them for a recipe. Note that you may wish to prepare mixtures of different-sized vegetables for different uses, or freeze a variety of amounts for different recipes.

A Final Note

The most important thing to remember when stocking your pantry is that great ingredients and flavor combinations make for great food. Always buy the highest quality products, as well as the flavor combinations that appeal to your taste buds. It's never a good idea to buy a brand or flavor that you don't like just because it's on sale. If a recipe calls for a garlic-flavored sauce and you always pass on the garlic, you're better off using a different-flavored sauce. Likewise, never cook with wine or spirits that you wouldn't drink by the glass. Follow this rule faithfully, and you'll be rewarded with fabulous tasting food every time.

Now that your pantry is stocked, let's get to the good stuff—the recipes that will make your life easier and your taste buds happy. It's time to turn the page and discover quick, easy recipes for slow-cooker foods—with just three ingredients or fewer!

CHAPTER 4

BEFORE YOU BEGIN

Information and Guidelines for Slow-Cooking Success

M aster chefs need read no further. But everyone else may want to learn what's what on a recipe page in this cookbook and peruse a short list of slow-cooking tips and techniques. As my grandmother always used to say, "Knowledge is power." In this case, it's also success in the kitchen.

The Parts of the Recipe

It's always a good idea to read a recipe through at least once before you start. That way, you'll know what ingredients to have on hand, how long the recipe should take to prepare and cook, and if your slow cooker needs any special attention during cooking. The recipes in this cookbook are set up to make this step easy for you. When reviewing a recipe, you'll find the usual—a list of ingredients, directions, and a cooking time range. You'll also discover a few other useful tidbits of information.

- Ingredient list and directions. These two items are an indispensable part of every recipe. This cookbook lists the ingredients in the order they're used and includes their metric equivalents. Before starting, make sure you have all the ingredients required. Perhaps it's not a bad idea to place everything on a countertop, to be really sure. With only three or fewer ingredients (not counting salt, black pepper, and water) in every recipe, no one's counter is too small for this step. It may even prevent false starts caused by unknowingly being out of or short of a pantry staple.

- Yield. Are you cooking in empty-nester quantities or entertaining a crowd? Do you love leftovers, or do you abhor them? The yield information makes it a snap to choose a recipe to suit any occasion. Given that we're all watching portion sizes these days, the serving sizes in these recipes are not overly conservative, but they're also not on the large side (unless they're specified as generous). Take particularly small or large appetites into consideration here.
- Tip. Most of the recipes in this cookbook are simple and straightforward. But just in case, some of the recipes include tips about an ingredient or cooking technique. Need to know how to do something? Look for a tip with the recipe.
- Note. Protein, carb, and calorie counts don't tell the whole story about many of the foods we eat. The notes with many of the recipes in this cookbook offer interesting tidbits about nutrition and ingredients. Read 'em, skip 'em, or exploit your newfound knowledge at the trivia game table. It's up to you.
- Cooking time and Attention. These items provide vital information at a glance. They make it easy to choose a recipe that fits the amount of time you have available for cooking the food. These items also eliminate unwelcome surprises—for instance, starting a recipe that needs to be stirred during cooking when you were planning to be gone all day. Recipes labeled as needing minimal attention are the fix it-and-forget-it type. All the other recipes have the briefest of summaries to explain their attention requirements. If you see anything other than "Minimal" listed for the attention required, you'll know to read the recipe directions for more information.
- Nutritional analysis. If you're on a diet or have a medical condition, check the very bottom of the recipe for the number of calories and grams of fat, protein, carbohydrate, and dietary fiber found in one average serving of the basic recipe.

Slow-Cooking Tips and Techniques

Now that you know what's included in the recipes in this cookbook, it's time to look at the slow-cooker tips and techniques that are essential for making good decisions when cooking. Slow cooking is different from conventional cooking, and while it doesn't demand an excess of talent, it does require you to know a few things. Apply the following tips and techniques to every recipe, and you'll enjoy slow-cooker success.

- Just like recipes for conventional cooking, the recipes in this cookbook provide a range of cooking times to account for variables such as the initial temperatures of the ingredients, room temperature, altitude, and variations in the temperature settings among the different slow-cooker models. Once you become accustomed to your slow cooker and have tried a recipe a few times, you'll have an idea of whether or not your food is apt to be done at the beginning or end of the given time range. This also helps you decide if it's appropriate to leave the slow cooker on unattended. You'll have a good idea of how much wiggle time you have if you become unexpectedly delayed and can't turn off the slow cooker when expected.

- Manufacturers recommend that slow cookers be between one-half and two-thirds full. An underfilled slow cooker may become too hot and burn the food, while an overfilled slow cooker may take too long to reach a safe temperature, increasing the potential for bacteria growth. Choose the properly sized slow cooker for each recipe, and don't double or halve a recipe unless your slow cooker can handle it. For more information, see "Slow Cooker Safety" on page 15.

- Most of the recipes in this cookbook do not require the meat to be browned because this is an added step. If you prefer the flavor and look of browned meat, however, sear your meat in a skillet with a little olive oil before placing it in the slow cooker. Just be aware that browned meat may shorten the cooking time slightly, since when you brown the meat, you're starting the cooking process.

- Never lift the slow-cooker lid during cooking unless instructed to do so. If you can't see inside the slow cooker because of condensation on the lid, jiggle the lid to make the droplets fall back into the cooker. Because slow cookers cook foods evenly and with moist heat, taking the lid off to stir or to monitor food is unnecessary and frequently counterproductive. In extreme situations, lifting the lid too much may cause your food to dry out. If this happens, add a few tablespoons of water or other liquid to correct the situation. More of a problem, however, is that lifting the lid will cause the temperature in the slow cooker to drop 10 to 15 degrees, which will take between 15 and 25 minutes to regain.

- If you lift the lid, you'll have to cook the food longer. How much longer will depend on when you lift the lid during the cooking process and for how long. If you lift the lid at the very beginning or end of cooking, you won't need to add as much cooking time as you would if you peek during the middle of cooking, when the food is at its highest temperature and needs the accumulated heat to finish cooking.

- It's hard to provide a rule of thumb for the many possibilities — from when a lid is accidentally knocked off the pot for a second or two, to when your child tries to help by removing the lid and stirring until you notice there's mischief afoot. The best solution is to add at least 15 minutes to the recommended cooking time and to use your best judgment or a meat thermometer to test your food for doneness at the end of the cooking time.

- Always taste a finished dish before serving it so you can adjust the seasonings if necessary. Long cooking can increase the intensity of some seasonings and decrease it in others. Many of the recipes in this cookbook use time-saving, prepared ingredients with varying amounts of salt and flavorings. Therefore, it's best to season a dish to taste once it's fully cooked. Many of the recipes include specific recommendations for seasonings and flavorings to punch up the dish.

As you can see, slow cooking is a method without difficult or time-intensive techniques. It's just that simple. You are now armed with the knowledge and the power to prepare a wide variety of foods the slow-cooker way. So, what are you waiting for? It's time to turn the page and discover 365 delicious ways to make cooking a quick-and-easy pleasure—with just three or fewer ingredients.

MULTI-INGREDIENT PRODUCTS AND CONVENIENCE

Three-ingredient speed and convenience often require the use of multi-ingredient products to give dishes deliciously complex flavors. The vast majority of these multi-ingredient products are manufactured by familiar national companies. Take a look, and you'll soon notice that multi-ingredient products are in vogue. The supermarket shelves are crowded with them:

- Tomato and pasta sauces with added flavorings such as garlic, onion, mushroom, and wine

- Soups, gravies, and seasonings with gourmet twists

- Sauces and marinades with garlic, herb, chili, or citrus flavorings

- Frozen and canned vegetable blends and dressed-up potatoes

- Shredded cheese blends, sometimes with added spices

Many of the recipes in this cookbook use multi-ingredient products, with the brand name included in the ingredient list if it's a hard-to-find or one-of-a-kind product. Even when a brand name is mentioned, feel free to make a substitution. The slow cooker is meant to free you from the drudgery of cooking. Shopping for pantry items should never be a chore, and trudging around town hunting for ingredients is contrary to the spirit of this cookbook.

Should you prefer to search out the few one-of-a-kind ingredients unavailable in your local grocery store, head for a large city supermarket, specialty or gourmet shop, or even the Internet. What you'll discover while shopping at these specialty stores or surfing the web may evolve into a three-ingredient recipe sensation of your own.

CHAPTER 5
BREAKFAST

Kick-start your day the night before. Throw a few ingredients into your slow cooker before you go to bed, and wake up to the sweet, nutty aroma of Banana-Nut Oatmeal (page 39) or Breakfast Apple Crunch (page 37). As it turns out, breakfast really is the most important meal of the day. Researchers have found that skipping breakfast increases the risks of developing diabetes, becoming obese, and even having a heart attack. People who consume whole-grain cereals and fruits for breakfast receive the greatest health benefits. The slow cooker is especially suitable for preparing oatmeal and fruit, as well as other breakfast favorites, so go for it tonight and enjoy a great start to your day tomorrow!

Basic Granola

Basic granola—or designer granola! Keep this recipe simple for a plain but delicious granola, or pump it up with antioxidants by tossing in your favorite combination of dried fruits, nuts, and seeds.

COOKING TIME: 2¹/₂ to 3¹/₂ hours   **ATTENTION:** Stir every 30 minutes

4 cups (300 g) old-fashioned rolled oats

¹/₂ cup (113 g) honey or maple syrup

3 tablespoons (45 ml) vegetable oil, enriched with vitamin E, if desired

Spray the inside of the slow cooker with cooking spray.

Put the rolled oats, honey, and vegetable oil in the slow cooker and mix well. Partially cover, propping the lid open with a twist of foil or a wooden skewer to allow the moisture to escape, and cook on LOW for 2¹/₂ to 3¹/₂ hours, or until the oat morsels are roasted dry and golden brown, stirring every 30 minutes.

Allow the granola to cool, then transfer it to an airtight container. Store it in the refrigerator.

YIELD: 5 servings

NUTRITIONAL ANALYSIS: One serving of the basic recipe contains 390 calories; 12 g fat; 10 g protein; 62 g carbohydrate; and 7 g dietary fiber.

ADD IT! When the granola has cooled, add in a total of 1 to 2 cups of raisins, shredded unsweetened coconut, chopped walnuts, slivered almonds, or shelled pumpkin or sunflower seeds. Mix and match your favorites!

NOTE: It's not easy to get a full day's requirement of vitamin E through food sources. Fortunately, manufacturers are starting to enrich vegetable oil with vitamin E. Enriched oil is a smart way to get your E because the body absorbs this fat-soluble vitamin best when it's consumed along with foods containing a fat such as vegetable oil. Vitamin E and vegetable oil—it's a natural!

Breakfast Apple Crunch

Apple Crunch for breakfast is appealing when the weather turns cold. The crunchy topping makes it all the more satisfying.

COOKING TIME: 5 to 6 hours on LOW, 2 to 3 hours on HIGH
ATTENTION: Minimal

One 21-ounce (595-g) can cinnamon-and-spice apple pie filling

2 cups (244 g) Basic Granola (page 36) plus a smidge more for garnish

1/2 cup (60 ml) water

4 tablespoons (56 g) lightly salted butter, cut into pieces

Spray the inside of the slow cooker with cooking spray.

Put the pie filling, granola, water, and butter in the slow cooker and mix well. Cover and cook on LOW for 5 to 6 hours or on HIGH for 2 to 3 hours.

To serve, divide the oatmeal among 5 cereal bowls. Sprinkle each serving with extra granola for added crunch.

YIELD: 5 generous servings

NUTRITIONAL ANALYSIS: One serving of the basic recipe contains 397 calories; 16 g fat; 5 g protein; 62 g carbohydrate; and 5 g dietary fiber.

ADD IT! Serve Breakfast Apple Crunch with milk or a dollop of whipped cream.

NOTE: The Golden Delicious apple is one of the best apples for cooking and baking. Interestingly enough, it's not related to the Red Delicious, which is the best apple for snacking. Other common cooking and baking apples are the Jonathan, Granny Smith, and Rome.

Maple and Brown Sugar Oatmeal

Maple, brown sugar, and oats—what a yummy way to start the day! This recipe tastes delicious as is or served with milk.

COOKING TIME: 8 to 9 hours   **ATTENTION:** Minimal

5 3/4 cups (1.38 L) water

3 cups (225 g) old-fashioned rolled oats

1/2 cup (75 g) dark brown sugar, packed

¹/₄ teaspoon salt

³/₄ teaspoon maple flavoring

Put the water, rolled oats, brown sugar, and salt in the slow cooker and mix well. Cover and cook on LOW for 8 to 9 hours.

Before serving, stir in the maple flavoring.

YIELD: 6 generous servings

NUTRITIONAL ANALYSIS: One serving of the basic recipe contains 202 calories; 3 g fat; 7 g protein; 39 g carbohydrate; and 4 g dietary fiber.

ADD IT! Toss in 1 cup finely chopped apple or ¹/₂ to 1 cup chopped walnuts with the uncooked rolled oats for an extra measure of yum.

NOTE: Everyone knows that an apple a day keeps the doctor away, but did you know that walnuts are one of the most heart-healthy nuts? A ¹/₂ cup of walnuts contains about the same amount of omega-3 fatty acids as 3 ounces of salmon.

Fruity Oatmeal

Oatmeal is heart-smart, and dried fruit is loaded with antioxidants. How fitting that dried fruit tastes marvelous with oatmeal.

COOKING TIME: 8 to 9 hours   **ATTENTION:** Minimal

2³/₄ cups (660 ml) water

1 cup (75 g) old-fashioned rolled oats

³/₄ cup (131 g) chopped mixed dried fruit

1¹/₂ teaspoons (3.5 g) ground cinnamon

Put the water, rolled oats, dried fruit, and cinnamon in the slow cooker and mix well. Cover and cook on LOW for 8 to 9 hours.

Before serving, stir the oatmeal, adding more water (or milk) if a thinner consistency is desired.

YIELD: 5 generous servings

NUTRITIONAL ANALYSIS: One serving of the basic recipe contains 102 calories; 1 g fat; 0 g protein; 3 g carbohydrate; and 3 g dietary fiber.

ADD IT! Sprinkle the cooked oatmeal with brown sugar or drizzle it with maple syrup for added flavor.

NOTE: In a recent study at Tufts University, dried plums ranked highest in antioxidants among all the fruits and vegetables, and raisins ranked second. You can find prepackaged bags of mixed dried fruits including these antioxidant powerhouses, plus dried apples, apricots, and a variety of other fruits, in the canned fruit aisle of your grocery store. For this recipe, you can also buy individual bags of your favorite dried fruits and make your own combinations. Whatever you choose to do, you'll really enjoy this healthy breakfast!

Banana-Nut Oatmeal

Try this recipe, and you'll never eat microwave oatmeal again. It's the real thing—warm, sweet, and nutty. Serve with milk or soymilk.

COOKING TIME: 7 to 8 hours　　　　　　**ATTENTION:** Minimal

1¹/₂ cups (360 ml) water

³/₄ cup (56 g) old-fashioned rolled oats

¹/₄ teaspoon salt

2 medium bananas, sliced just before serving

¹/₂ cup (63 g) slivered almonds or chopped walnuts

Put the water, rolled oats, and salt in the slow cooker and mix well. Cover and cook on LOW for 7 to 8 hours.

To serve, stir the oatmeal and divide it among 4 cereal bowls. Top each serving with one-fourth of the banana slices and 2 tablespoons (16 g) nuts.

YIELD: 4 servings

NUTRITIONAL ANALYSIS: One serving of the basic recipe contains 219 calories; 11 g fat; 7 g protein; 27 g carbohydrate; and 4 g dietary fiber.

TIP: If the banana slices don't make the oatmeal sweet enough, add some maple syrup.

NOTE: Bananas are a staple food and an income source for developing countries. They're also the main ingredient in a popular beer made in rural eastern Africa—banana beer. A close cousin, Banana Bread Beer, won as favorite beer for women during the Great British Beer Festival in 2003.

Raspberry Yogurt Oatmeal

Getting up early for a quick morning walk or run? Have this hot but refreshing breakfast waiting when you arrive home.

COOKING TIME: 7 to 8 hours   **ATTENTION:** Minimal

1½ cups (360 ml) water

¾ cup (56 g) old-fashioned rolled oats

¼ teaspoon salt

One to two 8-ounce (245-g) cartons raspberry yogurt

1 cup (110 g) fresh raspberries, washed and dried

Put the water, rolled oats, and salt in the slow cooker and mix well. Cover and cook on LOW for 7 to 8 hours.

To serve, stir the oatmeal and divide it among 4 cereal bowls. Fold one-fourth of the yogurt into each serving and top each serving with 1/2 cup of the fresh raspberries.

YIELD: 4 servings

NUTRITIONAL ANALYSIS: One serving of the basic recipe contains 144 calories; 5 g fat; 7 g protein; 19 g carbohydrate; and 4 g dietary fiber.

ADD IT! Fold 2 tablespoons (16 g) slivered almonds into each serving of cooked oatmeal along with the yogurt.

NOTE: Raspberries are an excellent source of vitamin C and potassium. In addition, studies show raspberries contain a phytochemical, ellagic acid, which may help prevent cancer. They also taste pretty good.

⌬ Honey-Nut Breakfast Rolls

The aroma of baking sweet rolls will encourage an atmosphere of ease and contentment in your home. Enjoy these rolls piping hot.

COOKING TIME: 3 to 4 hours　　　　　　　　**ATTENTION:** Minimal

½ cup (170 g) honey

One 16-ounce (455-g) can refrigerator-style buttermilk biscuits

¼ cup (31 g) chopped pecans, almonds, or walnuts

Coat the interior of the slow cooker's baking unit with cooking spray, and position the slow cooker's rack on the floor of the machine. If your slow cooker did not come with this equipment, use any baking pan and rack that fit inside the machine.

Put the honey in a small bowl. Dip the raw biscuits in the honey, then place them in the pan with their sides touching. Sprinkle the nuts over the raw biscuits. Place the pan in the slow cooker on the rack. Cover and cook on LOW for 3 to 4 hours; do not lift the lid during the first 2 to 3 hours.

Remove the pan from the slow cooker when it's cool enough to handle and serve the sweet rolls warm.

YIELD: 5 servings

NUTRITIONAL ANALYSIS: One serving of the basic recipe contains 478 calories; 17 g fat; 8 g protein; 77 g carbohydrate; and 3 g dietary fiber.

Breakfast Casserole

Breakfast is the most important meal of the day. Taste this easy-to-make casserole once, and you'll never skip breakfast again. It's addictively satisfying.

COOKING TIME: 8 to 9 hours   **ATTENTION:** Minimal

One 1-pound (455-g) bag frozen hash browns, partially thawed

3 cups (338 g) shredded cheddar or provolone cheese

12 large eggs

1 cup (240 ml) water

1/2 teaspoon salt

1/4 teaspoon freshly ground black pepper

Spray the inside of the slow cooker with cooking spray.

Put half of the hash browns in the slow cooker and spread them out evenly. Top the hash browns with half of the cheese. Repeat with the remaining hash browns and cheese.

In a large bowl, beat the eggs with a whisk, then mix in the water, salt, and pepper. Pour the egg mixture into the slow cooker over the hash browns and cheese. Cover and cook on LOW for 8 to 9 hours.

YIELD: 8 generous servings

NUTRITIONAL ANALYSIS: One serving of the basic recipe contains 358 calories; 22 g fat; 22 g protein; 16 g carbohydrate; and 2 g dietary fiber.

TIP: You don't have to thaw the hash browns unless they're rock-solid from sitting in your freezer. As long as you can sprinkle them into the slow cooker, you're good to go.

TIP: Leftover Breakfast Casserole is excellent served sandwich-style between two slices of toasted bread. Cheese lovers can add a slice of melted cheese.

ADD IT! Combine 12 ounces (120 g) bacon, cooked and crumbled, or 12 ounces (225 g) sausage, sliced and browned, with 1/2 cup sautéed chopped onion, and mix with the uncooked hash browns. For a richer casserole, substitute 1 cup milk for the water.

CHAPTER 6

BEVERAGES

There's nothing like a hot drink to warm a cold winter's night. There's nothing like a hot drink to celebrate an event. There's nothing like a coffee drink to start your day. So, it's settled. Break out that slow cooker and brew up a batch of Double Blackberry Brandy-Wine (page 46), Holiday Wassail (page 45), Cinnamon-Spiked Coffee (page 50)—or whatever makes you warm, happy, and raring to go!

☕ Spiced Apple Cider

Take pleasure in the spicy aroma of this wonderful beverage as it fills your home. The drink's prettiest when served warm in tall glass mugs and garnished with apple wedges.

COOKING TIME: 4 to 10 hours
ATTENTION: Sample after 4 hours, then every 30 minutes

1 gallon (3.8 L) apple cider or apple juice

1 cup (235 ml) cranberry juice

2 cinnamon sticks

Pour the apple cider and cranberry juice into the slow cooker and stir to combine. Add the cinnamon sticks and stir again. Cover and heat on LOW for 4 to 10 hours, sampling the cider after 4 hours, then every 30 minutes thereafter.

When the cinnamon flavor is just right, remove the cinnamon sticks and discard them. Ladle the cider into mugs and serve it warm.

YIELD: 18 servings

NUTRITIONAL ANALYSIS: One serving of the basic recipe (made with apple cider) contains 112 calories; .3 g fat; .1 g protein; 28 g carbohydrate; and .2 g dietary fiber.

ADD IT! Bundle 5 to 10 whole cloves and 2 to 3 whole allspice in a piece of cheesecloth and tie it with kitchen string. Float the bundled spices in the cider, then remove them along with the cinnamon sticks.

☕ Holiday Wassail

Add to your joy-filled holiday gathering with this steaming–hot fruity wassail. Float a pineapple ring in the slow cooker for a festive touch.

COOKING TIME: 4 to 6 hours
ATTENTION: Sample after 4 hours, then every 30 minutes

---

1 gallon (3.8 L) apple cider or apple juice

2 quarts (1.9 L) unsweetened pineapple juice

2 cinnamon sticks

Pour the apple cider and pineapple juice into the slow cooker and stir to combine. Add the cinnamon sticks and stir again. Cover and heat on LOW for 4 to 6 hours, sampling the wassail after 4 hours, then every 30 minutes thereafter.

When the cinnamon flavor is just right, remove the cinnamon sticks and discard them.

YIELD: 24 servings

NUTRITIONAL ANALYSIS: One serving of the basic recipe (made with apple cider) contains 124 calories; .3 g fat; .4 g protein; 31 g carbohydrate; and .3 g dietary fiber.

ADD IT! Add 1 cup (235 ml) strong black tea or your favorite herb tea.

TRY THIS! Enhance the holiday feeling by serving hot wassail in vintage Santa mugs.

☕ Double Blackberry Brandy-Wine

Enjoy the unforgettable flavor of blackberries with a hint of apple. Serve very hot in small cups garnished with raisins and slivered almonds.

COOKING TIME: 3 to 4 hours   **ATTENTION:** Minimal

---

1 bottle (750 ml) blackberry wine

1½ pints (710 ml) apple juice

1 cup (235 ml) blackberry brandy or liqueur

Pour the blackberry wine, apple juice, and blackberry brandy into the slow cooker and stir to combine. Cover and heat on LOW for 3 to 4 hours.

Serve the brandy-wine hot.

YIELD: 10 servings

NUTRITIONAL ANALYSIS: One serving of the basic recipe (made with blackberry brandy) contains 125 calories; .1 g fat; .2 g protein; 15 g carbohydrate; and .1 g dietary fiber.

ADD IT! For a spicy treat, add a cinnamon stick to the mixture as it's heating. Remove the cinnamon stick and discard it before serving the brandy-wine.

DID YOU KNOW? Blackberry brandy is brandy flavored with blackberries and contains only water, alcohol, and the essential oil of the berry. Blackberry liqueur is similar to blackberry brandy, but it contains less alcohol.

☕ Mulled Grape Cider

This warm, spicy cider fills your home with the tantalizing aroma of grapes. It looks pretty when served from the slow cooker garnished with lemon and orange slices.

COOKING TIME: 2 to 3 hours
ATTENTION: Sample after 1 hour, then every 30 minutes

1 quart (.95 L) grape juice

2 cinnamon sticks

1 lemon slice

Put the grape juice, cinnamon sticks, and lemon slice in the slow cooker and stir to combine. Cover and heat on HIGH for 2 to 3 hours, sampling the cider after 1 hour, then every 30 minutes thereafter.

When the cinnamon flavor is just right, remove the cinnamon sticks and discard them. Remove the lemon slice or keep it as a garnish. Serve the cider warm in mugs.

YIELD: 8 servings

NUTRITIONAL ANALYSIS: One serving of the basic recipe contains 77 calories; .1 g fat; .8 g protein; 19 g carbohydrate; and .1 g dietary fiber.

☕ Tropical Tea

Enjoy a little slice of tropical paradise any day. Serve tea in a tall glass, with an orange wedge as a garnish.

COOKING TIME: 2 to 3 hours
ATTENTION: Sample after 1 hour, then every 30 minutes

2 quarts (1.9 L) boiling water

8 black teabags

1½ pints (710 ml) pineapple-orange juice

1 cinnamon stick

Pour the boiling water into the slow cooker and add the teabags. Let the teabags steep for 5 minutes, then remove and discard them.

Add the pineapple-orange juice and cinnamon stick, and stir to combine. Cover and heat on LOW for 2 to 3 hours, sampling the tea after 1 hour, then every 30 minutes thereafter.

When the cinnamon flavor is just right, remove the cinnamon stick and discard it. Serve the tea immediately or keep it warm in the slow cooker.

YIELD: 10 servings

NUTRITIONAL ANALYSIS: One serving of the basic recipe contains 111 calories; .1 g fat; 3 g protein; 25 g carbohydrate; and .8 g dietary fiber.

TIP: Substitute orange-flavored tea or herb tea for the black tea.

☕ Raspberry Iced Tea

Yes, this is an iced tea recipe made in a slow cooker. You will need to make this ahead so that you have time to chill the beverage before serving.

PREP TIME: 10 minutes   **COOKING TIME:** 1½ hours
ADDITIONAL STEPS: Strain and chill the tea after cooking

8 black tea bags, or 1 cup (115 g) loose black tea

2 cups (500 g) frozen raspberries, plus some fresh ones for garnish

1 cup (200 g) sugar

Put the tea, raspberries, sugar, and 8 cups (1880 ml) water into the slow cooker. Stir. Cook for 1¹/₂ hours on HIGH. Strain the tea, pushing down on the solids in the strainer. Discard the tea and raspberries. Chill the brewed tea. Serve over ice with additional raspberries for garnish.

YIELD: 6 to 8 servings

NUTRITIONAL ANALYSIS: 166 calories; trace fat (0.5% calories from fat); 1 g protein; 43 g carbohydrate; 3 g dietary fiber; 0 mg cholesterol; 4 mg sodium. Exchanges: 1 fruit; 1¹/₂ other carbohydrates.

☕ Lemon-Mint Tea

This blend of lemon, chamomile, and mint refreshes and soothes at the same time. It's delicious sweetened with honey.

COOKING TIME: 1 to 2 hours　　　　　　　**ATTENTION:** Minimal

1¹/₂ **quarts (1.4 L) cold water**

6 black tea with lemon-flavor teabags

3 chamomile teabags

6 sprigs fresh mint

Pour the cold water into the slow cooker and add the teabags and fresh mint. Cover and heat on HIGH for 1 to 2 hours, or until the water begins to simmer.

Remove and discard the teabags and mint. Serve the tea immediately or keep it warm in the slow cooker.

YIELD: 6 servings

NUTRITIONAL ANALYSIS: One serving of the basic recipe contains 58 calories; 0 g fat; 3 g protein; 13 g carbohydrate; and .7 g dietary fiber.

IT'S GOOD FOR YOU This flavorful herb tea is not only delicious, it's ideal for settling an upset stomach or as a finishing touch to a big meal.

☕ Chai Tea

Traditionally served piping hot in little clay cups that are discarded after use, chai tea is fun to sip with a meal or dessert. Enjoy it with whipped cream and a sprinkle of ground cinnamon or cocoa.

COOKING TIME: 1 to 2 hours   **ATTENTION:** Minimal

4½ cups (1.1 L) cold water

6 chai teabags

½ cup plus 2 tablespoons (125 g) orange or clover honey

4½ cups (1.1 L) milk

Pour the cold water into the slow cooker and add the teabags. Cover and heat on HIGH for 1 to 2 hours, or until the water begins to simmer. Carefully remove the teabags with a slotted spoon.

Turn the slow cooker to LOW. Add the honey and stir until it has dissolved. Add the milk and stir again. Serve the tea immediately or keep it warm in the slow cooker.

YIELD: 12 servings

NUTRITIONAL ANALYSIS: One serving of the basic recipe contains 121 calories; 3 g fat; 5 g protein; 20 g carbohydrate; and .4 g dietary fiber.

ADD IT! Crush a large knob of fresh ginger and add it to the cold water along with the teabags. Remove when you remove the teabags.

☕ Cinnamon-Spiked Coffee

Zesty coffee with a whiff of cinnamon and a whisper of brown sugar. Garnish it with whipped cream and a cinnamon stick.

COOKING TIME: 2 to 3 hours
ATTENTION: Sample after 1 hour, then every 30 minutes

---

1 quart (.95 L) strong coffee

¼ cup (56 g) brown sugar, packed

1 cinnamon stick

Put the coffee, brown sugar, and cinnamon stick in the slow cooker and stir to combine. Cover and heat on LOW for 2 to 3 hours, sampling the coffee after 1 hour, then every 30 minutes thereafter.

When the cinnamon flavor is just right, remove the cinnamon stick and discard it. Serve the coffee black or with a generous helping of half-and-half.

YIELD: 4 servings

NUTRITIONAL ANALYSIS: One serving of the basic recipe contains 57 calories; 0 g fat; .3 g protein; 14 g carbohydrate; and 0 g dietary fiber.

☕ Raspberry Cappuccino

Perfect for a shower or bachelorette party—a raspberry-flavored explosion in a mug! It looks and tastes festive in an Irish coffee mug.

COOKING TIME: 30 to 60 minutes   **ATTENTION:** Minimal

4¹⁄₂ cups (1.1 L) strong coffee

2 cups (.47 L) half and half

1 cup (.24 L) raspberry liqueur

Combine the ingredients into the slow cooker and mix well. Cover and heat on LOW for 30 to 60 minutes, or until the flavors have melded.

Warm 10 mugs in the oven or microwave. Divide the espresso mixture among the warm mugs, then fill the mugs the rest of the way with the prepared whipped cream. Serve the cappuccino immediately.

YIELD: 10 servings

NUTRITIONAL ANALYSIS: One serving of the basic recipe contains 101 calories; 6 g fat; 2 g protein; 11 g carbohydrate; and 0 g dietary fiber.

ADD IT! Top the whipped cream with chocolate curls, dust it with ground cinnamon or cocoa powder, or drizzle it with raspberry sauce.

☕ Café Mocha

For an event or just to savor the day with your sweetheart, enjoy this chocolaty taste treat along with Belgian chocolates, Cinnamon Walnuts (page 74), or fresh strawberries dipped in dark chocolate.

COOKING TIME: 2 to 3 hours
ATTENTION: Stir occasionally; watch to keep from simmering

5 cups (1.2 L) strong coffee
Five to six 1-ounce (28-g) envelopes hot chocolate mix
Prepared whipped cream

Put the coffee and hot chocolate mix in the slow cooker and stir until the hot chocolate mix has completely dissolved. Cover and heat on LOW for 2 to 3 hours, or until the mixture is hot, stirring occasionally; do not let it simmer.

Serve the coffee in mugs, topped with dollops of the whipped cream.

YIELD: 6 servings

NUTRITIONAL ANALYSIS: One serving of the basic recipe (made with 5 envelopes hot chocolate mix and without whipped cream) contains 86 calories; .7 g fat; 1 g protein; 22 g carbohydrate; and 1 g dietary fiber.

ADD IT! Dust the whipped cream with ground cinnamon or cocoa powder.

IT'S GOOD FOR YOU Chocolate's health benefits have been making headlines. It's now being touted as a preventive for everything from heart disease to cancer—consumed in moderation, of course! So be good to your heart and your sweetheart, and serve up this rich chocolate concoction.

☕ Peppermint Hot Cocoa

This recipe is great for large groups.

COOKING TIME: 2 to 3 hours
ATTENTION: Add more ingredients after 30 minutes; watch to keep from simmering

1 gallon (3.8 L) cold milk
1 to 2 cups (235 to 470 ml) chocolate-flavored syrup
½ to 1 cup (120 to 235 ml) peppermint-flavored syrup

Pour the cold milk into the slow cooker. Cover and heat on LOW for 30 minutes, or until the milk is warm enough to dissolve the syrups.

Add the chocolate- and peppermint-flavored syrups and gently stir until the syrups have dissolved. Cover and continue heating on LOW for another $1^1/2$ to $2^1/2$ hours, or until the mixture is hot; do not let it simmer.

Serve the cocoa warm in mugs topped with whipped cream and crushed mint candies.

YIELD: 18 servings

NUTRITIONAL ANALYSIS: One serving of the basic recipe (made with 1 cup chocolate-flavored syrup and $^1/2$ cup peppermint-flavored syrup) contains 188 calories; 7 g fat; 8 g protein; 25 g carbohydrate; and .4 g dietary fiber.

TRY THIS! Instead of peppermint, try substituting raspberry or hazelnut syrup.

☕ Coquito Eggnog

It's good to create a new holiday tradition. Chilled coconut eggnog is a delicious tradition in Puerto Rico. Try it and see why.

COOKING TIME: 1 to 2 hours   **ATTENTION:** Watch to keep from simmering

2 quarts (1.9 L) eggnog

1 pint (475 ml) coconut milk

$^1/2$ teaspoon ground nutmeg

Pour the eggnog and coconut milk into the slow cooker and stir gently to combine. Cover and heat on LOW for 1 to 2 hours, or until the mixture is hot; do not let it simmer.

Ladle the eggnog into mugs, dust it with nutmeg, and serve it warm. To be traditional, refrigerate it for several hours and serve it chilled.

YIELD: 10 servings

NUTRITIONAL ANALYSIS: One serving of the basic recipe contains 383 calories; 27 g fat; 9 g protein; 30 g carbohydrate; and 1 g dietary fiber.

IT'S GOOD FOR YOU Coconut oil has been touted as the new weight-loss miracle food! Try cooking with coconut oil instead of your current cooking oil—unlike coconut milk and flesh, the oil won't add a coconut flavor to your food.

CHAPTER 7
DIPS AND APPETIZERS

Simplify, simplify, simplify. That's the mantra. It has a romantic appeal at first blush, but what does it really mean? Related to good eats, it can mean taking out a slow cooker or two for your next party. With a slow cooker you can prepare and cook an appetizer or dip quickly, plus keep it warm while serving it! No need for chafing dishes, warming trays, fuel for heating, matches, or a lighter. Better yet, simplify dinner—serve a hearty appetizer as the main course!

Beefy Cheese Dip

Prepare this dish with mild or spicy tomatoes—it's up to you. Serve it with tortilla chips and a side of guacamole on shredded lettuce.

COOKING TIME: 30 to 60 minutes	**ATTENTION:** Minimal

Two 16-ounce (455-g) jars double cheddar cheese sauce

1 pound (455 g) ground beef, browned and drained

One 10-ounce (280-g) can diced tomatoes with green chiles, undrained

Put the cheese sauce, browned ground beef, and diced tomatoes in the slow cooker and stir to combine. Cover and cook on LOW for 30 to 60 minutes, or until the mixture is hot and the cheese has melted.

Stir the dip and serve it immediately, or keep it warm in the slow cooker.

YIELD: 12 appetizer servings

NUTRITIONAL ANALYSIS: One serving of the basic recipe contains 195 calories; 14 g fat; 10 g protein; 7 g carbohydrate; and .7 g dietary fiber.

TRY THIS! Next time you're in a festive mood, call up some friends, whip up this dip and a batch of margaritas, put a favorite movie on, and kick back.

Chili con Queso Dip

Always the first to go at parties, this dip is wonderful with tortilla chips or with warm flour tortillas torn into bite-size pieces. The recipe is easily doubled.

COOKING TIME: 3 to 3½ hours
ATTENTION: Remove cover during final hour

1½ pounds (683 g) pasteurized processed cheese food, Mexican-flavored or plain, cut into cubes

One 19-ounce (540-g) can chunky-style chili, with or without beans

½ cup (30 g) chopped fresh cilantro

Salt and freshly ground black pepper

Put the cheese food, chili, and cilantro in the slow cooker and stir to combine. Season with salt and pepper to taste and stir again. Cover and cook on LOW for 2 to 2$\frac{1}{2}$ hours, or until the cheese has melted, stirring occasionally.

Uncover and cook for 1 more hour, or until the mixture is hot.

Stir the dip and serve it immediately, or keep it warm in the slow cooker.

YIELD: 12 appetizer servings

NUTRITIONAL ANALYSIS: One serving of the basic recipe (made with chili without beans) contains 339 calories; 23 g fat; 22 g protein; 16 g carbohydrate; and 1 g dietary fiber.

ADD IT! Garnish the dip with shredded cheddar cheese, chopped tomato, a dollop of sour cream, or chopped green onion for added visual appeal.

Sausage Nacho Dip

Sausage, cheese, and salsa combine for a marvelous dip to go with tortilla chips, soft tortilla triangles, or sourdough bread cubes. Sit back and watch it disappear.

COOKING TIME: 2$\frac{1}{2}$ to 3$\frac{1}{2}$ hours   **ATTENTION:** Stir occasionally

1 pound (455 g) bulk garlic sausage, browned and drained

1 pound (455 g) pasteurized processed cheese food, Mexican-flavored or plain, cut into cubes

One 16-ounce (455 g) jar mild or medium-hot chunky-style salsa

Salt and freshly ground black pepper

Put the browned sausage, cheese food, and salsa in the slow cooker and stir to combine. Cover and cook on LOW for 2$\frac{1}{2}$ to 3$\frac{1}{2}$ hours, or until the cheese has melted and the mixture is hot, stirring occasionally.

Season the dip with salt and pepper to taste and stir it again. Serve the dip warm from the slow cooker.

YIELD: 12 appetizer servings

NUTRITIONAL ANALYSIS: One serving of the basic recipe contains 358 calories; 30 g fat; 17 g protein; 10 g carbohydrate; and .6 g dietary fiber.

TIP: If you don't have sausage on hand, replace it with 1 pound (455 g) ground beef, browned and drained, combined with 1 small onion, chopped and sautéed.

🥬 Pepper Jack-Chicken Dip

The zesty cheese makes this change-of-pace dip a crowd pleaser. Serve with white tortilla chips or French bread cubes.

COOKING TIME: 2 to 3 hours   **ATTENTION:** Minimal

One 10¾-ounce (305-g) can condensed cream of chicken soup

One 10-ounce (280-g) can chicken breast, drained

8 ounces (225 g) hot pepper jack cheese, shredded

Salt and freshly ground black pepper

Put the condensed soup, chicken breast, and cheese in the slow cooker and stir to combine. Season with salt and pepper to taste and stir the mixture again. Cover and cook on LOW for 2 to 3 hours.

Stir the dip and serve it immediately, or keep it warm in the slow cooker.

YIELD: 8 appetizer servings

NUTRITIONAL ANALYSIS: One serving of the basic recipe contains 194 calories; 13 g fat; 16 g protein; 3 g carbohydrate; and .1 g dietary fiber.

ADD IT! Add ¼ to ½ teaspoon crushed red pepper along with the salt and black pepper to spice up the dip even more.

TRY THIS! If you're not a hot-pepper fan but still want a dip that packs a flavor punch, substitute extra-sharp white cheddar cheese for the pepper jack.

🥬 Crab Dip

Easy to make and oh-so-flavorful. Serve this dip in an edible bread bowl or with assorted crackers, raw vegetables, or blue corn chips.

COOKING TIME: 2 to 4 hours   **ATTENTION:** Minimal

One 8-ounce (225-g) package cream cheese, softened

1 scant cup (225 g) mayonnaise

1 pound (455 g) lump crabmeat, drained and cartilage removed

Put the softened cream cheese in a medium-size bowl. Add mayonnaise to taste and stir to combine. Transfer the mixture to the slow cooker. Add the crabmeat and gently stir, being careful not to shred the lumps. Cover and cook on LOW for 2 to 4 hours.

Stir the dip and serve it immediately, or keep it warm in the slow cooker for up to 2 hours.

YIELD: 8 appetizer servings

NUTRITIONAL ANALYSIS: One serving of the basic recipe contains 352 calories; 34 g fat; 14 g protein; .8 g carbohydrate; and 0 g dietary fiber.

ADD IT! Add 1 onion, finely minced, to the mayonnaise and cream cheese mixture. Add $1/2$ teaspoon Old Bay Seafood Seasoning for a special treat.

TRY THIS! Serve this decadent dip with an ice-cold glass of rose, sweet, or dry wine as you and your guests prefer. Great with icy mugs of beer, too!

⬤ Hot Artichoke Heart Dip

Smooth and creamy, tangy and zesty, this artichoke dip has become a cocktail party classic. Try serving it with pita crisps for dipping.

PREP TIME: 10 minutes   **COOKING TIME:** $1^1/2$ hours
ADDITIONAL STEPS: Process the ingredients to blend

2 (14-ounce or 395-g) cans artichoke hearts

2 (8-ounce or 225-g) packages cream cheese

$1^1/2$ cups (120 g) shredded Parmesan cheese, divided

Black pepper to taste

Drain the artichoke hearts and combine them with the cream cheese and half the Parmesan cheese in a food processor. Add black pepper to taste and process until smooth.

Scoop into the slow cooker and top with the remaining $3/4$ cup (60 g) cheese. Cook on HIGH for $1^1/2$ hours.

YIELD: 12 to 15 servings as a party dip

NUTRITIONAL ANALYSIS: 159 calories; 13 g fat (72.3% calories from fat); 7 g protein; 4 g carbohydrate; 0 g dietary fiber; 39 mg cholesterol; 357 mg sodium.

ADD IT! Stir in a clove or two of chopped garlic to add another dimension.

Hot Spinach Dip

It's funny how many people turn up their noses at spinach—unless it's served in this yummy dip. Our theory is that the cheese somehow cancels out the spinach.

PREP TIME: 10 minutes   **COOKING TIME:** 2 hours

ADDITIONAL STEPS: Add the cheese in the last hour

2 (10-ounce or 280-g) packages frozen chopped spinach

1 (16-ounce or 475-ml) jar Alfredo sauce with garlic

1 cup (80 g) shredded Parmesan cheese

Combine the frozen spinach and the Alfredo sauce in the slow cooker. (If you're using a small slow cooker, you may need to cut the frozen blocks of spinach in half.) Cook on HIGH for 1 hour. Stir to combine thoroughly. Sprinkle the Parmesan cheese on top and continue to cook, without stirring, for 1 hour.

YIELD: 6 to 8 servings as a party dip

NUTRITIONAL ANALYSIS: 168 calories; 13 g fat (66.8% calories from fat); 9 g protein; 6 g carbohydrate; 2 g dietary fiber; 39 mg cholesterol; 524 mg sodium.

ADD IT! Stir in a clove or two of chopped garlic to deepen the garlic flavor.

SERVING SUGGESTION: Serve with chips or slices of French bread for dipping.

Cheese Fondue

The classic cheeses for this dish are Emmental and Gruyère, but any favorite firm cheese will do. Some like to add a shot of Kirshwasser, a fiery cherry brandy, just before serving.

PREP TIME: 10 minutes   **COOKING TIME:** 2 hours

ADDITIONAL STEPS: Add the cheese after 1 hour, stir after 1$\frac{1}{2}$ hours

2 cups (475 ml) white wine

1 pound (455 g) Swiss cheese, cut into small cubes

$\frac{1}{4}$ cup (30 g) all-purpose flour

Salt and pepper to taste

Put the wine in the slow cooker and cook on HIGH for 1 hour. Dredge the cheese in the flour. Add the cheese and flour, plus salt and pepper to taste, to the hot wine. Do not stir. Cover and cook for $1/2$ hour. Stir until smooth. Continue to cook for $1/2$ hour more. Stir to make sure there are no chunks of unmelted cheese remaining.

Serving suggestion: Serve with bread and fruit (such as apple and pear pieces) for dunking.

YIELD: 4 to 6 servings

NUTRITIONAL ANALYSIS: 357 calories; 21 g fat (61.6% calories from fat); 22 g protein; 7 g carbohydrate; trace dietary fiber; 69 mg cholesterol; 201 mg sodium.

Broccoli and Cheese Dip

Enjoy how simple and easy it is to make this popular dip. Delicious with tortilla chips, crackers, and bread chunks.

COOKING TIME: 3 to 4 hours
ATTENTION: Stir occasionally during first 30 minutes; add more ingredients after 30 minutes

1 pound (455 g) pasteurized processed cheese food, cut into cubes

One 16-ounce (455-g) bag frozen broccoli florets, partially thawed

One 10³/₄-ounce (305-g) can condensed cream of broccoli soup

Salt

Put the cheese food in the slow cooker. Cover and heat on LOW for 30 minutes, or until the cheese has melted, stirring occasionally.

In a medium-size bowl, combine the broccoli florets and condensed soup. Add the broccoli-soup mixture to the melted cheese in the slow cooker and stir to blend. Season the mixture with salt to taste and stir it again. Cover and cook on LOW for $2^{1}/_{2}$ to $3^{1}/_{2}$ hours, or until the mixture is hot.

Stir the dip and serve it immediately, or keep it warm in the slow cooker.

YIELD: 10 appetizer servings

NUTRITIONAL ANALYSIS: One serving of the basic recipe contains 258 calories; 18 g fat; 16 g protein; 13 g carbohydrate; and 2 g dietary fiber.

ADD IT! Add 2 cloves garlic, minced, to the melted cheese. For a creamier dip, stir in $1/2$ cup (115 g) sour cream right before serving.

◉ White Cheese-Mushroom Dip

A tasty twist on the usual white-cheese dip. Serve with breadsticks or whole-wheat crackers.

COOKING TIME: $1^1/2$ to $2^1/2$ hours   **ATTENTION:** Stir occasionally

---

4 cups (452 g) shredded asadero cheese

1 cup (235 ml) milk or half-and-half

One 4-ounce (115-g) can marinated sliced mushrooms

Salt

Put the asadero cheese, milk, and mushrooms in the slow cooker and stir to combine. Season the mixture with salt to taste and stir it again. Cover and cook on LOW for $1^1/2$ to $2^1/2$ hours, or until the cheese has melted, stirring occasionally.

Stir the dip and serve it hot from the slow cooker, accompanied by breadsticks or crackers.

YIELD: 18 appetizer servings

NUTRITIONAL ANALYSIS: One serving of the basic recipe (made with milk) contains 102 calories; 8 g fat; 6 g protein; 1 g carbohydrate; and .2 g dietary fiber.

WATCH THIS: Make sure the cheese you choose is true asadero, not Muenster with the rind removed. This type of Mexican cheese, also called Chihuahua or Oaxaca cheese, melts without separating into oil and solids. This makes it perfect for slow-cooker dips. You can find it at the supermarket in balls, braids, or rounds.

🫑 Spicy Bagna Calda

This classic Italian recipe is great for dunking raw veggies or crusty Italian bread. The gentle heat in a slow cooker keeps the extra-virgin olive oil fragrant and flavorful.

PREP TIME: 10 minutes | **COOKING TIME:** 2 hours

4 anchovy fillets

12 cloves garlic, peeled

1 tablespoon (3.6 g) dried red pepper flakes

3 cups (705 ml) extra-virgin olive oil

Mince the anchovy fillets and, using the side of a chef's knife, mash them into a paste. Lightly smash the garlic cloves with the side of a chef's knife. Combine all the ingredients in the slow cooker and cook on LOW for 2 hours.

YIELD: 10 to 12 servings as a party dip

NUTRITIONAL ANALYSIS: 485 calories; 54 g fat (98.7% calories from fat); 1 g protein; 1 g carbohydrate; trace dietary fiber; 1 mg cholesterol; 50 mg sodium.

🫑 Pizza Dip

All your favorite pizza flavors in a dip. Yummy with tortilla chips, chunks of Italian bread, and breadsticks.

COOKING TIME: 30 to 60 minutes | **ATTENTION:** Minimal

One 8-ounce (225-g) package cream cheese, softened

One 14-ounce (398-g) jar pizza sauce

2 cups (224 g) shredded pizza-blend cheese

Spread the softened cream cheese in the bottom of the slow cooker. Pour the pizza sauce over the cream cheese, then sprinkle the cheese over the sauce. Cover and cook on LOW for 30 to 60 minutes, or until the cheese has melted.

Stir the dip and serve it immediately, or keep it warm in the slow cooker.

YIELD: 10 appetizer servings

NUTRITIONAL ANALYSIS: One serving of the basic recipe contains 178 calories; 15 g fat; 7 g protein; 5 g carbohydrate; and 0 g dietary fiber

ADD IT! Add 2 to 4 ounces (55 to 115 g) pepperoni, sliced and quartered, to the pizza sauce before adding it to the slow cooker.

TRY THIS! For extra decadence, serve this scrumptious dip with pizza breadsticks.

Layered Mexican Dip

Like all the dip recipes, this works best with a 1.5-quart-size slow cooker geared toward dips and such.

PREP TIME: 15 minutes   **COOKING TIME:** 1^1/$_2$ hours

2 (12-ounce or 390-g) cans refried beans, divided

2 (8-ounce or 200-g) packages whipped cream cheese with chives, divided

1 (16-ounce or 470-ml) jar salsa, divided

Spread 1 can of the refried beans on the bottom of the slow cooker. Top with half the cream cheese, then half the salsa. Repeat with the remaining 1 can of beans, 1 package cheese, and 8 ounces (235 ml) salsa. Cook on HIGH for 1^1/$_2$ hours.

YIELD: 10 to 12 as a party dip

NUTRITIONAL ANALYSIS: 197 calories; 13 g fat (59.7% calories from fat); 6 g protein; 14 g carbohydrate; 4 g dietary fiber; 45 mg cholesterol; 557 mg sodium.

ADD IT! Sprinkle the top with a layer of shredded Monterey Jack cheese for extra tang.

SERVING SUGGESTION: Serve with tortilla chips for dipping.

❧ Chili-Cheese Dip

A hot dip with a bit of a bite, sure to heat up any party. If you want to kick it up a notch, add a splash of hot sauce.

COOKING TIME: 3 to 3¹/₂ hours
ATTENTION: Stir occasionally; remove cover during final hour

---

1 pound (455 g) pasteurized processed cheese food, Mexican-flavored or plain, cut into cubes

One 12-ounce (340-g) jar hot chunky-style salsa

One 4-ounce (115-g) can chopped green chile peppers, drained

Salt and freshly ground black pepper

Put the cheese food, salsa, and green chiles in the slow cooker and stir to combine. Season the mixture with salt and pepper to taste and stir it again. Cover and cook on LOW for 2 to 2¹/₂ hours, or until the cheese has melted, stirring occasionally. Uncover and cook for 1 more hour, or until the mixture is hot.

Stir the dip and serve it immediately, or keep it warm in the slow cooker.

YIELD: 8 appetizer servings

NUTRITIONAL ANALYSIS: One serving of the basic recipe contains 300 calories; 21 g fat; 19 g protein; 14 g carbohydrate; and .9 g dietary fiber.

ADD IT! Garnish the dip with shredded cheddar cheese, chopped tomato, a dollop of sour cream, or chopped green onion for added visual appeal. Serve with tortilla chips or warm flour tortillas torn into bite-size pieces.

❧ Party Meatballs

Variety is the spice of life. At your next party, treat your guests to this tasty twist on an old favorite—sweet-and-spicy meatballs.

COOKING TIME: 3¹/₂ to 4¹/₂ hours on LOW, 1¹/₂ to 2¹/₂ hours on HIGH
ATTENTION: Minimal

1¹/₂ cups (480 g) raspberry jelly

¹/₂ cup (169 g) chili sauce

One 1-pound (455-g) bag frozen fully cooked meatballs, completely thawed

Put the raspberry jelly and chili sauce in the slow cooker and stir to combine. Add the meatballs and stir to coat them with the sauce. Cover and cook on LOW for 3½ to 4½ hours or on HIGH for 1½ to 2½ hours, or until the mixture is hot.

Before serving, stir the meatballs to coat them with sauce again.

YIELD: 6 appetizer servings

NUTRITIONAL ANALYSIS: One serving of the basic recipe contains 444 calories; 20 g fat; 10 g protein; 61 g carbohydrate; and 3 g dietary fiber.

TIP: This recipe can be easily doubled for big crowds.

❧ Cranberry Meatballs

The cranberries make this appetizer great for holiday parties. It's tasty enough for the rest of the year, too.

COOKING TIME: 3 to 4 hours   **ATTENTION:** Minimal

One 16-ounce (455-g) can whole-berry or jellied cranberry sauce

¾ cup (169) chili sauce

¼ cup (60 ml) water

Two 1-pound (455-g) bags frozen fully cooked meatballs, completely thawed

Put the cranberry sauce, chili sauce, and water in the slow cooker and stir to combine. Add the meatballs and stir to coat them with the sauce. Cover and cook on LOW for 3 to 4 hours.

Stir the meatballs again, and serve them warm from the slow cooker.

YIELD: 8 servings

NUTRITIONAL ANALYSIS: One serving of the basic recipe contains 439 calories; 30 g fat; 15 g protein; 31 g carbohydrate; and 4 g dietary fiber.

ADD IT! Add 2 packed tablespoons (28 g) brown sugar and 1 teaspoon lemon juice to the sauce.

Apple-Maple-Kielbasa Appetizer

Maple, applesauce, and sausage blend to perfection in this kielbasa appetizer. Serve with fancy toothpicks and cute cocktail napkins.

COOKING TIME: 6 to 8 hours　　　　　　　**ATTENTION:** Minimal

2 pounds (910 g) fully cooked Polska kielbasa sausage, sliced into ½-inch (1.3-cm) coins

One 16-ounce (455-g) jar natural applesauce

¾ cup (242 g) pure maple syrup

In a large skillet over medium heat, brown the sausage coins to render out the fat. Drain the coins between several layers of paper toweling.

Put the applesauce and maple syrup in the slow cooker and stir to combine. Add the sausage coins and stir to coat them with the sauce. Cover and cook on LOW for 6 to 8 hours, or until the mixture is hot.

YIELD: 12 appetizer servings

NUTRITIONAL ANALYSIS: One serving of the basic recipe contains 302 calories; 21 g fat; 10 g protein; 19 g carbohydrate; and .4 g dietary fiber.

IT'S GOOD FOR YOU Pure maple syrup is not just a delightful sweetener, extracted from the sap of sugar maple trees, which flow amber sap into buckets for up to a century. Maple syrup contains fewer calories than honey and is more nutritious. It's a decent source of calcium, iron, and the B vitamin thiamin. That's logical, really, as it takes up to 50 gallons (189 L) of sap to produce 1 gallon (3.78 L) of syrup.

Spicy Cocktail Franks

If you remember your father in long swoopy sideburns and your mom in polyester bell-bottoms, then you are from the Golden Age of the Cocktail Wiener. These yummy little dogs aren't as common at parties these days, but give them a try— they're still one of our favorite guilty pleasures! Don't forget to put out the tooth- picks so that guests can serve themselves.

PREP TIME: 10 minutes　　　　　　　**COOKING TIME:** 3 hours

2 medium onions

2 (1-pound or 455-g) packages cocktail franks

1 (12-ounce or 355-ml) jar chili sauce

Dice the onions into small pieces. Combine the onion, cocktail franks, and chili sauce in the slow cooker and stir. Cook on LOW for 3 hours.

YIELD: 10 to 12 servings as a party appetizer

NUTRITIONAL ANALYSIS: 255 calories; 22 g fat (78.2% calories from fat); 9 g protein; 5 g carbohydrate; 1 g dietary fiber; 38 mg cholesterol; 855 mg sodium.

✿ Classic Shrimp Cocktail

A slow cooker's gentle heat makes it perfect for poaching shrimp so that they remain plump, moist, and tender. Use good-size shrimp, at 21 to 25 per pound (455 g) or larger, that are shelled and deveined except for the tail.

PREP TIME: 10 minutes   **COOKING TIME:** 1 1/2 hours
ADDITIONAL STEPS: Chill the shrimp after poaching

2 cups (470 ml) white wine

3 tablespoons (22.5 g) pickling spice mixture

Salt and pepper to taste

2 pounds (910 g) shrimp, peeled and deveined, with the tail on

Combine the wine, pickling spice mixture, salt, pepper, and 4 cups (940 ml) of water in the slow cooker. Cook on HIGH for 1 hour. Add the shrimp and reduce to LOW. Cook for about 1/2 hour, until the shrimp are pink, opaque, and firm. Drain the shrimp and chill for at least 2 hours.

YIELD: 8 to 10 servings as an appetizer

NUTRITIONAL ANALYSIS: 137 calories; 2 g fat (18.2% calories from fat); 19 g protein; 2 g carbohydrate; trace dietary fiber; 138 mg cholesterol; 138 mg sodium.

SERVING SUGGESTION: These are delicious with lemon wedges and cocktail sauce.

Cajun Barbecue Shrimp

These shrimp cooked in spicy melted butter are always a hit. Our cholesterol couldn't take this dish on a daily basis, but it's lip-smacking good. Look for easy-peel shrimp at your grocery store.

PREP TIME: 10 minutes   **COOKING TIME:** 2 hours
ADDITIONAL STEPS: Add the shrimp in the last hour

2 sticks (1/2 pound or 225 g) butter

1/4 cup (30 g) Cajun spice mix

4 tablespoons (40 g) chopped garlic

2 pounds (910 g) shell-on shrimp, thawed if frozen

Combine the butter, Cajun spice mix, and garlic in the slow cooker. Cook on LOW for 1 hour. Add the shrimp, stirring to coat with the melted butter and spices. Turn the slow cooker on HIGH. Cook for 1/2 to 1 hour, until the shrimp are pink and firm.

YIELD: 8 to 10 as a party appetizer

NUTRITIONAL ANALYSIS: 275 calories; 20 g fat (65.8% calories from fat); 19 g protein; 4 g carbohydrate; 1 g dietary fiber; 188 mg cholesterol; 580 mg sodium.

ADD IT! Toss in a medium tomato, finely chopped.

SERVING SUGGESTION: Serve with bread to mop up the butter (and make sure there are plenty of napkins!).

Teriyaki Wings

Find a nice, thick Teriyaki sauce for this recipe and watch these goodies evaporate into thin air.

PREP TIME: 25 minutes   **COOKING TIME:** 2 hours 15 minutes
ADDITIONAL STEPS: Broil the wings; add pineapple in the last 15 minutes

3 pounds (1365 g) chicken wings

1 1/2 cups (355 ml) Teriyaki sauce

1 (16-ounce or 455-g) can pineapple chunks (in juice)

Preheat the broiler. Spread the wings on a baking pan and broil for 10 minutes. Turn and broil another 10 minutes, until crispy.

Combine the wings and the Teriyaki sauce in the slow cooker. Cook on HIGH for 2 hours. Drain the pineapple chunks and stir them gently into the wings. Continue to cook, with the cover off, for 15 minutes.

YIELD: 8 to 10 servings as an appetizer

NUTRITIONAL ANALYSIS: 214 calories; 12 g fat (49.7% calories from fat); 16 g protein; 11 g carbohydrate; trace dietary fiber; 57 mg cholesterol; 1710 mg sodium.

☙ Fruit Chutney

Consider making your Fruit Chutney separate from the holiday ham. Your vegetarian friends and relatives will love you for it.

COOKING TIME: 6 to 8 hours | **ATTENTION:** Minimal

One 12-ounce (340-g) jar fruit chutney

1 cup (175 g) chopped mixed dried fruit with raisins

1 tablespoon (14 ml) raspberry balsamic vinegar

Put the fruit chutney, mixed dried fruit with raisins, and balsamic vinegar in the slow cooker and stir to combine. Cover and cook on LOW for 6 to 8 hours, or until the flavors have melded.

Turn the heat OFF and allow the chutney to cool, then transfer the chutney to a covered bowl and store it in the refrigerator. Serve it at room temperature.

YIELD: 6 servings

NUTRITIONAL ANALYSIS: One serving of the basic recipe contains 181 calories; .3 g fat; .5 g protein; 46 g carbohydrate; and 3 g dietary fiber.

TRY THIS! Make Ham and Fruit Chutney. Put a fully cooked ham in the slow cooker, then combine all the other ingredients in a separate bowl and pour them over the ham. Cover and cook on LOW for 6 to 8 hours.

❀ Apple Butter

What's cooking for breakfast? Serve Apple Butter on your favorite breakfast bread, pancakes, or waffles, or with apple or pear wedges.

COOKING TIME: 10 to 11 hours
ATTENTION: Stir once an hour; mash apples and add another ingredient after 4$\frac{1}{2}$ to 5 hours

---

14 medium cooking apples (such as Jonathan, Granny Smith, or Rome), peeled or unpeeled, cored, and sliced

1 cup (235 ml) apple juice

2$\frac{1}{2}$ cups (473 g) Cinnamon Sugar (page 29)

Sterilize 2 glass jars with tight-fitting lids and set them aside. Spray the inside of the slow cooker with cooking spray.

Put the apples and apple juice in the slow cooker. Cover and cook on HIGH for 4$\frac{1}{2}$ to 5 hours, or until the apples are tender, stirring once an hour.

Turn the heat OFF and allow the slow cooker to cool enough so that you can handle the ceramic pot safely. Mash the apples with a fork until they're fairly smooth. If desired, strain them to remove the peels or pulse them in small batches in a blender or food processor, then return them to the slow cooker. Add the Cinnamon Sugar and stir to combine. Cover and cook on HIGH for another 5$\frac{1}{2}$ to 6 hours, stirring at least once an hour.

Once the apple butter has become thick and spreadable, turn the slow cooker OFF. Cool the apple butter to room temperature. Ladle the apple butter into the prepared jars and screw on the lids. Store the apple butter in the refrigerator.

YIELD: 16 servings

NUTRITIONAL ANALYSIS: One serving of the basic recipe contains 192 calories; 5 g fat; .3 g protein; 50 g carbohydrate; and 5 g dietary fiber.

ADD IT: Add $\frac{1}{4}$ teaspoon ground cloves and/or $\frac{1}{2}$ teaspoon ground ginger along with the Cinnamon Sugar for a spicier apple-butter flavor.

✿ Curried Party Mix

Soothe the crunchy munchies with this spicy party mix. Enjoy with plenty of your favorite beverage.

COOKING TIME: 4 to 6 hours
ATTENTION: Stir every 30 minutes; change heat setting after 30 minutes

3 tablespoons (42 g) butter, melted

1 teaspoon (2 g) curry powder

7 cups (343 g) bite-size square cereal, rice, corn, and/or oat flavors

Put the melted butter and curry powder in the slow cooker and stir to combine. Add the cereal and stir until the pieces are evenly coated. Cook uncovered on HIGH for 2 hours, stirring every 30 minutes.

Reduce the heat to LOW and cook for an additional 2 to 4 hours, or until the cereal becomes a golden color.

Line a baking sheet with several layers of paper toweling. Transfer the party mix to the baking sheet and allow it to cool.

When the party mix has completely cooled, serve it immediately or pour it into an airtight container for storage.

YIELD: 28 appetizer servings

NUTRITIONAL ANALYSIS: One serving of the basic recipe contains 61 calories; 2 g fat; 1 g protein; 12 g carbohydrate; and 2 g dietary fiber.

ADD IT! Increase the butter to 4 tablespoons (55 g), and add 1 cup (150 g) shelled mixed nuts and 1 cup (227 g) pretzel sticks along with the cereal. Increase the curry powder to taste. Lightly sprinkle the party mix with 1 teaspoon salt while it's cooling on the baking sheet.

Curried Almonds

Are you a party nut? Or do you just like serving them? Curried Almonds are a crunchy addition to chicken salad, curried rice, or your party table.

COOKING TIME: 3¹/₂ to 5 hours
ATTENTION: Change heat setting and uncover after 2 to 3 hours

8 tablespoons (1 stick, or 112 g) butter, melted

1 tablespoon (6 g) curry powder

1 teaspoon salt

8 cups (2 pounds, or 910 g) blanched whole almonds

Put the melted butter, curry powder, and salt in the slow cooker and stir to combine. Add the almonds and stir until they're evenly coated. Cover and cook on LOW for 2 to 3 hours.

Raise the heat to HIGH, remove the cover, and cook the mixture for another 1¹/₂ to 2 hours, stirring occasionally.

YIELD: 32 servings

NUTRITIONAL ANALYSIS: One serving of the basic recipe contains 235 calories; 21 g fat; 7 g protein; 7 g carbohydrate; and 4 g dietary fiber.

NOTE: Almonds have almost as much calcium as milk. If that isn't enough to drive you to the store for a bag o' nuts, almonds are also high in the antioxidants selenium and vitamin E.

Cajun Pecans

Try a spicy treat that's a little different—Cajun Pecans. It's a healthy snack with a kick.

COOKING TIME: 1¹/₂ to 2¹/₂ hours
ATTENTION: Change heat setting and remove cover after 15 minutes; stir occasionally

4 tablespoons (55 g) butter, melted

1 teaspoon Cajun seasoning

4 cups (1 pound, or 455 g) pecan halves

Put the melted butter and Cajun seasoning in the slow cooker and stir to combine. Add the pecan halves and stir until they're evenly coated. Cover and cook on HIGH for 15 minutes.

Reduce the heat to LOW and cook uncovered for an additional 1^1/$_2$ to 2 hours, stirring occasionally.

YIELD: 16 servings

NUTRITIONAL ANALYSIS: One serving of the basic recipe contains 206 calories; 21 g fat; 2 g protein; 5 g carbohydrate; and 2 g dietary fiber.

TIP: Pack these pecans into decorative glass jars for holiday gift-giving.

ADD IT! Add a splash of hot sauce—as much as you dare—to the melted butter for an extra hot Cajun taste.

Sugar and Spice Walnuts

Sugar and spice and nuts are nice! Cajun spice adds a hot surprise in place of the expected cinnamon. You can substitute pecans or almonds, if you prefer, with equally tasty results.

PREP TIME: 15 minutes   **COOKING TIME:** 2 hours
ADDITIONAL STEPS: Make the sugar syrup

2 cups (400 g) sugar

3 tablespoons (22.5 g) Cajun spice mix

1 pound (455 g) walnut halves

Turn the slow cooker on HIGH.

Combine the sugar, the spice mix, and ^{1}/$_2$ cup water in a small saucepan. Cook over high heat until the sugar is dissolved. Set aside.

Put the walnuts into a large bowl and pour the sugar syrup over them. Toss to coat the nuts thoroughly. Put them into the slow cooker and cook for 1 to 1^1/$_2$ hours, stirring every half hour, until the nuts are crispy and browned. Cool to room temperature.

YIELD: 8 to 10 servings as a party snack

NUTRITIONAL ANALYSIS: 438 calories; 26 g fat (49.8% calories from fat); 11 g protein; 47 g carbohydrate; 3 g dietary fiber; 0 mg cholesterol; 194 mg sodium.

❧ Cinnamon Walnuts

These exquisite nuts are the perfect complement to fresh peaches, pears, apples, and strawberries. Good together, and good for you.

COOKING TIME: 1$\frac{1}{2}$ to 2$\frac{1}{2}$ hours
ATTENTION: Change heat setting and remove cover after 15 minutes; stir occasionally

4 cups (1 pound, or 455 g) walnut halves

8 tablespoons (1 stick, or 112 g) butter, melted

$\frac{1}{2}$ cup (95 g) Cinnamon Sugar (page 27)

Put the walnut halves and melted butter in the slow cooker and mix well. Add the Cinnamon Sugar and stir until the walnut halves are evenly coated. Cover and cook on HIGH for 15 minutes.

Reduce the heat to LOW and cook uncovered for another 1$\frac{1}{2}$ to 2 hours, or until the nuts are coated with a glaze, stirring occasionally.

Transfer the walnuts to a bowl and allow them to cool completely.

YIELD: 16 appetizer servings

NUTRITIONAL ANALYSIS: One serving of the basic recipe contains 263 calories; 23 g fat; 8 g protein; 10 g carbohydrate; and 2 g dietary fiber.

ADD IT! When the walnuts are done but still in the slow cooker, sprinkle them with $\frac{1}{2}$ teaspoon apple pie spice and stir to coat them evenly.

● Hot and Spicy Nuts

Will you make these specialty nuts mild, scalding, or somewhere in between? Any way you serve them, make sure your guests have a cooling beverage accompaniment.

COOKING TIME: 2¹/₂ to 3¹/₂ hours
ATTENTION: Change heat setting and remove cover after 20 to 25 minutes; stir occasionally

---

5¹/₂ tablespoons (¹/₃ cup, or 75 g) butter, melted

2 teaspoons (6 g) mild or spicy Mexican seasoning

1¹/₂ cups (150 g) shelled whole pecans or walnut halves

Salt

Put the melted butter and Mexican seasoning in the slow cooker and stir to combine. Add the nuts and stir until they're evenly coated. Cover and cook on HIGH for 20 to 25 minutes.

Reduce the heat to LOW and cook uncovered for an additional 2 to 3 hours, stirring occasionally.

Transfer the nuts to a baking sheet and allow them to cool. Sprinkle them with salt to taste. Serve them warm or at room temperature.

YIELD: 12 servings

NUTRITIONAL ANALYSIS: One serving of the basic recipe (made with shelled whole pecans) contains 137 calories; 14 g fat; 1 g protein; 3 g carbohydrate; and 1 g dietary fiber.

ADD IT! Add ¹/₂ teaspoon onion or garlic powder along with the Mexican seasoning, or use onion or garlic salt in place of the plain salt.

CHAPTER 8
SOUPS

Nurturing, soothing, and satisfying—soup is a comfort food that's been feeding the human soul for centuries. More often than not, we eat comfort foods when we're happy, relaxed, and in a mood to reward ourselves. We feel good about choosing healthful foods such as soups that pass the "Mom test"—foods that bring back happy memories of Mom's cooking and nurturing care. A steaming bowl of healthful soup is quite a reward to your palate, especially when it's so easy to fix in the slow cooker. Try our Beef-Barley Soup (page 77), Chicken-Dumpling Soup (page 82), or Creamy Potato Soup (page 96) to start.

❥Beef-Barley Soup

Beef, barley, and vegetables combine for a soup sensation that can't be beat.
Serve in large bowls, and accompany with a green salad and crusty bread.

COOKING TIME: 5 to 6 hours   **ATTENTION:** Minimal

2 quarts (1.9 L) water

One 9-ounce (255-g) package vegetable-barley soup mix

2 pounds (910 g) beef chuck roast, cut into cubes

1 small onion, chopped

Salt and freshly ground black pepper

Put the water and soup mix in the slow cooker and stir until the soup mix
has dissolved. Add the beef cubes and chopped onion, season the mixture
with salt and pepper to taste, and stir again. Cover and cook on LOW for 5
to 6 hours.

YIELD: 10 servings

NUTRITIONAL ANALYSIS: One serving of the basic recipe contains 263 calories;
16 g fat; 16 g protein; 14 g carbohydrate; and 1 g dietary fiber.

TRY THIS! To clean your slow cooker, pour soapy water (about the same strength
as you use to hand-wash dishes) inside your slow cooker and let it cook on
HIGH for at least an hour before rinsing. One more proof that slow cooking is
super-convenient!

❥Beef Borscht

In this recipe, we take a prepared product and transform it into a hearty meal.
Serve with crusty pumpernickel bread and a crisp salad for a warming winter repast.

PREP TIME: 10 minutes   **COOKING TIME:** 7–8 hours
ADDITIONAL STEPS: Break up the meat after cooking

1 pound (455 g) beef stew meat

1 quart (945 ml) prepared borscht

1 cup (230 g) sour cream

Put the beef into the slow cooker and add the borscht. Cook on LOW for 7 to 8 hours. Break up the meat into shreds using tongs or a slotted spoon. Serve with a dollop of sour cream on top.

YIELD: 4 servings

NUTRITIONAL ANALYSIS: 388 calories; 22 g fat (51.2% calories from fat); 28 g protein; 19 g carbohydrate; 3 g dietary fiber; 88 mg cholesterol; 226 mg

Steak, Onion, and Mushroom Noodle Soup

Rich, fall-apart-tender chunks of beef taste mouth-wateringly delicious in an onion-mushroom broth. Ladle into soup bowls and serve with a grilled cheddar cheese sandwich.

COOKING TIME: 8$\frac{1}{2}$ to 11 hours
ATTENTION: Change heat setting and add another ingredient during final 30 to 60 minutes

5$\frac{1}{2}$ cups (1.3 L) water

Two 1.8-ounce (50-g) envelopes onion-mushroom soup mix

1 pound (455 g) round steak, cut into small pieces

8 ounces (225 g) dry egg noodles

Salt and freshly ground black pepper

Put the water and soup mix in the slow cooker and stir until the soup mix has dissolved. Add the steak pieces and stir again. Cover and cook on LOW for 8 to 10 hours.

Raise the heat to HIGH and add the egg noodles. Cover and cook for another 30 to 60 minutes, or until the egg noodles are tender and the soup has thickened.

Before serving, stir the soup and season it with salt and pepper to taste.

YIELD: 8 generous servings

NUTRITIONAL ANALYSIS: One serving of the basic recipe contains 237 calories; 9 g fat; 15 g protein; 24 g carbohydrate; and 1 g dietary fiber.

☙Italian Meatball Soup

This soup couldn't be easier to make. Just drop the ingredients in the slow cooker, and you'll find a tasty soup waiting for you when you return from your long day.

COOKING TIME: 6 to 8 hours   **ATTENTION:** Minimal

1 quart (.95 L) hot water

6 beef bouillon cubes

Two 14-ounce (398-g) cans diced tomatoes with garlic, undrained

1-pound (455-g) bag frozen fully cooked Italian-style meatballs, completely thawed

Put the hot water and bouillon cubes in the slow cooker and stir until the bouillon cubes have dissolved. Add the diced tomatoes and meatballs and stir again. Cover and cook on LOW for 6 to 8 hours.

YIELD: 10 servings

NUTRITIONAL ANALYSIS: One serving of the basic recipe contains 161 calories; 12 g fat; 7 g protein; 7 g carbohydrate; and 2 g dietary fiber.

ADD IT! Add a 16-ounce (455-g) bag frozen mixed vegetables, thawed, along with the diced tomatoes and meatballs.

TRY THIS! Crusty Italian bread, a crisp green salad, and a glass of Chianti makes this a perfect weekday meal.

☙Chicken Soup with Pasta

This cozy concoction is delicious and popular with grown-ups and small-fry alike.

PREP TIME: 20 minutes   **COOKING TIME:** 6–8 hours

1 pound (455 g) boneless, skinless chicken breasts

1 (16-ounce or 455-g) bag frozen vegetable and pasta blend

2 quarts (1890 ml) chicken stock or broth

Salt and pepper to taste

Cut the chicken into small cubes and put the pieces into the slow cooker. Add the vegetable and pasta blend and the stock. Season with salt and pepper, and cook for 6 to 8 hours on LOW. Adjust the seasoning and serve.

☕Chicken, Broccoli, and Ale Soup

This easy soup is sure to please, and it makes a delicious dinner with some warm rolls and a green salad.

PREP TIME: 15 minutes   **COOKING TIME:** 6–8 hours

1 pound (455 g) boneless, skinless chicken breasts

1 (16-ounce or 455-g) package frozen broccoli in cheese sauce

1 (12-ounce or 355-ml) bottle beer

Salt and pepper to taste

Cut the chicken into small pieces and put into the slow cooker. Add the broccoli and the beer, along with 4 cups (940 ml) water. Cook for 6 to 8 hours on LOW. Stir well, breaking up some of the broccoli into the soup. Season with salt and pepper to taste.

YIELD: 4 to 6 servings

NUTRITIONAL ANALYSIS: 132 calories; 2 g fat (16.5% calories from fat); 19 g protein; 6 g carbohydrate; 2 g dietary fiber; 46 mg cholesterol; 61 mg sodium.

ADD IT! Stir in 1 cup (115 g) of shredded cheddar cheese for even more cheesy tang.

❧Chicken Noodle Soup

This one has some additional steps, but the results are all you could want in a chicken soup. It's guaranteed to cure common colds, evening grumps, and general sick-of-winter blues.

PREP TIME: 45 minutes   **COOKING TIME:** 10 hours
ADDITIONAL STEPS: Remove the chicken meat from the bones after cooking; par-cook the noodles; add the noodles and vegetables during the last 2 hours of cooking

1 chicken (about 3 pounds or 1365 g)

½ pound (225 g) egg noodles

1 (16-ounce or 455-g) bag frozen mixed vegetables

Salt and pepper to taste

Cut the chicken into 4 pieces, removing the skin. Put the chicken, along with the neck, into the slow cooker. Season with salt and pepper. Add 10 cups (2350 ml) water and cook on LOW for 8 hours.

Remove the chicken from the cooker and allow to cool. Leave the broth in the cooker. Bring a pot of salted water to a boil and cook the noodles for 6 minutes. Drain the noodles and add them to the cooker. Add the vegetables. When the chicken is cool enough to handle, remove the meat from the bones, discarding the bones. Discard the neck. Shred the chicken meat and return it to the cooker. Cook for another 2 hours on LOW. Adjust the seasoning and serve.

YIELD: 8 to 10 servings

NUTRITIONAL ANALYSIS: 248 calories; 16 g fat (57.3% calories from fat); 19 g protein; 8 g carbohydrate; 2 g dietary fiber; 91 mg cholesterol; 90 mg sodium.

⬤Chicken-Dumpling Soup

This soup is absolutely delicious and oh-so-simple to make. A true one-pot meal.

COOKING TIME: 2 to 3 hours
ATTENTION: Change heat setting and prepare and add another ingredient during final 30 to 60 minutes

Three 19-ounce (540-g) cans ready-to-eat chunky chicken noodle soup

1 cup (120 g) all-purpose buttermilk baking mix

5 to 6 tablespoons (75 to 90 ml) milk

Put the chicken noodle soup in the slow cooker, cover, and cook on LOW for 1 to 1¹/₂ hours, or until the soup is very hot.

Raise the heat to HIGH. When the soup begins to simmer (in about 20 minutes), and not before, put the baking mix and milk in a medium-size bowl and stir just until the baking mix is moistened; do not overmix or the dumplings will be tough. Uncover the slow cooker and, using a tablespoon, drop the dough by spoonfuls into the hot soup; leave space around each dumpling, since the dumplings will expand and merge as they cook. Cover and cook for another 30 to 60 minutes, or until the dumplings are done; do not lift the lid or the dumplings will not finish cooking.

YIELD: 6 generous servings

NUTRITIONAL ANALYSIS: One serving of the basic recipe (made with 5 tablespoons milk) contains 171 calories; 6 g fat; 6 g protein; 24 g carbohydrate; and .8 g dietary fiber.

SPEED IT UP! For faster-to-the-table Chicken-Dumpling Soup, preheat the canned chicken noodle soup in a microwave-safe bowl according to the soup-label directions. Carefully ladle the hot soup into the slow cooker and turn the heat to HIGH, then begin preparing the dumplings. You'll have an extra dish to wash, but you'll save yourself 1 to 1¹/₂ hours in heating time.

Grandma's Turkey Noodle Soup

A tasty and healthful way to use up leftover turkey and stuffing after the holidays.

COOKING TIME: 10½ to 12½ hours
ATTENTION: Change heat setting, strain broth, debone meat, and add more ingredients during final 15 to 30 minutes

1½ quarts (1.4 L) hot water

6 chicken bouillon cubes

2 to 3 pounds (.9 to 1.4 kg) leftover turkey, including meat, skin, bones, and stuffing

Salt and freshly ground black pepper

1 cup (160 g) fresh or frozen egg noodles

Put the hot water and bouillon cubes in the slow cooker and stir until the bouillon cubes have dissolved. Add the turkey meat, skin, bones, and stuffing, and stir again. Cover and cook on LOW for 10 to 12 hours.

Turn the heat OFF and allow the slow cooker to cool enough so that you can handle the ceramic pot safely. Transfer the contents of the slow cooker to a large bowl, then strain off the broth and return it to the ceramic pot. Remove the turkey meat from the bones, chop it into bite-size pieces, and return it to the slow cooker. Stir the mixture and season it with salt and pepper to taste. Turn the heat to HIGH, stir in the egg noodles, and cook for another 15 to 30 minutes, or until the noodles are tender.

YIELD: 8 servings

NUTRITIONAL ANALYSIS: One serving of the basic recipe (made with 2 pounds turkey meat) contains 170 calories; 8 g fat; 83 g protein; 4 g carbohydrate; and .1 g dietary fiber.

ADD IT! Add 1½ cups (340 g) frozen Seasoning-Blend Vegetables (page 29) and 2 to 3 fresh broccoli stalks (without the florets) along with the turkey meat, skin, bones, and stuffing for a more flavorful broth.

Easy Manhattan Clam Chowder

As good New Englanders, we must uphold the Yankee Oath of Fealty we took at birth regarding clam chowder: Milk-based chowder is, and always will be, superior. That said, we like the red kind, too. Here is an easy way to have some.

PREP TIME: 20 minutes   **COOKING TIME:** 6–8 hours

2 pounds (910 g) boiling potatoes, such as Yukon Gold

2 (12-ounce or 355-ml) bottles clam juice

2 (14-ounce or 425-ml) cans red clam sauce

Salt and pepper to taste

Peel the potatoes and cut them into small cubes. Put the potatoes into the slow cooker. Add the clam juice, the red clam sauce, and 3 cups (705 ml) water. Cook for 6 to 8 hours on LOW, until the potatoes are nice and soft. Season with salt and pepper to taste.

YIELD: 4 to 6 servings

NUTRITIONAL ANALYSIS: 309 calories; 10 g fat (27.5% calories from fat); 10 g protein; 48 g carbohydrate; 3 g dietary fiber; 16 mg cholesterol; 1129 mg sodium.

ADD IT! Stir $1/2$ cup (50 g) chopped celery into the mix.

Spicy Clam Chowder

The rich taste of this clam chowder provides the ultimate in satisfaction. Hot, buttered cornbread is a delicious and traditional accompaniment.

COOKING TIME: 2 to 3 hours
ATTENTION: Change heat setting and add another ingredient during final 30 minutes; watch to keep from boiling

Three 19-ounce (540-g) cans ready-to-eat chunky potato soup

One 10-ounce (280-g) can baby clams, drained, with $1/2$ cup (60 ml) juice reserved

$1/2$ teaspoon Old Bay Seafood Seasoning

Salt and freshly ground black pepper

Put the potato soup, reserved clam juice, and Old Bay Seafood Seasoning in the slow cooker and stir to combine. Cover and cook on LOW for 1½ to 2½ hours.

Add the clams and cook the soup for another 30 minutes, or until the clams are hot. To hasten the warming of the clams, raise the heat to HIGH, but do not allow the soup to boil or the clams will become tough.

Before serving, stir the soup and season it with salt and pepper to taste.

YIELD: 6 generous servings

NUTRITIONAL ANALYSIS: One serving of the basic recipe contains 162 calories; 4 g fat; 17 g protein; 15 g carbohydrate; and 1 g dietary fiber.

ADD IT! For a richer chowder, add 4 tablespoons (55 g) butter, melted, along with the salt and pepper. Garnish each serving with crumbled bacon.

DID YOU KNOW? The original slow cooker, the Rival Crock Pot, was introduced in 1971. It was developed from a baked-bean cooker called The Beanery. To date, over 100 million Crock Pots have been sold! A host of sophisticated slow cookers have come on the market in recent years from Rival and other companies like Hamilton Beach, Cuisinart, Proctor-Silex, Nesco, Russell Hobbs, and Breville. These new models include oval slow cookers, sleek chrome versions, and cookers with pre-programmable features.

ᴗ Quick Shrimp Bisque

Bisques make an elegant starter for a dinner party, and this one is ready to go when you are—no last-minute work necessary. Bon appétit!

PREP TIME: 15 minutes **COOKING TIME:** 4 hours
ADDITIONAL STEPS: Blend the soup after cooking

2 (10-ounce or 285-ml) bottles clam juice

2 (10-ounce or 280-g) bottles shrimp in cocktail sauce

2 (8-ounce or 235-ml) cans evaporated milk

Salt and pepper to taste

Put the clam juice, the shrimp and cocktail sauce, and the evaporated milk into the slow cooker. Cook for 4 hours on LOW. Blend with an immersion blender or in batches in a blender or food processor. Adjust the seasoning with salt and pepper.

YIELD: 4 to 6 servings

NUTRITIONAL ANALYSIS: 245 calories; 7 g fat (27.7% calories from fat); 25 g protein; 19 g carbohydrate; trace dietary fiber; 166 mg cholesterol; 598 mg sodium.

Tomato Salmon Bisque

This is a rich and delicious soup that is so easy to make. Try to find a really good-quality tomato soup to use as a base for the recipe—we recommend those soups that come in cardboard cartons, generally found in the natural foods section of the grocery store.

PREP TIME: 10 minutes   **COOKING TIME:** 3–4 hours
ADDITIONAL STEPS: Blend the soup and stir in the cheese at the end of cooking

1 quart (945 ml) tomato soup (not condensed)

1 (12-ounce or 340-g) can salmon

2 cups (225 g) shredded cheddar cheese

Salt and pepper to taste

Put the tomato soup and the salmon into the slow cooker. Cook for 3 to 4 hours on LOW. Blend the soup with an immersion blender or blend in batches in a blender or food processor. Stir in the cheese until it has melted and the soup is smooth. Adjust the seasoning with salt and pepper.

YIELD: 4 to 6 servings

NUTRITIONAL ANALYSIS: 287 calories; 17 g fat (53.6% calories from fat); 22 g protein; 12 g carbohydrate; trace dietary fiber; 71 mg cholesterol; 1011 mg sodium.

ADD IT! Sprinkle a bit of chopped dill over each bowl before serving.

❤Barbecue 15-Bean Soup

This soup really is easy, delicious, and chock full of protein. Serve with crusty bread and garlic butter.

COOKING TIME: 8 to 10 hours on LOW, 4 to 5 hours on HIGH
ATTENTION: Add another ingredient during final hour

One 20-ounce (560-g) package ham-flavored 15-bean soup mix

1 quart (.95 L) water

1 cup (250 g) barbecue sauce

2 medium onions, chopped

Salt and freshly ground black pepper

Set aside the soup mix seasoning packet and put the beans in a large colander. Pick through the beans to remove any debris, then rinse them under running water. Put the beans in the slow cooker, cover them with water, and let them soak for 6 to 8 hours, or overnight.

Pour the beans back into the colander, discarding the used water, and rinse them under running water. Return the beans to the slow cooker and add 1 quart (.95 L) fresh water. Add the barbecue sauce and chopped onions, and stir to combine. Cover and cook on LOW for 8 to 10 hours or on HIGH for 4 to 5 hours. (Cooking the beans on LOW will bring out the best flavor.)

An hour before the soup is done, add the contents of the soup mix seasoning packet and stir. Just before serving, season the soup with salt and pepper to taste.

YIELD: 8 generous servings

NUTRITIONAL ANALYSIS: One serving of the basic recipe contains 103 calories; 2 g fat; 6 g protein; 17 g carbohydrate; and .9 g dietary fiber.

ADD IT! Add 1 pound (455 g) ham, diced, along with the barbecue sauce and chopped onions, and substitute vegetable stock for the water. Reduce the salt accordingly.

Bean and Pasta Soup

We use a mix available in most markets that gives you a wide variety of beans in one soup. You need to start the night before to soak the beans.

PREP TIME: 30 minutes   **COOKING TIME:** 7–8 hours

ADDITIONAL STEPS: Presoak the beans; par-cook the pasta and add for the last 2 hours of cooking

1 pound (455 g) 15-bean soup mix

1 (64-ounce or 1880-ml) can vegetable juice cocktail, such as V-8

4 ounces (115 g) mini-tube pasta (ditalini)

Salt and black pepper to taste

Starting at least 12 hours before you plan to make the soup, pick over the beans to remove any debris (such as small stones) and put them into a pan or bowl. Cover with water to twice the depth of the beans. Allow them to soak for at least 12 hours.

Drain the beans and put them into the slow cooker. Add the vegetable juice and 2 cups (475 ml) water. Cook for 6 hours.

Bring a pot of salted water to a boil and add the pasta. Cook the pasta for 6 to 7 minutes, drain, and add to the soup. Continue cooking for 1 to 2 hours, until the beans are soft.

Adjust the seasoning with salt and pepper.

YIELD: 6 to 8 servings

NUTRITIONAL ANALYSIS: 286 calories; 1 g fat (3.5% calories from fat); 16 g protein; 55 g carbohydrate; 16 g dietary fiber; 0 mg cholesterol; 621 mg sodium.

ADD IT IN! A couple of cloves of chopped garlic, some diced onion, a few chopped carrots, and chopped celery—all would make this soup even yummier.

Bean and Vegetable Soup

A good bean soup must be one of the most satisfying meals there is. This vegetable blend we spotted has a nice variety of veggies and beans, such as broccoli, carrots, green beans, white beans, garbanzo beans, and kidney beans. All of this adds up to a bowlful of healthy and tasty soup goodness.

PREP TIME: 30 minutes

COOKING TIME: 6–8 hours

ADDITIONAL STEPS: Cook the bacon

½ pound (225 g) bacon, chopped into ½-inch (1-cm) dice

1 (16-ounce or 455-g) package Rancho Fiesta Vegetable Blend

2 quarts (1890 ml) chicken stock or broth

Cook the bacon in a skillet, the microwave, or the oven. Drain the fat from the bacon and put the bacon into the slow cooker, along with the vegetable blend and the chicken stock. Cook for 6 to 8 hours on LOW.

YIELD: 6 to 8 servings

Nutritional analysis: 206 calories; 14 g fat (67.7% calories from fat); 10 g protein; 5 g carbohydrate; 2 g dietary fiber; 24 mg cholesterol; 2727 mg sodium.

ADD IT IN! Sprinkle a little finely grated Parmesan cheese on top of each bowl of soup before serving.

Creamy Black Bean and Tomato Soup

This tangy soup has a Tex-Mex flair that takes it from merely good to simply terrific.

PREP TIME: 15 minutes

COOKING TIME: 6–8 hours

2 (14-ounce or 395-g) cans diced tomatoes with lime juice, cilantro, and jalapeños

1 (16-ounce or 455-g) can black beans

1 (8-ounce or 235-ml) can evaporated milk

Salt and pepper to taste

Put all the ingredients plus 2 cups (470 ml) water into the slow cooker. Stir. Cook for 6 to 8 hours on LOW. Adjust the seasoning with salt and pepper to taste.

YIELD: 6 to 8 servings

NUTRITIONAL ANALYSIS: 101 calories; 3 g fat (23.5% calories from fat); 6 g protein; 14 g carbohydrate; 3 g dietary fiber; 8 mg cholesterol; 602mg sodium.

Vegetarian White Bean and Escarole Soup

Escarole is one of those dark green leafy vegetables so beloved by nutritional experts and so neglected by many cooks. This take on a classic Italian soup will help you bring this delicious vegetable into your mainstream menu.

PREP TIME: 20 minutes   **COOKING TIME:** 6–8 hours

1 small head escarole

2 quarts (1890 ml) vegetable stock or broth

1 (20-ounce or 560-g) can large white beans

Salt and pepper to taste

Chop the escarole into small pieces and wash it well. Drain and add the escarole to the slow cooker. Add the vegetable stock. Pour the beans into a colander. Rinse, drain, and add them to the cooker. Season with salt and pepper to taste. Cook on LOW for 6 to 8 hours.

YIELD: 6 to 8 servings

NUTRITIONAL ANALYSIS: 257 calories; 4 g fat (14.2% calories from fat); 12 g protein; 44 g carbohydrate; 8 g dietary fiber; 2 mg cholesterol; 1642 mg sodium.

ADD IT IN! If you're not a vegetarian, you can use chicken stock or broth if you prefer. Try stirring in some fresh chopped thyme for a deeper burst of flavor.

Cabbage Soup with Kielbasa

Rich in vitamin C, cabbage is both good and good for you, as this recipe attests. Try to find a low-fat sausage for even healthier eating.

PREP TIME: 30 minutes   **COOKING TIME:** 6–8 hours

1 pound (455 g) kielbasa sausage

1/2 head green cabbage

1 (64-ounce or 1880-ml) can vegetable juice cocktail, such as V-8

Cut the kielbasa into ½-inch-thick rings and put them into the slow cooker. Finely shred the cabbage; you should have about 4 cups (280 g). Add the cabbage to the cooker. Pour the vegetable juice over all. Cook for 6 to 8 hours on LOW.

YIELD: 6 to 8 servings

NUTRITIONAL ANALYSIS: 220 calories; 16 g fat (62.8% calories from fat); 9 g protein; 12 g carbohydrate; 2 g dietary fiber; 38 mg cholesterol; 1224 mg sodium.

Sausage and Vegetable Soup

Rich tomato broth simmered with Italian sausage and vegetables makes for a delicious and hearty meal.

PREP TIME: 30 minutes   **COOKING TIME:** 6–8 hours

1 pound (455 g) sweet Italian sausage links

1 (16-ounce or 455-g) package Italian vegetable blend

1 (64-ounce or 1880-ml) can tomato juice

Salt and pepper to taste

Slice the sausages into ½-inch (1-cm) rounds and put them into the slow cooker. Add the vegetables and the tomato juice. Cook on LOW for 6 to 8 hours on LOW. Adjust the seasoning with salt and pepper.

YIELD: 6 to 8 servings

NUTRITIONAL ANALYSIS: 271 calories; 18 g fat (58.3% calories from fat); 12 g protein; 18 g carbohydrate; 5 g dietary fiber; 43 mg cholesterol; 1260 mg sodium.

ADD IT IN! Use vegetable juice cocktail, such as V-8, instead of tomato juice.

Onion Soup

Fragrant, piping-hot onion soup—what a wonderful way to greet a chilly night! This soup is delicious as a first course, or it can be a light meal with a salad and crusty bread.

PREP TIME: 30 minutes   **COOKING TIME:** 8 hours
ADDITIONAL STEPS: Add wine and broth after 4 hours

2 pounds (910 g) yellow or Spanish onions

3 tablespoons (45 g) butter

1 cup (235 ml) red wine

1 (64-ounce or 1880-ml) can beef broth

Salt and pepper to taste

Peel the onions and slice them very thin. Put the onions and the butter into the slow cooker. Cook on LOW for 4 hours, until the onions are very soft and a little caramelized. Add the red wine and the beef broth. Cook for another 4 hours on LOW. Adjust the seasoning with salt and pepper to taste.

YIELD: 6 to 8 servings

NUTRITIONAL ANALYSIS: 157 calories; 4 g fat (28.9% calories from fat); 11 g protein; 14 g carbohydrate; 2 g dietary fiber; 12 mg cholesterol; 1246 mg sodium.

ADD IT IN! Some cheese melted on top of the soup gives it that French onion soup feel.

Lentil, Barley, and Sausage Soup

This thick, hearty stew is a protein powerhouse. Serve with mixed vegetables and crusty bread.

COOKING TIME: 8 to 10 hours   **ATTENTION:** Minimal

Two 19-ounce (540-g) cans ready-to-eat lentil soup

1 pound (455 g) fresh Italian sausage, browned and drained

1½ cups (355 ml) water

1 cup (200 g) uncooked pearl barley

Salt

Put the lentil soup, browned sausage, water, and barley in the slow cooker and stir to combine. Cover and cook on LOW for 8 to 10 hours.

Before serving, stir the soup and season it with salt to taste.

YIELD: 8 servings

NUTRITIONAL ANALYSIS: One serving of the basic recipe contains 360 calories; 20 g fat; 16 g protein; 31 g carbohydrate; and 4 g dietary fiber.

ADD IT! Substitute vegetable broth for the water, and add 2 cloves garlic, minced.

DON'T TRY THIS! Once you've added all the ingredients, don't stir slow-cooked soups. Lifting the lid throws off the cooking time.

🍲Lentil and Tomato Soup

Lentils are one of those foods that don't jump right out at most meal planners, but they also seem to garner rave reviews when they do make an appearance at the dinner table. Not only are they packed with iron and protein, but they are also far cheaper than many other protein sources. (T-bone steak, we're looking at you.)

PREP TIME: 10 minutes   **COOKING TIME:** 6–8 hours

1½ quarts (1425 ml) chicken stock or broth

2 cups (400 g) dried lentils

1 (14-ounce or 395-g) can diced tomatoes with onion and celery

Salt and pepper to taste

Wash the lentils in a colander and pick them over for any small pebbles. Add all of the ingredients to the slow cooker. Cook for 6 to 8 hours on LOW, until the lentils are soft. Adjust the seasoning with salt and pepper to taste.

YIELD: 6 to 8 servings

NUTRITIONAL ANALYSIS: 188 calories; 1 g fat (3.2% calories from fat); 15 g protein; 30 g carbohydrate; 15 g dietary fiber; 0 mg cholesterol; 1689 mg sodium.

ADD IT IN! Add in 1 cup (130 g) chopped carrots.

Split Pea and Ham Soup

This country classic is always a hit at the dinner table, even with folks who generally eschew anything green.

PREP TIME: 20 minutes   **COOKING TIME:** 6–8 hours

½ pound (225 g) cooked ham

1 medium onion

1 pound (455 g) split green peas

Salt and pepper to taste

Cut the ham into ¼-inch (6-mm) cubes and put them into the slow cooker. Peel the onion and dice it into small pieces. Add the onion to the ham. Rinse the peas and pick through them to remove any small stones or other debris. Add the peas and 8 cups (1880 ml) water to the slow cooker. Cook for 6 to 8 hours on LOW. The peas should be very soft. Stir the soup to break up some of the peas and thicken the soup. Adjust the seasoning with salt and pepper.

YIELD: 6 to 8 servings

NUTRITIONAL ANALYSIS: 250 calories; 4 g fat (13.0% calories from fat); 19 g protein; 36 g carbohydrate; 15 g dietary fiber; 16 mg cholesterol; 383 mg sodium.

Wild Rice Soup

Wild Rice Soup makes an elegant statement. Enjoy this nutty-tasting soup with an open-face cheese sandwich garnished with bacon.

COOKING TIME: 8 to 10 hours on LOW, 4 to 5 hours on HIGH
ATTENTION: Minimal

Three 10¾-ounce (305-g) cans condensed cream of mushroom soup

3 soup cans (918 ml) water

1½ cups (340 g) frozen Seasoning-Blend Vegetables (page 29), thawed

½ cup (80 g) wild rice, boiled for 20 minutes and drained

Salt and freshly ground black pepper

Put the condensed soup, water, Seasoning-Blend Vegetables, and partially cooked wild rice in the slow cooker and stir to combine. Season the mixture with salt and pepper to taste and stir it again. Cook on LOW for 8 to 10 hours or on HIGH for 4 to 5 hours.

YIELD: 8 servings

NUTRITIONAL ANALYSIS: One serving of the basic recipe contains 144 calories; 9 g fat; 3 g protein; 14 g carbohydrate; and 2 g dietary fiber.

ADD IT! Substitute 1 quart (.95 L) chicken bouillon for the 3 soup cans water, and add 1 pound (455 g) bacon, cooked and crumbled.

DID YOU KNOW? Wild rice isn't really rice—it's a type of aquatic grass that's native to North America.

Wild Rice-Cheese Soup

Cheese, potato, and wild-rice flavors merge in this delicious, satisfying soup. Serve with your favorite soup crackers.

COOKING TIME: 2 to 3$^{1}/_{2}$ hours
ATTENTION: Stir twice during first 30 minutes; change heat setting and add another ingredient after first 30 minutes

7 cups (1.6 L) water

One 9.3-ounce (263-g) package Fantastic Foods Creamy Potato Simmer Soup

2 cups (455 g) shredded pasteurized processed cheese food

1 cup (160 g) wild rice, boiled for 40 minutes and drained

Salt and freshly ground pepper to taste

Put the water and soup mix in the slow cooker and stir until the soup mix has dissolved. Add the cheese food and stir well. Cover and cook on HIGH for 30 minutes, or until the cheese has melted, stirring every 15 minutes.

Add the partially cooked wild rice to the slow cooker and stir again. Reduce the heat to LOW, cover, and cook for 1$^{1}/_{2}$ to 3 hours, or until the flavors have melded.

Stir the soup and season it with salt and pepper to taste. Serve the soup warm with crusty bread.

YIELD: 10 servings

NUTRITIONAL ANALYSIS: One serving of the basic recipe contains 348 calories; 20 g fat; 21 g protein; 27 g carbohydrate; and 1 g dietary fiber

ADD IT! Substitute 7 cups (1.6 L) chicken bouillon for the water, and add 1 pound (455 g) bacon, cooked and crumbled.

☕Creamy Potato Soup

This creamy soup benefits from the essence of the herbs in the soup mix. Ladle into bowls, garnish with fresh chives, and serve with crusty bread.

COOKING TIME: 4 to 5 hours on HIGH
ATTENTION: Add another ingredient during final hour

1½ quarts (1.4 L) water

One 9.3-ounce (263-g) package Fantastic Foods Creamy Potato Simmer Soup

4 large potatoes, peeled and cut into 1-inch (2.5-cm) cubes

One 12-ounce (355-ml) can evaporated milk

Salt and freshly ground black pepper

Put the water and soup mix in the slow cooker and stir until the soup mix has dissolved. Add the potato cubes and stir again. Cover and cook on HIGH for 4 to 5 hours.

An hour before the soup is done, stir in the evaporated milk. Just before serving, season the soup with salt and pepper to taste and stir it again.

YIELD: 8 generous servings

NUTRITIONAL ANALYSIS: One serving of the basic recipe contains 223 calories; 9 g fat; 11 g protein; 33 g carbohydrate; and 2 g dietary fiber.

ADD IT! Add 5½ tablespoons (½ cup, or 75 g) butter, melted, along with the evaporated milk for a richer-tasting soup.

Potato Minestrone

A satisfying, comfort-food twist on a vegetarian staple. Serve with bruschetta topped with diced tomatoes and chopped fresh basil.

COOKING TIME: $8\frac{1}{2}$ to $10\frac{1}{2}$ hours on LOW, $4\frac{1}{2}$ to $6\frac{1}{2}$ hours on HIGH
ATTENTION: Add another ingredient during final 30 minutes

Three 19-ounce (540-g) cans ready-to-eat minestrone soup

4 large potatoes, peeled and cut into 1-inch (2.5-cm) cubes

One 10-ounce (280-g) package frozen chopped spinach, thawed and drained

Put the minestrone soup and potato cubes in the slow cooker and stir to combine. Cover and cook on LOW for 8 to 10 hours or on HIGH for 4 to 6 hours.

Add the thawed spinach to the slow cooker and stir again. Cover and cook for another 30 minutes, or until the spinach is hot.

YIELD: 10 generous servings

NUTRITIONAL ANALYSIS: One serving of the basic recipe contains 100 calories; 2 g fat; 5 g protein; 17 g carbohydrate; and 2 g dietary fiber.

ADD IT! To pump up the protein content, add a 16-ounce (455-g) can kidney or garbanzo beans, rinsed and drained.

SAFETY FIRST! Never immerse a slow cooker in water. If your slow cooker has a stoneware insert, you can remove and wash it as you would any piece of crockery. But clean the appliance itself with a damp rag—and make sure you unplug it first!

⬗Asparagus Soup

Tender, flavorful baby asparagus in a delicate broth. Add a dollop of sour cream for garnish.

COOKING TIME: 5¹/₂ to 7 hours
ATTENTION: Change heat setting, process soup, and add another ingredient during final 30 to 60 minutes

1¹/₂ **pounds (683 g) fresh baby asparagus, washed and dried**

1 **quart (.95 L) vegetable broth**

¹/₄ **teaspoon salt**

¹/₄ **teaspoon freshly ground black pepper**

Prepare the asparagus by cutting off the tips and setting them aside. Snap off the tough lower ends and discard them. Cut the remaining stems into 1-inch (2.5-cm) pieces and put them in the slow cooker. Add the vegetable broth, salt, and pepper, and stir to combine. Cover and cook on LOW for 5 to 6 hours.

Turn the heat OFF and allow the slow cooker to cool enough so that you can handle the ceramic pot safely. Using a blender or food processor, purée the soup in small batches, returning the puréed soup to the slow cooker. Add the raw asparagus tips and stir to combine. Cover and cook on HIGH for 30 to 60 minutes, or until the asparagus tips are tender.

Serve the soup hot, garnished with a sprinkling of freshly ground black pepper.

YIELD: 6 servings

NUTRITIONAL ANALYSIS: One serving of the basic recipe contains 122 calories; 3 g fat; 5 g protein; 20 g carbohydrate; and 3 g dietary fiber.

ADD IT! For a richer soup, add any combination of the following along with the asparagus tips: 1 cup (225 g) diced potatoes, ¹/₂ cup (75 g) chopped scallions, 1 to 2 cloves garlic, minced. Increase the cooking time by 1 hour.

Pumpkin Soup

This harvest favorite is a wonderful treat when the leaves start to turn. You can substitute any winter squash for the pumpkin with equally delightful results.

PREP TIME: 15 minutes   **COOKING TIME:** 6–8 hours
ADDITIONAL STEPS: Puree soup after cooking

2 medium onions

2 (14-ounce or 395-g) cans pumpkin puree

1 quart (945 ml) apple cider

Salt and pepper to taste

Peel the onions and dice them into small pieces. Put the chopped onion into the slow cooker. Add the pumpkin and the cider. Cook for 6 to 8 hours on LOW. Puree using an immersion blender, or puree in batches in a blender or food processor. Season with salt and pepper to taste. Add water to thin the soup, if necessary

YIELD: 6 to 8 servings

NUTRITIONAL ANALYSIS: 102 calories; trace fat (3.7% calories from fat); 1 g protein; 25 g carbohydrate; 3 g dietary fiber; 0 mg cholesterol; 10 mg sodium.

ADD IT IN! Add $1/2$ teaspoon (1.1 g) nutmeg to the soup.

Broccoli-Cheese Soup

Smooth and satisfying, this soup is a lovely light meal or a delicious accompaniment. Serve with soft honey wheat rolls.

COOKING TIME: $4^{1}/2$ to $6^{1}/2$ hours
ATTENTION: Change heat setting and add another ingredient during final 15 to 30 minutes

2 large stalks fresh broccoli, washed and dried

Two $10^{3}/4$-ounce (305-g) cans condensed cream of celery soup

1 cup (235 ml) water

1 pound (455 g) pasteurized processed cheese food, cut into cubes

Salt and freshly ground black pepper

Prepare the broccoli by cutting off the florets and setting them aside. Cut off the tough lower ends and discard them. Cut the remaining stems into rounds or chunks of uniform size and set them aside. The florets and stem pieces should total about $2^1/2$ cups (175 g).

Put the condensed soup and water in the slow cooker and stir to combine. Add the broccoli stem pieces and cheese, and stir again. Cover and cook on LOW for 4 to 6 hours, or until the stem pieces are tender but not overcooked.

Turn the heat to HIGH, add the broccoli florets, and stir. Cover and cook for another 15 to 30 minutes, or just until the florets are tender. Season the soup with salt and pepper to taste and serve it immediately.

YIELD: 8 servings

NUTRITIONAL ANALYSIS: One serving of the basic recipe contains 340 calories; 24 g fat; 20 g protein; 17 g carbohydrate; and 2 g dietary fiber.

TIP: To save time, steam the broccoli florets before adding them to the soup, and keep the heat on LOW.

ADD IT! For a richer soup, substitute milk for the water.

Golden Onion Soup

Rich and creamy, this soup is the perfect comfort food for a bone-chilling day. Enjoy with crusty French bread.

COOKING TIME: $5^1/2$ to $6^1/2$ hours on LOW, $2^1/2$ to $3^1/2$ hours on HIGH
ATTENTION: Minimal

3 cups (680 g) thinly sliced onion

4 tablespoons (55 g) butter

Three 2.6-ounce (73-g) envelopes golden onion soup mix

7 cups (1.6 L) water

In a large skillet over medium heat, sauté the onion in the butter until the onion is translucent; do not allow it to burn.

Put the water and soup mix in the slow cooker and stir until the soup mix has dissolved. Add the sautéed onion and stir again. Cover and cook on LOW for $5^1/2$ to $6^1/2$ hours or on HIGH for $2^1/2$ to $3^1/2$ hours.

YIELD: 8 servings

NUTRITIONAL ANALYSIS: One serving of the basic recipe contains 111 calories; 7 g fat; 2 g protein; 12 g carbohydrate; and 2 g dietary fiber.

ADD IT! Add ¼ cup (60 ml) dry vermouth or cognac along with the water.

TRY THIS! Add a dollop of sour cream or crème fraiche and a sprinkle of chopped chives to each bowl just before serving.

Cheddar Cheese Soup

This rich and creamy soup is fun and fabulous when served in an edible bread bowl. Add heaping servings of steamed California vegetables for a satisfying, balanced meal.

COOKING TIME: 1½ to 2 hours   **ATTENTION:** Watch to keep from boiling

1 pint (475 ml) hot water

2 chicken or vegetable bouillon cubes

Two 10¾-ounce (305-g) cans condensed cheddar cheese soup

3 tablespoons (42 ml) cooking sherry

Put the hot water and bouillon cubes in the slow cooker and stir until the bouillon cubes have dissolved. Add the condensed soup and stir again. Cover and cook on LOW for 1½ to 2 hours, or until the soup is hot; do not allow it to boil.

Before serving, add the sherry and stir to combine.

YIELD: 5 servings

NUTRITIONAL ANALYSIS: One serving of the basic recipe contains 137 calories; 7 g fat; 5 g protein; 9 g carbohydrate; and .8 g dietary fiber.

☕Hot and Sour Chinese Vegetable Soup

This is not the same recipe as the hot and sour soup found in your favorite restaurant, but it's quite tasty in its own right.

PREP TIME: 15 minutes   **COOKING TIME:** 8 hours
ADDITIONAL STEPS: Add the vegetables for the final hour of cooking

---

1 (64-ounce or 1880-ml) can beef broth

1 (10-ounce or 285-ml) jar Szechuan stir-fry sauce

1 (16-ounce or 455-g) package frozen Szechuan or stir-fry vegetables

Salt and pepper to taste

Combine the beef broth and the stir-fry sauce in the slow cooker. Cook for 7 hours on LOW. Add the vegetables and cook for an additional hour. Adjust the seasoning with salt and pepper.

YIELD: 6 to 8 servings

NUTRITIONAL ANALYSIS: 106 calories; 0 g fat (0.0% calories from fat); 13 g protein; 14 g carbohydrate; 1 g dietary fiber; 0 mg cholesterol; 2294 mg sodium.

CHAPTER 9

SAUCES, DRESSINGS, AND TOPPINGS

Sauces, dressings, and toppings are the accessories of the food world. They add a dash of color, a little excitement, and lots of flavor. Enjoy decorating meat, main dishes, breakfast foods, and desserts with these edible accessories, and you'll have a truly gourmet look for your table.

Red Pasta Sauce

This is a delicious way to serve a family favorite. Serve over spaghetti or linguini, with a romaine salad and garlic breadsticks on the side.

COOKING TIME: 2 to 4 hours on LOW, 1 to 2 hours on HIGH
ATTENTION: Minimal

One 28-ounce (795-g) jar mushroom-and-garlic-flavored pasta sauce

⅓ cup (78 ml) dry red wine

⅛ teaspoon crushed red pepper

Salt and freshly ground black pepper

Put the pasta sauce and red wine in the slow cooker and stir to combine. Cover and cook on LOW for 2 to 4 hours or on HIGH for 1 to 2 hours.

Before serving, stir the crushed red pepper into the sauce. Season the sauce with salt and black pepper to taste and stir it again.

YIELD: 6 servings

NUTRITIONAL ANALYSIS: One serving of the basic recipe contains 10 calories; trace fat; trace protein; .2 g carbohydrate; and trace dietary fiber.

TRY THIS! Spray a little nonstick cooking spray inside your slow cooker insert before adding ingredients, and gunk wipes off easily after cooking.

Ginger-Apricot-Cranberry Sauce

A holiday favorite with a kick. Apricots and fresh ginger add an interesting heat to this chilled standard, as cold and refreshing as the winter wind.

COOKING TIME: 3 to 4 hours   **ATTENTION:** Minimal

One 6-ounce (168-g) package dried apricots

One 16-ounce (455-g) can whole-berry cranberry sauce

2 tablespoons (28 ml) water

1 tablespoon (6 g) minced fresh ginger

Cut the dried apricots into 3 strips each and put them in the slow cooker. Add the cranberry sauce, water, and minced ginger, and stir to combine.

Cover and cook on LOW for 3 to 4 hours, or until the apricots are tender and all the flavors have melded.

Allow the sauce to cool to room temperature, then transfer it to an airtight container and refrigerate it until it's very cold. To serve, spoon the sauce into a chilled serving bowl and serve it immediately.

YIELD: 6 servings

NUTRITIONAL ANALYSIS: One serving of the basic recipe contains 182 calories; .2 g fat; 1 g protein; 47 g carbohydrate; and 3 g dietary fiber.

TRY THIS! Reduce the sugar in this dish by substituting from-scratch cranberry sauce for the canned version. Put a 12-ounce (340-g) bag of fresh cranberries, 1/2 cup (60 ml) reduced-sugar cranberry juice, and 1/2 cup plus 1 tablespoon (14 g) Splenda granular no-calorie sweetener in the slow cooker and stir to combine. Cover and cook on HIGH for 3 to 4 hours, or until the cranberries have popped and the syrup has thickened.

Cranberry-Rhubarb Sauce

The slightly sweet and tangy flavor of rhubarb is enhanced by the addition of cranberries. Serve over ice cream or as an accompaniment to fish, scallops, or pork tenderloin.

COOKING TIME: 4 to 5 hours   **ATTENTION:** Minimal

1½ pounds (683 g) fresh rhubarb, cut into ½-inch (1.3-cm) pieces

12 ounces (340 g) fresh cranberries

1½ cups (300 g) sugar

½ cup (120 ml) water

¼ teaspoon salt

Put the rhubarb pieces, fresh cranberries, sugar, water, and salt in the slow cooker and stir to combine. Cover and cook on LOW for 4 to 5 hours.

Allow the sauce to cool to room temperature, then transfer it to an airtight container and refrigerate it until it's very cold. Serve it chilled.

YIELD: 6 servings

NUTRITIONAL ANALYSIS: One serving of the basic recipe contains 239 calories; 0 g fat; 1 g protein; 61 g carbohydrate; and 4 g dietary fiber.

TRY THIS! To create a rich, exotic flavor, stir in a tablespoon or two (to taste) of peach or apricot chutney in the last half-hour of cooking.

Easy Barbecue Sauce

When you're caught short and don't have time to run to the store, this quick and easy recipe for barbecue sauce will do the trick.

COOKING TIME: 1 to 2 hours ————— **ATTENTION:** Minimal

3 cups (720 g) ketchup

¼ cup (63 g) honey mustard sauce

¼ cup (60 ml) apple cider vinegar

⅛ teaspoon freshly ground black pepper

Put the ketchup, honey mustard sauce, apple cider vinegar, and pepper in the slow cooker and stir to combine. Cover and cook on LOW for 1 to 2 hours, or until the flavors have melded.

YIELD: 6 servings

NUTRITIONAL ANALYSIS: One serving of the basic recipe contains 150 calories; 3 g fat; 2 g protein; 35 g carbohydrate; and 2 g dietary fiber.

ADD IT! Add 1 clove garlic, minced. To sweeten the sauce, add honey to taste.

Favorite Barbecue Sauce

Ready for a change? Take your favorite barbecue sauce and reinvent it!

COOKING TIME: 1 to 2 hours ————— **ATTENTION:** Minimal

2 cups (500 g) bottled barbecue sauce

½ cup (170 g) honey

Put the bottled barbecue sauce and honey in the slow cooker and stir to combine. Cover and cook on LOW for 1 to 2 hours, or until the flavors have melded.

YIELD: 5 servings

NUTRITIONAL ANALYSIS: One serving of the basic recipe contains 178 calories; 2 g fat; 2 g protein; 41 g carbohydrate; and 1 g dietary fiber.

❧Dressed-Up Barbecue Sauce

Sometimes on holiday weekends, all that the supermarket shelves yield is store-brand barbecue sauce. Try this little pick-me-up, and your family will think you picked up gourmet barbecue sauce instead.

COOKING TIME: 1 to 2 hours	**ATTENTION:** Minimal

2 cups (500 g) barbecue sauce

¼ cup (56 g) dark brown sugar, packed

4 tablespoons (55 g) butter, melted

⅛ teaspoon freshly ground black pepper

Put the bottled barbecue sauce, brown sugar, melted butter, and pepper in the slow cooker and stir to combine. Cover and cook on LOW for 1 to 2 hours or until the flavors have melded.

YIELD: 5 servings

NUTRITIONAL ANALYSIS: One serving of the basic recipe contains 198 calories; 11 g fat; 2 g protein; 24 g carbohydrate; and 1 g dietary fiber.

ADD IT! Add 1 clove garlic, minced, and 1 tablespoon (15 g) hot sauce for an extra kick.

TRY THIS! This sauce also makes a phenomenal layer in a ground beef (or chicken) dip. Pour it over cooked and drained ground beef or chicken in a casserole dish, top with grated Monterey jack or Swiss cheese, and all you need is tortilla chips for dipping—and maybe some beer or margaritas!

Sweet Savory Sauce

A special sauce that's easy to make and tastes great with just about anything. Try drowning cooked cocktail franks, hot dogs, pork morsels, meatballs, or chicken wings in a slow cooker full of this sauce. A real crowd pleaser.

COOKING TIME: 1½ to 2½ hours   **ATTENTION:** Minimal

1 cup (225 g) chili sauce

1 cup currant (320 g) jelly

1 tablespoon (15 g) Dijon mustard

Put the chili sauce, currant jelly, and mustard in the slow cooker and stir to combine. Cover and cook on LOW for 1½ to 2½ hours, or until the flavors have melded.

Serve the sauce warm from the slow cooker.

YIELD: 5 servings

NUTRITIONAL ANALYSIS: One serving of the basic recipe contains 177 calories; 0 g fat; 1 g protein; 46 g carbohydrate; and 2 g dietary fiber.

ADD IT! For a richer sauce, add 1 ounce (28 ml) dry red wine.

SPEED IT UP! If this sauce will be served with appetizer meats, heat the meat in the sauce and serve it from the slow cooker. This sauce is enough for 1 to 1½ pounds (455 to 683 g) of meat.

Mustard Sauce

A quick-and-easy solution to humdrum pork chops and ribs.

COOKING TIME: 1 to 2 hours   **ATTENTION:** Minimal

1 cup (225 g) brown sugar, packed

1 cup (240 g) honey mustard

1 cup (235 ml) apple cider vinegar or beer

Put the brown sugar, honey mustard, and apple cider vinegar in the slow cooker and stir to combine. Cover and cook on LOW for 1 to 2 hours, or until all the flavors have melded. Use this sauce as a pork or rib finishing sauce, as a table sauce, or on sandwiches.

YIELD: 6 servings

NUTRITIONAL ANALYSIS: One serving of the basic recipe (made with apple cider vinegar) contains 174 calories; 2 g fat; 2 g protein; 41 g carbohydrate; and 1 g dietary fiber.

≈Herb Stuffing

It's a cinch to prepare stuffing outside the turkey using your slow cooker.

COOKING TIME: 4 to 5 hours   **ATTENTION:** Minimal

1½ cups (340 g) frozen Seasoning-Blend Vegetables (page 29)

4 tablespoons (55 g) butter

One 14-ounce (398-g) package bread cube style herb-seasoned stuffing mix

1½ pints (710 ml) water

Spray the inside of the slow cooker with cooking spray.

In a large skillet over medium heat, sauté the Seasoning-Blend Vegetables in the butter until the onion is translucent. Place the sautéed vegetables in the slow cooker along with the stuffing mix and stir to combine. Sprinkle the water over the vegetable-and-stuffing mixture and mix lightly. Cover and cook on LOW for 4 to 5 hours.

YIELD: 8 servings

NUTRITIONAL ANALYSIS: One serving of the basic recipe contains 259 calories; 8 g fat; 6 g protein; 41 g carbohydrate; and 3 g dietary fiber.

ADD IT! Substitute 1½ cups (355 ml) applesauce or chicken bouillon for an equal amount of the water. Garnish the stuffing with toasted chopped walnuts.

✺Curried Fruit Topping

You can prepare hot curried fruit using a variety of fruits. Some of the most popular are peaches, pineapples, pears, cherries, and apricots. Enjoy with yogurt for breakfast or with ice cream any time.

COOKING TIME: 6 to 8 hours on LOW, 3 to 4 hours on HIGH
ATTENTION: Minimal

4 cups (856 g) assorted canned fruits, drained

¾ cup (169 g) brown sugar, firmly packed

1 tablespoon (6 g) curry powder

¼ teaspoon salt

Layer the different canned fruits, one type of fruit per layer, on the bottom of the slow cooker. Combine the brown sugar, curry powder, and salt in a small bowl and sprinkle the mixture over the fruits. Cover and cook on LOW for 6 to 8 hours or on HIGH for 3 to 4 hours.

YIELD: 8 servings

NUTRITIONAL ANALYSIS: One serving of the basic recipe contains 172 calories; 0 g fat; .6 g protein; 45 g carbohydrate; and 2 g dietary fiber.

ADD IT! Toast ½ cup (63 g) slivered almonds in 8 tablespoons (1 stick, or 112 g) butter and layer them on the bottom of the slow cooker along with the fruits.

Apricot Preserves

Whether it's summer or winter, the taste of Apricot Preserves is always a welcome treat. Slather it on hot, buttered toast, drizzle it over ice cream, or use it in recipes.

COOKING TIME: 2$\frac{1}{2}$ to 5 hours
ATTENTION: Stir every 45 to 60 minutes; remove cover during final 1 to 2 hours

1 pound (455 g) dried apricots, finely chopped in a food processor

3$\frac{1}{2}$ cups (885 ml) unsweetened apple juice

1 cup (200 g) sugar

Sterilize a glass jar with a tight-fitting lid and set it aside.

Put the apricot pieces, apple juice, and sugar in the slow cooker and stir to combine. Cover and cook on HIGH for 1$\frac{1}{2}$ to 3 hours, stirring every 45 to 60 minutes. Uncover and cook for an additional 1 to 2 hours, or until the mixture has thickened, stirring occasionally.

Ladle the preserves into the prepared jar and allow them to cool. Screw on the lid and store the preserves in the refrigerator.

YIELD: 8 servings

NUTRITIONAL ANALYSIS: One serving of the basic recipe contains 283 calories; 0 g fat; 2 g protein; 73 g carbohydrate; and 5 g dietary fiber.

TRY THIS! Next time you need a quick and delicious frosting on a layer cake, spread these preserves over the bottom layer, add a layer of whipped cream, then the top cake layer, another layer of preserves, and another layer of whipped cream. Serve immediately. Yum!

CHAPTER 10

MAIN DISHES: BEEF, PORK, AND OTHER MEATS

Bring out the tender, juicy flavor of meat—and do it the easy way. The slow cooker reigns supreme when it comes to preparing meats and meaty stews. Inexpensive tougher cuts almost magically become fall-apart tender. And how delightful that delicious gravies and sauces develop on their own while the meat cooks. The slow cooker captures the abundance of juices and tasty bits of meat as the roast or stew is slowly cooked to perfection. For tricks to make a superior gravy or sauce to accompany your meal, check out the "Tips" or the "Try This" suggestions with the recipes.

Beef Burgundy in Hunter Sauce

Simple yet elegant roast beef coddled in a sensational mushroom-onion-wine sauce. Enjoy with garlic potatoes and dinner rolls.

COOKING TIME: 8 to 10 hours   **ATTENTION:** Minimal

One 3- to 4-pound (1.4- to 1.8-kg) beef roast

¾ cup (175 ml) water

½ cup (120 ml) dry red wine

One 1.1-ounce (31-g) envelope hunter sauce mix

Put the beef roast in the slow cooker. Combine the water, red wine, and sauce mix in a small bowl and pour the mixture over the roast. Cover and cook on LOW for 8 to 10 hours, or until the roast is done.

YIELD: 12 servings

NUTRITIONAL ANALYSIS: One serving of the basic recipe (made with a 3-pound beef roast) contains 251 calories; 18 g fat; 18 g protein; 2 g carbohydrate; and 0 g dietary fiber.

TIP: If you don't have hunter sauce mix on hand, substitute onion-mushroom soup mix.

ADD IT IN! For an instant side dish, stir 8 ounces (225 g) thickly sliced fresh mushrooms into the sauce mixture. Garnish the finished roast with chopped fresh parsley.

DID YOU KNOW? Hunter sauce, also called chasseur sauce, is a brown sauce made with tomato purée and flavored with mushrooms, onion, and a hint of white wine. This robust sauce was created in the early 1600s to tenderize tough old game birds. You'll enjoy hunter sauce for its rich, full-bodied taste, but you really won't need it to tenderize your slow-cooked roast

Belgian Beef Stew

This recipe is a riff on Beef Carbonnade, a classic Belgian stew traditionally served with steamed or boiled, buttered potatoes. Use a bottle of good Belgian ale for a full, rich flavor. Like most stew recipes in this book, low and slow is the key. A high temperature results in tough meat.

PREP TIME: 10 minutes   **COOKING TIME:** 7–8 hours

3 pounds (1365 g) stew meat

2 (12-ounce or 355-ml) jars onion gravy

1 (12-ounce or 355-ml) bottle beer

Salt and pepper to taste

Place the stew meat into the slow cooker. Add the gravy and beer. Cook on LOW for 7 to 8 hours. Adjust the seasoning with salt and pepper.

This stew is even better done a day ahead and then reheated for 1 to 2 hours on LOW.

YIELD: 4 to 6 servings

NUTRITIONAL ANALYSIS: 749 calories; 47 g fat (59.1 % calories from fat); 64 g protein; 9 g carbohydrate; 11 g dietary fiber; 227 mg cholesterol; 1109 mg sodium.

ADD IT IN: Peel and slice 4 or 5 onions and layer them under the beef. Stir in 1 tablespoon (15 g) strong mustard for a tad more zest.

Beef Braised in Red Wine

We could always tell when our mother was attempting something a little more gourmet than usual, because she cooked with wine. And we responded with whine. Now, of course, we think something like this is terrific comfort food.

PREP TIME: 10 minutes   **COOKING TIME:** 8 hours
ADDITIONAL STEPS: Reduce the cooking juices to make a sauce

1 beef pot roast, such as chuck eye (3 to 4 pounds or 1365 to 1820 g)

Salt and pepper to taste

2 cups (470 ml) red wine

6 or 7 cloves garlic, peeled

Put the beef into the slow cooker. Season with salt and pepper. Add the red wine and the garlic. Cook for about 8 hours on LOW. Remove the beef from the cooker and keep it warm. Degrease the cooking juices and put them into a saucepan. Reduce the juices over high heat until you have about 1½ cups (355 ml). Slice the beef thin and serve moistened with some of the reduced pan juices.

YIELD: 4 to 6 servings

NUTRITIONAL ANALYSIS: 837 calories; 57 g fat (61.8% calories from fat); 75 g protein; 5 g carbohydrate; trace dietary fiber; 256 mg cholesterol; 161 mg sodium.

🐄 Beef and Noodle Bake

This cozy dinner may be straight out of the Richie and Fonzie Time Capsule, but it's still delicious.

PREP TIME: 25 minutes   **COOKING TIME:** 3 hours
ADDITIONAL STEPS: Half-cook the noodles and add them to the slow cooker in the last hour

2 pounds (910 g) ground beef

2 (12-ounce or 340-g) cans diced tomatoes with onion

1 pound (455 g) egg noodles

Break up the ground beef into the slow cooker. Add the diced tomatoes and cook on HIGH for 1 hour. Stir to break up the meat into very small bits. Cook for another hour.

Bring a large pot of salted water to a boil and add the egg noodles. Cook for half the recommended time on the package—about 6 minutes. Drain the noodles well and add them to the slow cooker. Stir the noodles and the beef mixture together. Cook for another hour.

YIELD: 6 to 8 servings

NUTRITIONAL ANALYSIS: 586 calories; 33 g fat (50.7% calories from fat); 28 g protein; 44 g carbohydrate; 2 g dietary fiber; 150 mg cholesterol; 97 mg sodium.

ADD IT IN! Stir ⅔ cup (80 g) grated cheddar cheese into the mixture.

Simple Ground Beef Stroganoff

Serve this luscious stroganoff over rice or egg noodles.

PREP TIME: 10 minutes   **COOKING TIME:** 2 hours on HIGH, 4 hours on LOW
ADDITIONAL STEPS: Add sour cream at the end of cooking

1 pound (455 g) ground beef

1 (12-ounce or 355-ml) can mushroom gravy

1 cup (230 g) sour cream

Salt and pepper to taste

Break up the beef into small pieces and put into the slow cooker. Add the gravy. Cook for 2 hours on HIGH or 4 hours on LOW. Stir in the sour cream and adjust the seasoning to taste.

YIELD: 4 servings

NUTRITIONAL ANALYSIS: 518 calories; 44 g fat (77.6% calories from fat); 22 g protein; 7 g carbohydrate; trace dietary fiber; 122 mg cholesterol; 593 mg sodium.

ADD IT IN! Slice up 10 or so white (button) mushrooms and stir them into the ground beef mixture.

Stewed Beef Short Ribs

Short ribs are a cut of beef that's naturally suited to the slow cooker. Because short ribs are a fatty cut of meat, it's best to cook this recipe ahead, leaving time to degrease the cooking liquid and produce a flavorful sauce.

PREP TIME: 15 minutes   **COOKING TIME:** 7–8 hours
ADDITIONAL STEPS: Remove the ribs and degrease the sauce

3 medium-size onions

3 pounds (1365 g) beef short ribs

Salt and pepper to taste

1 (12-ounce or 355-ml) jar beef gravy

Peel and slice the onions thin. Put the onion slices into the slow cooker. Put the short ribs on top of the onions and sprinkle with salt and pepper to taste. Pour the gravy over the ribs. Cook on LOW for 7 to 8 hours. Remove the ribs from the cooker and keep them warm. Degrease the cooking liquid and put it and the braised onions into a saucepan. Reduce over high heat until you have about 2 cups (470 ml) of liquid. Serve the short ribs with some of the sauce over them.

YIELD: 4 servings

NUTRITIONAL ANALYSIS: 1142 calories; 94 g fat (74.8% calories from fat); 60 g protein; 11 g carbohydrate; 2 g dietary fiber; 244 mg cholesterol; 663 mg sodium.

Orange-Onion Pot Roast

Here's a classic pot roast with a twist. Beef and orange are great flavor buddies, and the onions make a tasty accompaniment.

PREP TIME: 20 minutes   **COOKING TIME:** 8 hours
ADDITIONAL STEPS: Brown the pot roast before adding it to the slow cooker; degrease the pan juices

3 medium-size onions

Cooking oil

1 beef pot roast (about 3 pounds or 1365 g)

Salt and pepper to taste

1 cup (320 g) orange marmalade

Peel the onions and slice thin. Put the onions into the slow cooker. Heat a sauté pan over medium-high heat and add a couple of tablespoons (30 ml) of oil. Season the pot roast with salt and pepper and sear in the sauté pan on all sides to brown. Put the beef into the slow cooker and spread the marmalade over it. Add ¹/₂ cup (120 ml) water. Cook on LOW for 8 hours. Remove the beef from the cooker and slice thin. Degrease the pan juices and serve the beef with some of the onions and pan juices.

YIELD: 4 to 6 servings

NUTRITIONAL ANALYSIS: 625 calories; 35 g fat (51.0% calories from fat); 37 g protein; 40 g carbohydrate; 4 g dietary fiber; 131 mg cholesterol; 145 mg sodium.

Sweet and Spicy German-Style Pot Roast

The gingersnaps in this recipe cook down into a delicious sauce. The smaller members of our food-testing panel generally view any condiments other than ketchup with deep suspicion, but they gobbled up this sauce with shouts of happy glee.

PREP TIME: 10 minutes

COOKING TIME: 8 hours

ADDITIONAL STEPS: Degrease the sauce

1 beef pot roast (about 3 pounds or 1365 g)

10 to 12 gingersnaps

½ cup (125 g) steak sauce

Put the beef into the slow cooker. Crumble the gingersnaps over the beef and pour the steak sauce over all. Cook on LOW for 8 hours. Remove the beef from the slow cooker and keep it warm. Degrease the cooking liquid and stir until smooth. Slice the beef and serve with some of the sauce over it.

YIELD: 6 servings

NUTRITIONAL ANALYSIS: 543 calories; 37 g fat (62.1% calories from fat); 37 g protein; 14 g carbohydrate; 1 g dietary fiber; 131 mg cholesterol; 496 mg sodium.

Spicy Pot Roast with Onions

The rich sauce adds spice and excitement, and puts the finishing touch on this tender roast. Serve the roast with a green salad and crusty bread.

COOKING TIME: 8 to 10 hours **ATTENTION:** Minimal

---

2 onions, quartered

One 2-pound (910-g) beef roast

One 2.25-ounce (63-g) envelope French's onion-flavored Chili-O Seasoning Mix

½ cup (120 ml) water

Put the onion quarters in the slow cooker and place the pot roast on top of them. In a small bowl, dissolve the seasoning mix in the water, then pour the mixture over the pot roast. Cover and cook on LOW for 8 to 10 hours, or until the roast is done.

To serve, remove the roast from the slow cooker and place it on a platter. Let it rest for 10 minutes, then carve it into ½-inch (6-mm) slices.

YIELD: 8 servings

NUTRITIONAL ANALYSIS: One serving of the basic recipe contains 287 calories; 18 g fat; 18 g protein; 10 g carbohydrate; and .8 g dietary fiber.

ADD IT IN! Add 4 medium tomatoes, peeled and chopped into 1-inch (2.5-cm) pieces, and ½ cup (61 g) baby carrots. Arrange the vegetables around the sides of the slow cooker to help them cook faster.

TRY THIS! To make a great gravy, dissolve 3 tablespoons (24 g) flour in ½ cup (120 ml) water and add the mixture to the juices left in the slow cooker after removing the pot roast. Season the gravy with salt and freshly ground black pepper to taste.

🐄 Slow-Cooker Brisket

Brisket is a very tasty cut of meat that's making a big comeback in trendy restaurants. Cooked slowly with moist heat, it's succulent and full-flavored.

COOKING TIME: 8 to 10 hours   **ATTENTION:** Minimal

One 3- to 4-pound (1.4- to 1.8-kg) beef brisket, or a size that fits inside your covered slow cooker

Salt and freshly ground black pepper

One 2-ounce (55-g) envelope onion soup mix

One .9-ounce (25-g) envelope brown gravy mix

1¹/₂ cups (355 ml) water

Put the brisket in the slow cooker fat side up. Season the beef brisket with salt and pepper. In a small bowl, dissolve the soup mix and gravy mix in the water, then pour the mixture over the brisket. Cover and cook on LOW for 8 to 10 hours, or until the brisket is done.

To serve, remove the roast from the slow cooker and place it fat side up on a platter. Let it rest for 10 to 15 minutes, then carve it diagonally across the grain into thin slices.

YIELD: 10 servings

NUTRITIONAL ANALYSIS: One serving of the basic recipe (made with a 3-pound beef brisket) contains 451 calories; 37 g fat; 24 g protein; 5 g carbohydrate; and .6 g dietary fiber.

ADD IT IN: Peel enough potatoes, carrots, and onions to feed your dinner crowd, cut them into uniform-size chunks, and arrange them around the sides of the slow cooker.

🐄 Braised Beef Brisket

This dish is the tender and flavorful pot roast of your dreams! You can substitute another cut of beef for the brisket, such as chuck eye. You can also sear the beef before adding it to the slow cooker, if you wish.

PREP TIME: 10 minutes   **COOKING TIME:** 7–8 hours
ADDITIONAL STEPS: Reduce the cooking juices to make a sauce

1 beef brisket, flat cut (about 4 pounds or 1820 g)

Salt and pepper to taste

1 cup (235 ml) red wine

1 cup (250 g) mushroom marinara sauce

Put the brisket into the slow cooker and sprinkle with salt and pepper. Pour the wine and tomato sauce over. Cook on LOW for 7 to 8 hours.

Remove the beef from the slow cooker and keep it warm. Degrease the pan juices and reduce them to about 1^1/$_2$ cups (355 ml) in a saucepan over medium-high heat. Serve the beef sliced with some of the gravy.

YIELD: 4 to 6 servings

NUTRITIONAL ANALYSIS: 1112 calories; 84 g fat (70.4% calories from fat); 57 g protein; 23 g carbohydrate; 0 g dietary fiber; 221 mg cholesterol; 2711 mg sodium.

ADD IT IN! Peel and mince 3 or 4 cloves of garlic and add them to the mixture.

Corned Beef and Cabbage

Here's a no-muss, no-fuss way to make your St. Patrick's Day favorite. (Leprechauns and shamrocks not included.)

PREP TIME: 20 minutes   **COOKING TIME:** 8–9 hours
ADDITIONAL STEPS: Add the cabbage and potatoes in the last 2–3 hours

---

1 corned beef (about 4 pounds or 1820 g)

1 small head green cabbage (about 2 pounds or 910 g)

6 medium boiling potatoes (about 2 pounds or 910 g)

Put the corned beef and any spice package that comes with it into the slow cooker. Add water to barely cover the meat. Cook on LOW for 6 hours.

Cut the cabbage into 6 wedges. Peel the potatoes. Add the vegetables to the slow cooker and cook for 2 to 3 hours more.

Remove the corned beef from the cooker. Slice it thin. Remove the cabbage and potatoes from the pot and allow the cabbage to drain. Serve slices of corned beef with a piece of the cabbage and a potato.

YIELD: 6 servings

NUTRITIONAL ANALYSIS: 693 calories; 45 g fat (59.1% calories from fat); 47 g protein; 23 g carbohydrate; 2 g dietary fiber; 162 mg cholesterol; 375 mg sodium.

ADD IT IN! We like to pour a little malt vinegar over our cabbage for a zesty kick.

🐄 Dry Rub Slow-Cooked Beef Ribs

Look for the meatiest beef ribs you can find. There are many varieties of dry rubs on the market, so use your favorite.

PREP TIME: 15 minutes   **COOKING TIME:** 8 hours

3 to 4 pounds (1365 to 1820 g) beef back ribs

1 cup (100 g) beef steak/BBQ rub

4 medium-size onions

Cut the beef into individual ribs. Toss the ribs in a large bowl with the rub until the meat is well coated. Peel the onions and cut them into thin slices. Put the onions into the slow cooker and add the ribs. Cook on LOW for 8 hours. Serve the ribs with some of the onions, if desired.

YIELD: 4 servings

NUTRITIONAL ANALYSIS: Per Serving (not including BBQ rub, which varies a lot): 1463 calories; 123 g fat (76.4% calories from fat); 76 g protein; 9 g carbohydrate; 2 g dietary fiber; 322 mg cholesterol; 248 mg sodium.

🐄 Steak Roll-Ups with Asparagus

The essence of elegance, yet so simple to prepare and cook. Serve with Caesar salad, French bread, and herbed butter.

COOKING TIME: 5 to 7 hours   **ATTENTION:** Minimal

6 cube steaks

¼ teaspoon salt

½ teaspoon freshly ground black pepper

18 baby asparagus spears, trimmed

12 very small new potatoes, scrubbed

Season the cube steaks with the salt and pepper. Position three spears of asparagus on top of each cube steak, then roll up the steaks jelly-roll style. Secure the ends of the rolled-up cube steaks with toothpicks.

Put the potatoes in the slow cooker and place the rolled-up cube steaks seam sides down on top of them. Cover and cook on LOW for 5 to 7 hours.

YIELD: 6 servings

NUTRITIONAL ANALYSIS: One serving of the basic recipe contains 410 calories; 14 g fat; 26 g protein; 46 g carbohydrate; and 5 g dietary fiber.

ADD IT IN! Substitute adobo seasoning for the salt and pepper.

🐄 Cheesesteaks

Just add sub rolls for a great game-day feast!

PREP TIME: 20 minutes   **COOKING TIME:** 3 hours
ADDITIONAL STEPS: Add the cheese in the last hour

4 medium-size onions

2 pounds (910 g) shaved sandwich steak

Salt and pepper to taste

1 pound (455 g) processed cheese, such as Velveeta

Peel and slice the onions. Break the onion rounds into rings and put them into the slow cooker. Add the steak and season with salt and pepper. Cook for 2 hours on HIGH. Add the cheese and cook for another hour on LOW. Stir until the cheese is smooth.

YIELD: 6 to 8 servings

NUTRITIONAL ANALYSIS: 590 calories; 43 g fat (64.1% calories from fat); 39 g protein; 15 g carbohydrate; 1 g dietary fiber; 147 mg cholesterol; 1519 mg sodium.

Swiss Steak

This classic dish is wonderful served with spaetzle, noodles, or boiled potatoes.

PREP TIME: 30 minutes   **COOKING TIME:** 3 hours on HIGH, 6 hours on LOW
ADDITIONAL STEPS: Brown the steaks before putting them into the slow cooker

2 pounds (910 g) round steak, cut about 1 inch (2.5 cm) thick

Salt and pepper to taste

1 cup (125 g) all-purpose flour

¼ cup (60 ml) cooking oil

1 (12-ounce or 340-g) can diced tomatoes with celery and onion

Cut the steak into 4 equal-size pieces. Pound the steak lightly with a meat tenderizer. Season with salt and pepper and dredge the meat in the flour. Heat a sauté pan over medium-high heat and add the oil. Sauté the beef until well browned, then turn and repeat on the other side. Put the browned meat into the slow cooker. Add the diced tomatoes and cook for 3 hours on HIGH or 6 hours on LOW. Serve the steak with some of the sauce over it.

YIELD: 4 servings

NUTRITIONAL ANALYSIS: 685 calories; 42 g fat (55.4% calories from fat); 47 g protein; 28 g carbohydrate; 2 g dietary fiber; 134 mg cholesterol; 121 mg sodium.

🐂 Stuffed Beef Round Steak

This is a simpler take on the classic Italian dish braciola. The round steak is cut very thin, stuffed, tied, and braised in a flavorful marinara sauce. Slices of meat are served with the cooking sauce. In New England, round steak is often sold thinly cut specifically for this dish. If you can't find it this way at your market, ask the butcher to cut the meat thin for you. We recommend using the LOW temperature setting for a more tender dish.

PREP TIME: 45 minutes   **COOKING TIME:** 7–8 hours
ADDITIONAL STEPS: Cook the stuffing; prepare the meat

1 (12-ounce or 340-g) package stovetop stuffing mix

1 thin-cut top round steak (about 2 pounds or 910 g)

Salt and pepper to taste

Cooking oil

2 cups (490 g) marinara sauce

Additional materials: **Butcher twine**

Prepare the stuffing mix according to package directions and set aside to cool.

Lay the steak on a cutting board and cover with plastic wrap. With the side of a cleaver or with a meat mallet, gently pound the meat to a uniform thickness. Sprinkle with salt and pepper.

Spread the stuffing onto the meat and roll up the meat. Tie the roll with butcher's twine. Heat a sauté pan large enough to hold the steak over medium-high heat. Add a couple of tablespoons (30 ml) of oil and sear the beef on all sides.

Transfer the beef to the slow cooker and add the marinara sauce. Cook for 7 to 8 hours on LOW. Remove the meat from the slow cooker and remove the twine. Cut rounds about ½ inch (1 cm) thick. Serve with some of the cooking sauce, passing the remaining sauce at the table.

YIELD: 4 to 6 servings

NUTRITIONAL ANALYSIS: 555 calories; 22 g fat (36.3% calories from fat); 36 g protein; 50 g carbohydrate; 3 g dietary fiber; 90 mg cholesterol; 1320 mg sodium.

ADD IT IN: Feel free to add embellishments on top of the stuffing, such as Italian cold cuts, provolone cheese, or even peeled and sliced hard-boiled eggs laid end to end.

Three-Alarm Chili

When it turns cold and wet outside, there's nothing better to warm the bones than Three-Alarm Chili. Serve with your choice of shredded cheese and plenty of beverages to quench the fire.

COOKING TIME: 6 to 8 hours   **ATTENTION:** Minimal

2 pounds (910 g) beef chuck, cut into 1-inch (2.5-cm) cubes

1/2 teaspoon salt

1/4 teaspoon freshly ground black pepper

One 2.25-ounce (63-g) envelope French's Texas-style Chili-O Seasoning Mix

One 14 1/2-ounce (413-g) can Mexican-flavored stewed tomatoes with jalapeños, garlic, and cumin

Put the beef cubes in the slow cooker and season them on all sides with the salt and pepper. Sprinkle the beef cubes with the seasoning mix, then top them with the stewed tomatoes. Cover and cook on LOW for 6 to 8 hours.

Before serving, stir the chili and season it with additional salt and freshly ground black pepper.

YIELD: 8 servings

NUTRITIONAL ANALYSIS: One serving of the basic recipe contains 291 calories; 18 g fat; 19 g protein; 12 g carbohydrate; and .8 g dietary fiber.

ADD IT IN! Add 5 to 10 drops Tabasco sauce along with the seasoning mix and stewed tomatoes—if you dare!

Taco Filling

This easy recipe is the basis for a great taco feast. These spice mixes are found in most Latin markets.

PREP TIME: 10 minutes **COOKING TIME:** 3 hours on HIGH, 5–7 hours on LOW
ADDITIONAL STEPS: Break up the meat halfway through cooking

2 pounds (910 g) ground beef

Salt and pepper to taste

1 (1-ounce or 30-g) package Menudo or other Mexican spice mix

1 (6-ounce or 175-ml) can tomato sauce

Break up the beef into small chunks and add to the slow cooker. Season with salt and pepper to taste and add the spice mix. Be sure to crush any large herb leaves with your fingers. Add the tomato sauce. Cook on HIGH for 1½ hours or on LOW for 3 to 4 hours. Using a slotted spoon, break up the meat until it is in fine pieces. Continue to cook on HIGH for 1½ hours or on LOW for another 2 to 3 hours.

YIELD: 6 to 8 servings

NUTRITIONAL ANALYSIS: 364 calories; 30 g fat (75.5% calories from fat); 19 g protein; 3 g carbohydrate; 1 g dietary fiber; 96 mg cholesterol; 207 mg sodium.

Slow-Cooked Teriyaki Steak

Peanut oil paired with teriyaki sauce adds just the right accent. Serve with rice and sauce from the slow cooker.

COOKING TIME: 8 to 10 hours　　　　　　　　**ATTENTION:** Minimal

1 pound (455 g) beef stir-fry strips

1 to 2 tablespoons (14 to 28 ml) peanut oil

1 cup (235 ml) teriyaki sauce

¼ cup (60 ml) water

In a large skillet over medium heat, brown the beef strips in the peanut oil. Drain the browned meat and place it in the slow cooker.

In a small bowl, combine the teriyaki sauce and water, then pour the mixture over the beef strips. Cover and cook on LOW for 8 to 10 hours.

YIELD: 4 servings

NUTRITIONAL ANALYSIS: One serving of the basic recipe (made with 1 tablespoon peanut oil) contains 375 calories; 25 g fat; 25 g protein; 12 g carbohydrate; and trace dietary fiber.

ADD IT IN! Brown the beef strips with any or all of the following: ½ cup (33 g) chopped onion, 1 teaspoon minced fresh ginger, 1 clove garlic, minced. Place the cooked seasonings in the slow cooker along with the meat.

DID YOU KNOW? The mild flavor of peanut oil really makes a difference when you're cooking an Asian-inspired dish. A good cold-pressed peanut oil will have the aroma of freshly roasted peanuts. Preserve the flavor and aroma by storing the oil in the refrigerator or in another cold, dark location.

🐄 Lazy-Day Cheeseburgers

Lazy days can produce the most delicious meals. Enjoy this cheesy burger mixture on onion buns.

COOKING TIME: 6 to 7 hours   **ATTENTION:** Minimal

1¼ **pounds (569 g) ground beef**

¼ **teaspoon salt**

⅛ **teaspoon freshly ground black pepper**

8 **ounces (225 g) pasteurized processed cheese food, grated**

8 **onion-flavored sandwich buns**

In a large skillet over medium heat, brown the ground beef. Drain the browned meat and season with the salt and pepper. Put the browned meat in the slow cooker, add the cheese, and stir to combine. Cover and cook on LOW for 6 to 7 hours.

Spoon the burger mixture onto the buns, and serve the sandwiches with plenty of dinner napkins.

YIELD: 8 servings

NUTRITIONAL ANALYSIS: One serving of the basic recipe contains 454 calories; 31 g fat; 23 g protein; 22 g carbohydrate; and .9 g dietary fiber.

ADD IT IN! Brown the ground beef with ½ cup (43 g) chopped onion and 1 clove garlic, minced.

TRY THIS! Add a blast of flavor by putting a dollop of gourmet ketchup or mustard, chutney, or green chile sauce (or some sliced jalapeños) on top of the burger mixture. A red cabbage or broccoli slaw makes a crunchy, colorful accompaniment.

Gumbo-Joe Hot Sandwich Filling

Not your ordinary sloppy sandwich. Try, instead, a little something Cajun for your sandwich bun.

COOKING TIME: 4 to 6 hours on LOW, 2 to 3 hours on HIGH
ATTENTION: Minimal

One 10³/₄-ounce (305-g) can condensed chicken gumbo soup

¹/₂ cup (120 g) ketchup

2 pounds (910 g) ground beef, browned and drained

Salt and freshly ground black pepper

Put the condensed soup and ketchup in the slow cooker and stir to combine. Add the browned meat and stir again. Cover and cook on LOW for 4 to 6 hours or on HIGH for 2 to 3 hours.

Stir the mixture and season it with salt and pepper to taste. Serve it on toasted sandwich buns, with a side of coleslaw.

YIELD: 10 servings

NUTRITIONAL ANALYSIS: One serving of the basic recipe contains 314 calories; 25 g fat; 17 g protein; 6 g carbohydrate; and .3 g dietary fiber.

ADD IT IN! Add ¹/₂ cup (113 g) frozen Seasoning-Blend Vegetables (page 29), 2 tablespoons (30 g) prepared yellow mustard, and 1/2 teaspoon Cajun seasoning to the soup-and-ketchup mixture.

DID YOU KNOW? No one is sure whether the word "gumbo" derives from an African word for okra, "gombo," or a Choctaw word for the spice file (made from dried sassafras leaves), "kombo." Both are ingredients in what we know as gumbo.

🐄 Fiesta Meatballs

Jalapeños and cumin lend a distinctive southwestern flare to this party favorite. Serve over Spanish rice or Yellow Rice (page 310 and 307), with a side of tortilla chips. Leftover meatballs on buns make awesome next-day sandwiches.

COOKING TIME: $3^1/_2$ to $4^1/_2$ hours on LOW, 1 to 2 hours on HIGH
ATTENTION: Minimal

One $14^1/_2$-ounce (413-g) can Mexican-flavored stewed tomatoes with jalapeños, garlic, and cumin

1 small green bell pepper, chopped

$^1/_4$ teaspoon salt

$1^1/_4$ pounds (569 g) frozen fully cooked meatballs, completely thawed

Put the stewed tomatoes, chopped green pepper, and salt in the slow cooker and stir to combine. Add the thawed meatballs and stir again. Cover and cook on LOW for $3^1/_2$ to $4^1/_2$ hours or on HIGH for 1 to 2 hours, or until the sauce is hot and thickened.

YIELD: 5 servings

NUTRITIONAL ANALYSIS: One serving of the basic recipe contains 378 calories; 30 g fat; 16 g protein; 15 g carbohydrate; and 4 g dietary fiber.

TRY THIS! Pass the crudités! To add some crunch (not to mention vitamins) to your fiesta, make a platter of red, yellow, and orange pepper rings, cherry tomatoes, broccoli bites, and sliced cucumbers. Let family and friends help themselves. End the meal with refreshing sliced melon.

🐄 Simple Veal Stew

This recipe is great as is, or it can be embellished in many ways. Try adding diced carrots, or some tomato, garlic, or fresh herbs. It's great over pasta, polenta, risotto, or mashed potatoes.

PREP TIME: 10 minutes   **COOKING TIME:** 7–8 hours

2 pounds (910 g) stew veal

1 cup (235 ml) red wine

1 (12-ounce or 355-ml) can mushroom gravy

Salt and pepper to taste

Put the veal, red wine, and gravy into the slow cooker and stir them together. Season with salt and pepper to taste (remember, the gravy will already add some salt). Cook on LOW for 7 to 8 hours.

YIELD: 6 to 8 servings over pasta or rice

NUTRITIONAL ANALYSIS: 388 calories; 25 g fat (61.3% calories from fat); 32 g protein; 3 g carbohydrate; trace dietary fiber; 113 mg cholesterol; 595 mg sodium.

🐄 Roast Veal Shoulder

Veal shoulder makes a delicious slow-cooker roast. The bacon adds flavor and needed moisture to this lean meat. You can discard the bacon after cooking, if you wish.

PREP TIME: 10 minutes   **COOKING TIME:** 6–8 hours

1 boneless rolled veal shoulder roast (3 to 4 pounds or 1365 to 1820 g)

Salt and pepper to taste

4 slices bacon

½ cup (120 ml) white wine

Put the veal roast into the slow cooker. Season the meat with salt and pepper. Drape the bacon on top of the meat. Pour the wine over all. Cook on LOW for 6 to 8 hours. Remove the meat from the cooker and remove and discard the bacon. Remove the twine from the roast and slice. The cooking liquid can be reduced to make a simple sauce, or it can be a base for gravy.

YIELD: 6 to 8 servings

NUTRITIONAL ANALYSIS: 265 calories; 11 g fat (41.6% calories from fat); 36 g protein; trace carbohydrate; 0 g dietary fiber; 150 mg cholesterol; 200 mg sodium.

ADD IT IN: Sprinkle the roast with some chopped fresh rosemary for an added flavor dimension.

🐄 Osso Buco

This classic Italian dish is traditionally served with risotto and topped with gremolata, a sprightly garnish made of minced garlic, lemon zest, and parsley.

PREP TIME: 25 minutes   **COOKING TIME:** 8 hours
ADDITIONAL STEPS: Brown the veal before adding it to the slow cooker

4 pounds (1820 g) veal shanks, cut about 2 inches (5 cm) long

Salt and pepper to taste

Cooking oil

1 cup (250 g) garlic marinara sauce

½ cup (120 ml) white wine

Heat a sauté pan over medium-high heat. Season the shanks with salt and pepper. Put a couple of tablespoons (30 ml) of oil into the sauté pan and sear the veal on each side until browned, working in batches, if necessary, to avoid crowding the pan. Put the veal into the slow cooker and add the marinara sauce and wine. Cook for 8 hours on LOW. Carefully remove the veal from the cooker. Serve the shanks topped with some of the sauce.

YIELD: 4 to 6 servings

NUTRITIONAL ANALYSIS: 391 calories; 10 g fat (25.3% calories from fat); 64 g protein; 4 g carbohydrate; 1 g dietary fiber; 236 mg cholesterol; 363 mg sodium.

ADD IT IN: Add several handfuls of baby carrots, along with a small, diced onion, to deepen the flavor.

Brats in Beer

Bratwurst sausages are a classic barbecue item in the Midwest, and with good reason. Slow cooking helps bring the taste of barbecue indoors.

PREP TIME: 10 minutes   **COOKING TIME:** 2 hours on HIGH, 4 hours on LOW

1 pound (455 g) bratwursts

1 (12-ounce or 355-ml) can beer

Put the bratwursts into the slow cooker. Add the beer and enough water to cover the sausages. Cook for 2 hours on HIGH or 4 hours on LOW.

YIELD: 4 to 6 servings

NUTRITIONAL ANALYSIS: 251 calories; 20 g fat (75.3% calories from fat); 11 g protein; 4 g carbohydrate; trace dietary fiber; 45 mg cholesterol; 424 mg sodium.

SERVING SUGGESTION: Serve the sausages on rolls.

Sausage with Apples and Onions

This dish is so adaptable it can be served on nearly any occasion. Serve it with pancakes for a hearty breakfast, or pair it with mashed potatoes for a delicious dinner.

PREP TIME: 30 minutes
COOKING TIME: 2–3 hours on HIGH, 6–8 hours on LOW
ADDITIONAL STEPS: Sauté the apples, onions, and sausages

2 pounds (910 g) apples

4 medium-size onions

Cooking oil

Salt and pepper to taste

1 pound (455 g) breakfast sausage links

Peel and core the apples and cut them into 1/4-inch-thick (6-mm-thick) slices. Peel the onions and julienne them 1/4 inch (6 mm) thick. Heat a large sauté pan over medium-high heat. Add enough oil to coat the pan and add the apples and onions. Season with salt and pepper to taste. Sauté, tossing occasionally, until lightly browned. Put the sautéed apples and onions into the slow cooker. Add the sausage links to the sauté pan and brown on all sides for a few minutes. Add them to the slow cooker. Cook on HIGH for 2 to 3 hours or on LOW for 6 to 8 hours.

YIELD: 4 to 6 servings

NUTRITIONAL ANALYSIS: 426 calories; 31 g fat (64.6% calories from fat); 10 g protein; 28 g carbohydrate; 5 g dietary fiber; 51 mg cholesterol; 507 mg sodium.

Sausage Gravy

This is delicious served over fresh biscuits for a great Southern-style breakfast treat. Start the dish the night before, and the aroma will have you leaping out of bed in the morning.

PREP TIME: 10 minutes   **COOKING TIME:** 8 hours
ADDITIONAL STEPS: Add flour and milk after 1 hour

1 pound (455 g) bulk breakfast sausage

1/2 cup (60 g) all-purpose flour

2 cups (470 ml) milk

Salt and pepper to taste

Break up the sausage into small bits and put into the slow cooker. Cook on HIGH for 1 hour. Stir well to break the sausage into small "pebbles." Stir in the flour until absorbed. Stir in the milk. Add salt and pepper to taste. Turn the cooker to LOW and cook for 6 to 7 hours.

YIELD: 4 to 6 servings

NUTRITIONAL ANALYSIS: 403 calories; 33 g fat (74.9% calories from fat); 13 g protein; 12 g carbohydrate; trace dietary fiber; 63 mg cholesterol; 545 mg sodium.

SERVING SUGGESTION: Make some quick biscuits to serve as a base for the sausage gravy.

Slow-Cooker Sausage and Lima Beans

The mild flavor of limas and the spicy flavor of sausage are perfect counterparts. Serve with biscuits and honey butter.

COOKING TIME: 8 to 10 hours   **ATTENTION:** Minimal

2 cups (475 ml) hot water

2 beef bouillon cubes

1 to 1½ pounds (455 to 683 g) smoked sausage, sliced into ½-inch (1.3-cm) coins

One 15-ounce (417-g) can baby lima beans, drained

½ teaspoon freshly ground black pepper

Put the hot water and bouillon cubes in the slow cooker and stir until the bouillon cubes have dissolved. Add the sausage coins and lima beans, and stir again. Cover and cook on LOW for 8 to 10 hours.

Before serving, stir the mixture and season it with the pepper.

YIELD: 8 servings

NUTRITIONAL ANALYSIS: One serving of the basic recipe (made with 1 pound smoked sausage) contains 371 calories; 18 g fat; 19 g protein; 35 g carbohydrate; and 11 g dietary fiber.

ADD IT IN! Add ½ cup (60 g) chopped green onion, 1 clove garlic, minced, and hot sauce to taste along with the sausage coins and lima beans.

DID YOU KNOW? Lima beans, also called butter beans, are a favorite southern staple. Fordhooks are the large variety and slightly stronger in taste. Baby limas are a smaller, milder variety, not just small Fordhooks. Choose your beans accordingly!

Pork Roast with 40 Cloves of Garlic

Succulent pork roast with mellow, sweet garlic tastes great sliced thin and served with gravy. Enjoy with a baked-apple dessert.

COOKING TIME: 6 to 8 hours | **ATTENTION:** Minimal

---

40 cloves garlic, peeled

One 2- to 3-pound (.9- to 1.4-kg) boneless pork loin roast, boneless

One 10³/₄-ounce (305-g) can condensed cream of mushroom soup

Put the garlic cloves in the slow cooker, spreading them out to form a single layer. Place the pork roast on top of the garlic cloves and pour the condensed soup over the pork. Cover and cook for 6 to 8 hours on LOW, or until the roast is done.

YIELD: 8 servings

NUTRITIONAL ANALYSIS: One serving of the basic recipe (made with a 2-pound pork roast) contains 230 calories; 14 g fat; 19 g protein; 8 g carbohydrate; and .4 g dietary fiber.

TRY THIS! You can purchase jars of whole garlic cloves in oil, or you can peel your own. If you've never peeled garlic before, try this method: Press the head of garlic on your countertop until the cloves begin to separate. Remove 40 cloves and toss them into a pot of boiling water for just a few seconds. Allow them to cool, then slip off their peels. Slice the root end off each clove, and you're done!

To make a great gravy, dissolve 3 tablespoons (24 g) flour in ¹/₂ cup (120 ml) water and add the mixture to the juices left in the slow cooker after the pork roast has been removed. Season the gravy with salt and freshly ground black pepper to taste.

🐷 Cherry-Glazed Pork Roast

Pork pairs well with so many fruits. Here, we use cherries for a tart and tasty flavor twist.

PREP TIME: 10 minutes **COOKING TIME:** 3 hours on HIGH, 6–7 hours on LOW
ADDITIONAL STEPS: Degrease the pan liquids and make a sauce

1 boneless pork loin roast (about 3 pounds or 1365 g)

Salt and pepper to taste

1 (12-ounce or 340-g) jar cherry preserves

2 tablespoons (30 ml) balsamic vinegar

4 tablespoons (½ stick or 55 g) unsalted butter

Season the roast with salt and pepper and place it in the slow cooker. Spread the cherry preserves over the pork and add ½ cup (120 ml) water to the slow cooker. Cook on HIGH for about 2 hours, or for 6 to 7 hours on LOW, until a meat thermometer inserted into the thickest part reads 165°F. Remove the roast from the cooker and keep it warm. Degrease the pan juices. Put the degreased juice into a saucepan and add the balsamic vinegar. Bring to a boil and reduce to about ½ cup (120 ml). Swirl in the butter to make an emulsified sauce. Adjust the salt and pepper to taste. Serve slices of the roast with some of the sauce over it.

YIELD: 6 to 8 servings

NUTRITIONAL ANALYSIS: 321 calories; 22 g fat (61.8% calories from fat); 25 g protein; 5 g carbohydrate; trace dietary fiber; 100 mg cholesterol; 137 mg sodium.

🐖 Easy Maple Barbecue Pulled Pork

Pulled pork is a classic Southern barbecue treat. Here, we add a Northern twist with maple syrup.

PREP TIME: 10 minutes   **COOKING TIME:** 8¹/₂–9 hours
ADDITIONAL STEPS: Cool and shred the pork

1 pork shoulder roast (about 5 pounds or 2275 g)

2 cups (500 g) barbecue sauce, divided

¹/₂ cup (170 g) maple syrup

Put the pork, 1 cup (250 g) of the barbecue sauce, and the maple syrup into the slow cooker. Cook for 8 hours on LOW. Remove the pork from the cooker and allow to cool enough to handle. Shred the meat, discarding the bones. Degrease the liquid from the slow cooker. Add the shredded meat and the liquid back into the slow cooker along with the remaining 1 cup (250 g) barbecue sauce. Cook for another ¹/₂ to 1 hour.

YIELD: 8 to 10 servings

NUTRITIONAL ANALYSIS: 481 calories; 32 g fat (60.1% calories from fat); 30 g protein; 17 g carbohydrate; 1 g dietary fiber; 121 mg cholesterol; 520 mg sodium.

SERVING SUGGESTION: Serve with red beans and rice, or on a bun as a sandwich.

🐖 Pulled-Pork Barbecue

Fall-apart goodness that you shred with a fork. Serve on a sandwich bun, accompanied by coleslaw and potato salad.

COOKING TIME: 8 to 10 hours   **ATTENTION:** Minimal

One 3-pound (1.4-kg) pork loin roast, boneless, or a size that fits inside your covered slow cooker

1¹/₂ cups (375 g) barbecue sauce

In a large skillet over medium heat, sear the pork roast on all sides. Place the pork roast in the slow cooker and drizzle it with the barbecue sauce. Cover and cook on LOW for 8 to 10 hours.

Shred the pork roast with a fork and serve it on sandwich buns.

NUTRITIONAL ANALYSIS: One serving of the basic recipe contains 287 calories; 17 g fat; 26 g protein; 6 g carbohydrate; and .7 g dietary fiber.

DID YOU KNOW? Pulled pork, pork smoked until the meat was tender enough to pull apart by hand, was the first barbecue. Nowadays it's also considered okay to pull it into shreds with a fork!

Adobo Stew

What a big payoff for such a small amount of effort! Enjoy this peppery, tender stew with rice and mixed vegetables.

COOKING TIME: 6 to 8 hours   **ATTENTION:** Minimal

1½-pound (683-g) beef or pork roast, cut into 1-inch (2.5-cm) cubes

½ cup (120 ml) water

½ cup (120 ml) apple cider vinegar

¼ cup (60 ml) soy sauce

¼ teaspoon freshly ground black pepper

Put the beef or pork cubes in the slow cooker. In a small bowl, combine the water, apple cider vinegar, soy sauce, and pepper, then pour the mixture over the meat. Cover and cook on LOW for 6 to 8 hours.

Before serving, stir the stew and season it with additional freshly ground black pepper. Serve the stew with rice, either with or without the sauce.

YIELD: 5 servings

NUTRITIONAL ANALYSIS: One serving of the basic recipe (made with beef roast) contains 295 calories; 21 g fat; 22 g protein; 3 g carbohydrate; and 0 g dietary fiber.

ADD IT IN! If you like the taste of garlic, substitute garlic-flavored soy sauce for the plain soy sauce. If you don't have this gourmet soy sauce on hand, add 2 cloves garlic, minced, to the stew along with the plain soy sauce. For an authentic touch, substitute coconut milk for the water. Throw in a bay leaf for good measure, as long as you remember to remove it before serving the stew.

DID YOU KNOW? Adobo is the national dish of the Philippines. It's a stew of pork, beef, or chicken cooked in soy sauce and vinegar, with garlic and lots of black pepper. Our version calls for less black pepper, but if you get a hankering to be really authentic, feel free to keep that pepper mill grinding.

⭐ Creamy Pork Tenderloin

Garlic-flavored mushrooms and pork make for a tasty and tender main dish. Serve with baked potatoes and a green salad.

COOKING TIME: 8 to 10 hours	**ATTENTION:** Minimal

1¼ pounds (569 g) pork tenderloin
1 teaspoon adobo seasoning, with salt and with or without black pepper
Two 10¾-ounce (305-g) cans condensed cream of mushroom soup
Salt and freshly ground black pepper

Season the pork tenderloin on all sides with the adobo seasoning, then place the tenderloin in the slow cooker. Pour the condensed soup over the tenderloin, covering it completely. Cover and cook on LOW for 8 to 10 hours.

Place the tenderloin on a platter and season it with salt and pepper to taste. Serve it with the extra gravy on the side.

YIELD: 5 servings

NUTRITIONAL ANALYSIS: One serving of the basic recipe contains 264 calories; 13 g fat; 26 g protein; 9 g carbohydrate; and .4 g dietary fiber.

ADD IT IN! For a more garlicky sauce, substitute condensed cream of mushroom with roasted garlic soup for the plain soup.

DID YOU KNOW? Adobo seasoning is definitely in the running for best-kept-secret ingredient. A traditional and popular spice mix from Mexico, it's well balanced, spicy, and rich in flavor, but not hot. Adobo seasoning comes in various combinations—with or without salt and/or black pepper—so read the label before you buy. What you can count on it containing is garlic, onion, Mexican oregano, cumin, and cayenne red pepper.

🐖 Plantain-Stuffed Pork Tenderloin Braised in Tomatillo Sauce

This dish involves a little more prep work than many in this book, but it is very much worth it. Serve with rice, black beans, and warm tortillas.

PREP TIME: 45 minutes **COOKING TIME:** 2 hours on HIGH, 4–5 hours on LOW
ADDITIONAL STEPS: Prepare the pork tenderloin rolls

2 pork tenderloins (about 1½ pounds or 685 g)

Salt and pepper to taste

1 medium-size ripe plantain

Cooking oil

1 (16-ounce or 455-g) jar tomatillo salsa (also called salsa verde)

***Additional materials:* Butcher twine**

Trim any fat and silver skin (the thin, pearlescent membrane) from the tenderloins. Cut them in half across. Split each half lengthwise, leaving one side still attached. Lay out the meat pieces on a cutting board and lightly pound them to a uniform thickness. Season the meat with salt and pepper.

Peel the plantain and cut it into slices. Heat a sauté pan over medium-high heat and add a couple of tablespoons (30 ml) of oil. Sauté the plantain until lightly browned. Allow to cool.

Put some of the plantain in the center of each piece of pork and roll them up, tucking in the ends. Tie the rolls with butcher's twine. Reheat the sauté pan over medium-high heat and add a little more oil. Sear the tenderloin rolls in the sauté pan until browned on each side.

Put the pork rolls into the slow cooker and add the tomatillo sauce. Cook for 2 hours on HIGH or 4 to 5 hours on LOW. Remove the pork from the cooker and remove the twine. Slice the rolls and put the slices on each of 4 plates. Spoon some of the sauce over the meat.

YIELD: 4 servings

NUTRITIONAL ANALYSIS: 299 calories; 6 g fat (18.7% calories from fat); 36 g protein; 22 g carbohydrate; 1 g dietary fiber; 111 mg cholesterol; 459 mg sodium.

ADD IT IN! Sprinkle some chopped fresh cilantro in with the salsa verde.

🐖 Smoked Shoulder Braised in Cider

Pork and apples are classic flavor buddies. In this recipe, cider, cloves, and pepper add a deeper, more complex taste to the beloved combination.

PREP TIME: 10 minutes   **COOKING TIME:** 8–10 hours

1 smoked pork shoulder (about 5 pounds or 2275 g)

2 cups (470 ml) apple cider

4 whole cloves

Pepper to taste

Put the pork shoulder into the slow cooker. Add the cider, cloves, and pepper to taste. Cook on LOW for 8 to 10 hours. Remove the pork shoulder from the cooker and slice.

YIELD: 6 to 8 servings

NUTRITIONAL ANALYSIS: 542 calories; 39 g fat (65.6% calories from fat); 37 g protein; 9 g carbohydrate; 1 g dietary fiber; 151 mg cholesterol; 148 mg sodium.

ADD IT IN: Core, peel, and slice 3 or 4 apples and add them to the cooker for some applesauce.

🐖 Mexican Pork Tinga

A tinga is a slow-cooked meat that is then pulled into shreds and typically heaped onto tostadas.

PREP TIME: 10 minutes   **COOKING TIME:** 10^1/$_2$ hours
ADDITIONAL STEPS: Allow the meat to cool enough to handle after cooking

1 pork shoulder (about 5 pounds or 2275 g)

1 (16-ounce or 455-g) jar roasted tomato salsa

1 cup (235 ml) Malta Goya or similar malt drink, or beer

Put the pork shoulder into the slow cooker and pour the salsa and malt drink over it. Cook on LOW for 10 hours. Remove the meat from the cooker, leaving the juices in the pot and the cooker on LOW. Allow the meat to cool, and then shred it with your hands or with tongs. Return the shredded meat to the slow cooker, stir into the sauce, and reheat for ^{1}/$_2$ hour.

NUTRITIONAL ANALYSIS: 424 calories; 31 g fat (67.3% calories from fat); 30 g protein; 4 g carbohydrate; 1 g dietary fiber; 121 mg cholesterol; 309 mg sodium.

SERVING SUGGESTION: Serve with tostadas and a variety of Mexican toppings.

Pork and Black Bean Stew

Serve with tortillas, fresh cilantro, and lime wedges for an authentic Mexican treat.

PREP TIME: 20 minutes   **COOKING TIME:** 2–3 hours on HIGH, 5–6 hours on LOW

2 pounds (910 g) lean pork, such as loin

2 (14-ounce or 395-g) cans black beans

1 (16-ounce or 455-g) jar salsa

Salt and pepper to taste

Trim the fat from the pork. Cut the pork into 1-inch (2.5-cm) cubes and put them into the slow cooker. Drain the beans and add them to the pork. Add the salsa and stir. Cook for 2 to 3 hours on HIGH or 5 to 6 hours on LOW. Adjust the seasoning with salt and pepper to taste.

YIELD: 6 to 8 servings

NUTRITIONAL ANALYSIS: 196 calories; 5 g fat (22.6% calories from fat); 20 g protein; 17 g carbohydrate; 6 g dietary fiber; 36 mg cholesterol; 580 mg sodium.

Smoked Ham Hocks with White Beans

If you're going to cook beans in a slow cooker, you must presoak them. You can do this by soaking the beans in cool water overnight, then draining them and adding them to the recipe. A faster method is to cover the beans with plenty of water in a saucepan, bring them to a boil, remove them from the heat, keep them covered, and allow them to stand for 1 hour. Drain the beans and proceed with the recipe.

PREP TIME: 10 minutes   **COOKING TIME:** 8–10 hours

1 pound (455 g) great Northern or other white beans, presoaked

2 pounds (910 g) smoked ham hocks

4 cups (940 ml) chicken stock or broth

Pepper to taste

Put the beans and the ham hocks into the slow cooker. Add the chicken stock and enough water so you have about twice as much liquid as beans. Cook on LOW for 8 to 10 hours, until the beans are tender and the liquid is absorbed. Check and add liquid during the cooking as needed to keep the beans from going dry.

YIELD: 4 servings

NUTRITIONAL ANALYSIS: 1006 calories; 44 g fat (40.3% calories from fat); 76 g protein; 72 g carbohydrate; 23 g dietary fiber; 241 mg cholesterol; 2304 mg sodium.

ADD IT IN! Stir in 1 or 2 tablespoons (2.5 to 5 g) chopped fresh thyme to add another flavor dimension.

Red Beans and Ham Hocks

Grab a couple of slices of cornbread, some rice, and a seat at the picnic table under the old oak tree for a down-home meal of Red Beans and Ham Hocks. Can't you hear "What a Wonderful Life" playing in the distance?

COOKING TIME: 8 to 10 hours on LOW, 5 to 6 hours on HIGH
ATTENTION: Minimal

Two 15-ounce (417-g) cans red beans, drained

1¹/₂ cups (340 g) frozen Seasoning-Blend Vegetables (page 29), thawed

2 to 3 pounds (.9 to 1.4 kg) smoked ham hocks

Water

Salt and freshly ground black pepper

Put the red beans and Seasoning-Blend Vegetables in the slow cooker. Arrange the ham hocks on top of the beans and vegetables, then add enough water to cover everything. Cover and cook on LOW for 8 to 10 hours or on HIGH for 5 to 6 hours.

Before serving, stir the ham hocks, beans, and vegetables, and season the mixture with salt and pepper to taste.

YIELD: 10 servings

NUTRITIONAL ANALYSIS: One serving of the basic recipe (made with 2 pounds smoked ham hocks) contains 559 calories; 18 g fat; 42 g protein; 58 g carbohydrate; and 24 g dietary fiber.

ADD IT IN! Put 1 clove garlic, minced, and 1 bay leaf along with the beans and vegetables.

DID YOU KNOW? A ham hock is the lower part of a hog's hind leg.

Ham and Potato Bake

Here's a good way to use up that leftover Easter ham.

PREP TIME: 30 minutes   **COOKING TIME:** 2 hours on HIGH, 4 hours on LOW

4 pounds (1820 g) potatoes

1 pound (455 g) ham, thinly sliced

1 (16-ounce or 475-ml) jar Alfredo sauce

Peel the potatoes and slice them ¼ inch (6 mm) thick. Put a layer of potatoes in the slow cooker, top with some ham, and repeat until the ingredients are all used, ending with potatoes on top. Pour the Alfredo sauce over all and cook for 4 hours on LOW or 2 hours on HIGH.

YIELD: 4 to 6 servings

NUTRITIONAL ANALYSIS: 523 calories; 22 g fat (36.9% calories from fat); 23 g protein; 60 g carbohydrate; 5 g dietary fiber; 86 mg cholesterol; 1417 mg sodium.

ADD IT IN: Sprinkle ½ cup (40 g) of shredded Parmesan cheese on top of the casserole.

Orange-Glazed Ham

This is an easy way to bake a ham and leave the oven available for the rest of the dinner.

PREP TIME: 10 minutes   **COOKING TIME:** 3–4 hours on HIGH , 7–8 hours on LOW

1 semi-boneless ham (about 6 pounds or 2730 g)

1 (12-ounce or 340-g) jar orange marmalade

4 or 5 whole cloves

Place the ham in the slow cooker. Slather the marmalade over the ham and stick the cloves into the ham. Cook on HIGH for 3 to 4 hours or on LOW for 7 to 8 hours.

YIELD: 8 to 10 servings

NUTRITIONAL ANALYSIS: 590 calories; 29 g fat (44.9% calories from fat); 48 g protein; 33 g carbohydrate; 1 g dietary fiber; 155 mg cholesterol; 3615 mg sodium.

Ham and Cabbage Casserole

This would be perfect with some noodles or spaetzle on the side for a nice, cozy winter dinner!

PREP TIME: 30 minutes   **COOKING TIME:** 2–3 hours on HIGH, 6–7 hours on LOW

1 small head green cabbage

1 pound (455 g) boneless ham, sliced

1 (10-ounce or 285-ml) can condensed cream of cheddar soup

Core and shred the cabbage and place in alternating layers with the ham slices in the slow cooker. Pour the cream of cheddar soup over all. Cook for 2 to 3 hours on HIGH or 6 to 7 hours on LOW.

YIELD: 4 to 6 servings

NUTRITIONAL ANALYSIS: 168 calories; 10 g fat (54.3% calories from fat); 14 g protein; 5 g carbohydrate; trace dietary fiber; 49 mg cholesterol; 1181 mg sodium.

ADD IT IN! Layer in some shredded cheddar to intensify the cheese flavor.

Holiday Ham

This quick-and-easy ham will get raves. Don't let on how little time it really took to prepare!

COOKING TIME: 6 to 8 hours   **ATTENTION:** Minimal

2$\frac{1}{2}$- to 4-pound (1.1- to 1.8-kg) ham, depending on slow cooker size

2 cups (498 g) canned pineapple chunks, undrained

$\frac{1}{2}$ cup (161 g) pure maple syrup

Put the ham in the slow cooker. Pour the pineapple chunks over the ham and then drizzle on the maple syrup. Cover and cook on LOW for 6 to 8 hours.

Serve the ham with the pineapple chunks on the side.

YIELD: 10 servings

NUTRITIONAL ANALYSIS: One serving of the basic recipe (made with a 2$\frac{1}{2}$-pound ham) contains 278 calories; 12 g fat; 20 g protein; 22 g carbohydrate; and .4 g dietary fiber.

Coddled Ham

Indulge yourself with this easy-to-prepare ham. With very little effort, you can prepare a wonderful meal and win yourself a day away from the kitchen.

COOKING TIME: 6 to 10 hours on LOW, 3 to 5 hours on HIGH
ATTENTION: Minimal

½ cup (120 ml) water

½ cup (120 ml) ham glaze

One 3- to 4-pound (1.4- to 1.8-kg) fully cooked ham, or a size that fits inside your covered slow cooker

Pour the water into the slow cooker. Rub the ham glaze over the ham, wrap and seal the ham in aluminum foil, and place it in the water. Cover and cook on LOW for 6 to 10 hours or on HIGH for 3 to 5 hours, or until the ham is hot throughout; do not overcook the ham or it may fall apart when sliced.

YIELD: 12 servings

NUTRITIONAL ANALYSIS: One serving of the basic recipe (made with a 3-pound ham) contains 227 calories; 12 g fat; 20 g protein; 9 g carbohydrate; and 0 g dietary fiber.

🐖 Easiest Ribs

The unusual blend of flavors in this recipe creates a tasty and memorable main dish. Serve with buttered corn-on-the-cob and coleslaw.

COOKING TIME: 8 to 9 hours   **ATTENTION:** Minimal

1 slab pork ribs in a size that fits inside your covered slow cooker

One 12-ounce (340-g) bottle chili sauce

One 10-ounce (280-g) jar currant jelly

Put the ribs in the slow cooker. In a medium-size bowl, combine the chili sauce and currant jelly, then pour the mixture over the ribs. Cover and cook on LOW for 8 to 9 hours.

YIELD: 8 servings

NUTRITIONAL ANALYSIS: One serving of the basic recipe (made with 4 pounds pork ribs) contains 531 calories; 28 g fat; 41 g protein; 27 g carbohydrate; and 1 g dietary fiber.

🐖 Chinese-Style Ribs

This is everybody's favorite—tender ribs bathed in the classic red glaze, and without the expense of takeout!

PREP TIME: 20 minutes   **COOKING TIME:** 4 hours on HIGH, 8–9 hours on LOW

2 racks spareribs (about 4 pounds or 1890 g)

Salt and pepper to taste

1 (12-ounce or 355-ml) jar Chinese pork glaze

Cut the ribs into 2 or 3 rib sections. Sprinkle the meat with salt and pepper to taste. Put the ribs into a bowl, add the pork glaze, and toss to coat. Put the ribs into the slow cooker and cook for about 4 hours on HIGH or 8 to 9 hours on LOW.

YIELD: 4 to 6 servings

NUTRITIONAL ANALYSIS: 757 calories; 44 g fat (53.4% calories from fat); 33 g protein; 55 g carbohydrate; 1 g dietary fiber; 146 mg cholesterol; 727 mg sodium.

Country-Style Pork Ribs with Paprikash Sauce

PREP TIME: 10 minutes **COOKING TIME:** 5–6 hours
ADDITIONAL STEPS: Add yogurt to the sauce after cooking

2 pounds (910 g) country-style pork ribs

4 tablespoons (30 g) paprika

Salt and pepper to taste

1 cup (230 g) plain yogurt

Put the ribs into the slow cooker. Combine the paprika and salt and pepper to taste, then add enough water to make a paste. Rub the paste on the ribs. Add ½ cup (120 ml) water to the slow cooker and cook the ribs on LOW for 5 to 6 hours. Remove the ribs from the slow cooker and keep them warm. Put 1 cup (235 ml) of the sauce into a saucepan and bring to a boil. Stir in the yogurt. Serve the ribs with the yogurt sauce.

YIELD: 4 to 6 servings

NUTRITIONAL ANALYSIS: 307 calories; 24 g fat (70.6% calories from fat); 18 g protein; 4 g carbohydrate; 1 g dietary fiber; 78 mg cholesterol; 92 mg sodium.

ADD IT IN! Add a can of chopped tomatoes with herbs and some chopped celery to deepen the flavor.

Roast Pork Loin with Honey Mustard

This recipe produces a juicy, tender, and delectable pork roast.

PREP TIME: 30 minutes **COOKING TIME:** 6–7 hours
ADDITIONAL STEPS: Brown the meat before adding to the slow cooker

1 pork loin roast, bone-in (about 5 pounds or 2275 g)

Salt and pepper to taste

Cooking oil

3 medium-size onions

1 cup (250 g) honey mustard

Season the pork roast with salt and pepper. Heat a large sauté pan over medium-high heat and add a couple of tablespoons (30 ml) of oil. Add the roast. Sear the meat, fatty side down, until nicely browned.

Skin the onions and slice them into $1/2$-inch-thick (1-cm) slices. Put the onions into the slow cooker. Put the pork roast on top of the onions and smear the honey mustard on the pork. Cook for 6 to 7 hours on LOW. Serve the pork with the braised onions from the pan, or use the onions and accumulated juices to make a gravy, if desired.

YIELD: 4 to 6 servings

NUTRITIONAL ANALYSIS: 380 calories; 16 g fat (38.4% calories from fat); 51 g protein; 8 g carbohydrate; 1 g dietary fiber; 119 mg cholesterol; 643 mg sodium. Exchanges: 0 Grain(Starch); 7 Lean Meat; 1 Vegetable; $1/2$ Fat.

Thai Curry Pork

This luscious dish is perfect served with steamed jasmine rice. (You'll want to spoon the sauce over the rice as well as the ribs.) Feel free to add more curry paste if you want a spicier dish.

PREP TIME: 10 minutes   **COOKING TIME:** 8 hours
ADDITIONAL STEPS: Add more coconut milk in the last $1/2$ hour

2 pounds (910 g) country-style pork ribs

2 tablespoons (32 g) Thai red curry paste

1 cup (235 ml) coconut milk, divided

Place the country-style ribs in the slow cooker and rub the curry paste on the meat. Add $1/2$ cup (120 ml) of the coconut milk and cook on LOW for 7 to 8 hours. Add the remaining $1/2$ cup (120 ml) coconut milk in the final $1/2$ hour of cooking.

YIELD: 4 servings

NUTRITIONAL ANALYSIS: 583 calories; 51 g fat (79.3% calories from fat); 26 g protein; 4 g carbohydrate; 2 g dietary fiber; 111 mg cholesterol; 339 mg sodium.

Stuffed Pork Chops

The rice and vegetable stuffing practically makes these chops a meal in themselves.

PREP TIME: 30 minutes   **COOKING TIME:** 4–5 hours
ADDITIONAL STEPS: Brown the pork chops before adding to the slow cooker

4 (1-inch- or 2.5-cm-thick) pork chops (about 2 pounds or 910 g)

1 (8-ounce or 225-g) package cooked rice with vegetables

Salt and pepper to taste

Cooking oil

1 cup (235 ml) chicken stock or broth

Cut a pocket in the side of each chop, and stuff each one with some of the rice mixture. Close the pocket by securing with a toothpick. Heat a large sauté pan over medium-high heat. Season the chops with salt and pepper and add a couple of tablespoons (30 ml) of oil to the hot pan. Add the chops and brown on each side, about 5 minutes per side, working in batches, if necessary, to avoid crowding the pan.

Put the chops into the slow cooker and add the stock. Cook on LOW for 4 to 4½ hours. You can degrease the pan juices and reduce them for a sauce, if desired.

YIELD: 4 servings

NUTRITIONAL ANALYSIS: 403 calories; 22 g fat (52.1 % calories from fat); 36 g protein; 10 g carbohydrate; 1 g dietary fiber; 112 mg cholesterol; 689 mg sodium.

Barbecued Pork Chops

Succulent and saucy, these pork chops will melt in your mouth. Enjoy with green vegetables and 7-grain bread.

COOKING TIME: 8 to 10 hours   **ATTENTION:** Minimal

Four ½-inch (1.9-cm)–thick pork loin chops

One 8-ounce (225-g) can tomato sauce

½ cup (125 g) hickory smoke–flavored barbecue sauce

½ teaspoon freshly ground black pepper

Put the pork chops in the slow cooker. In a medium-size bowl, combine the tomato sauce, barbecue sauce, and pepper, then pour the mixture over the pork chops. Cover and cook on LOW for 8 to 10 hours.

YIELD: 4 servings

NUTRITIONAL ANALYSIS: One serving of the basic recipe contains 169 calories; 6 g fat; 20 g protein; 8 g carbohydrate; and 1 g dietary fiber.

ADD IT IN! Add $^1/_2$ cup (28 g) minced onion, 1 teaspoon dried oregano, and 2 cloves garlic, minced, to the sauce mixture.

TRY THIS! This recipe also makes delicious barbecued chicken wings. Add 8 to 12 wings instead of the chops and enjoy!

🐖 Pork Chops and Vegetables in Mushroom Gravy

A truly smooth and savory one-pot meal. Mushrooms pair well with the vegetables and the pork.

COOKING TIME: $7^1/_2$ to $8^1/_2$ hours on LOW, $3^1/_2$ to $4^1/_2$ hours on HIGH
ATTENTION: Minimal

6 cups (720 g) frozen stew vegetables, thawed

6 pork loin chops, trimmed

Salt and freshly ground black pepper

One $10^3/_4$-ounce (305-g) can condensed cream of mushroom soup

$^1/_4$ cup (60 ml) water

Put the vegetables in the slow cooker. Lightly season the pork chops with salt and pepper on both sides and place them on top of the vegetables. In a small bowl, combine the condensed soup and water, then pour the mixture over the pork chops. Cover and cook on LOW for $7^1/_2$ to $8^1/_2$ hours or on HIGH for $3^1/_2$ to $4^1/_2$ hours.

YIELD: 6 servings

NUTRITIONAL ANALYSIS: One serving of the basic recipe contains 212 calories; 7 g fat; 13 g protein; 28 g carbohydrate; and 8 g dietary fiber.

ADD IT IN! Substitute white wine or chicken broth for the water.

TRY THIS! Enjoy these rich, satisfying chops with a crusty loaf of bread, a spinach salad, and your favorite wine.

Pork Chops with Sage-Mushroom Sauce

Sage and mushrooms combine to give pork chops a new flavor your guests won't soon forget. Serve with wild rice and sourdough bread.

COOKING TIME: 8 to 10 hours | **ATTENTION:** Minimal

---

8 thick boneless pork chops

1¼ (8 g) teaspoons salt

¼ teaspoon freshly ground black pepper

¼ teaspoon ground sage

One 10¾-ounce (305-g) can condensed cream of mushroom soup

In a large nonstick skillet, sear each pork chop on both sides, adding a small amount of water to the pan, if necessary; do not discard the pan juices. Drain the seared chops, season them on both sides with the salt and pepper, and place them in the slow cooker. Sprinkle the chops with the sage.

Pour the condensed soup into the skillet, stir to combine it with the pan juices, and pour the mixture over the pork chops. Cover and cook on LOW for 8 to 10 hours.

YIELD: 8 servings

NUTRITIONAL ANALYSIS: One serving of the basic recipe contains 264 calories; 17 g fat; 24 g protein; 2 g carbohydrate; and .1 g dietary fiber.

TRY THIS! It's easy to grow your own fresh sage. Buy a plant with plain gray-green leaves (they taste better than the multicolored varieties), and plant it in a well-drained, sunny spot. Harvest individual leaves as needed.

Pineapple Pork Chops Teriyaki

Sweet-and-sour pork chops are a luscious, tender treat. Serve over rice and top with the pineapple sauce.

COOKING TIME: 6 to 8 hours | **ATTENTION:** Minimal

---

6 pork chops, browned, if desired

One 15-ounce (417-g) can pineapple tidbits, undrained

3 tablespoons (45 ml) teriyaki sauce

Put the pork chops in the slow cooker. In a medium-size bowl, combine the pineapple tidbits and teriyaki sauce, then pour the mixture over the pork chops. Cover and cook on LOW for 6 to 8 hours.

Serve the pork chops with the pineapple sauce.

YIELD: 6 servings

NUTRITIONAL ANALYSIS: One serving of the basic recipe contains 282 calories; 15 g fat; 24 g protein; 13 g carbohydrate; and .5 g dietary fiber.

ADD IT IN! Add ½ teaspoon minced fresh ginger and 1 clove garlic, minced, to the pineapple-teriyaki mixture. Serve the pork chops garnished with chopped green onion.

IT'S GOOD FOR YOU: The enzyme bromelain in pineapple fights inflammation, so it helps relieve a host of problems from bruises and swelling to rheumatoid arthritis. It also promotes faster healing. And pineapple is also a great source of vitamin C.

Creamy Pork Chops

This recipe makes a rich mushroom sauce that pairs well with both mashed potatoes and rice. Add a green vegetable and yeasty dinner rolls for a complete meal.

COOKING TIME: 8 to 10 hours   **ATTENTION:** Minimal

One 10³/₄-ounce (305-g) can condensed golden mushroom soup

¹/₃ cup (78 ml) good white wine or cooking wine

4 pork chops

Put the condensed soup and wine in the slow cooker and stir to combine. Add the pork chops and turn them to coat them with the sauce. Cook on LOW for 8 to 10 hours.

Before serving, turn the pork chops in the sauce again. Serve them with the extra sauce on the side.

YIELD: 4 servings

NUTRITIONAL ANALYSIS: One serving of the basic recipe (made with good white wine) contains 324 calories; 21 g fat; 24 g protein; 6 g carbohydrate; and .3 g dietary fiber.

TIP: To make a great gravy, dissolve 3 tablespoons (24 g) flour in ¹/₂ cup (120 ml) water and add the mixture to the juices left in the slow cooker after the pork chops have been removed. Season the gravy with salt and freshly ground black pepper to taste.

ADD IT IN! Add 4 to 6 ounces (115 to 168 g) sliced fresh or canned mushrooms to the soup-and-wine mixture.

DID YOU KNOW? Always use good-quality spirits when cooking. If you wouldn't want to drink it by the glass, you certainly don't want it smothering your pork chops.

🐖 Pork Chops Braised with Sauerkraut

You'll swear you're in Alsace! Serve with mashed potatoes and warm homemade applesauce for a cozy dinner.

PREP TIME: 30 minutes   **COOKING TIME:** 5–6 hours
ADDITIONAL STEPS: Brown the chops before adding to the slow cooker

4 center-cut pork chops (about 2 pounds or 910 g)

Salt and pepper to taste

Cooking oil

1 (16-ounce or 455-g) package sauerkraut

1 cup (235 ml) white wine

Season the chops with salt and pepper to taste. Heat a large sauté pan over medium-high heat. Add a couple of tablespoons (30 ml) of oil, then add the chops, turning them after a few minutes to brown both sides.

Put the chops into the slow cooker. Rinse the sauerkraut for a minute under cold water in a colander and allow to drain. Add the rinsed sauerkraut to the slow cooker. Add the wine. Cook for 5 to 6 hours on LOW.

YIELD: 4 servings

NUTRITIONAL ANALYSIS: 412 calories; 22 g fat (55.0% calories from fat); 36 g protein; 5 g carbohydrate; 3 g dietary fiber; 112 mg cholesterol; 841 mg sodium.

Honey Dijon Pork Cutlets

There is nothing better than coming home after work to a meal that's two-thirds of the way prepared. Here, just add some biscuits or rice and you are good to go.

PREP TIME: 10 minutes   **COOKING TIME:** 3 hours on HIGH, 6 hours on LOW
ADDITIONAL STEPS: Add the vegetables 1 hour before the dish is done

2½ pounds (1140 g) pork sirloin cutlets

1 cup (235 ml) honey Dijon marinade

1 (14-ounce or 395-g) bag frozen baby potato vegetable blend, thawed

Put the pork cutlets into the slow cooker and pour the honey Dijon marinade over them. Cook on HIGH for 2 hours or on LOW for 5 hours. Add the thawed vegetables and cook for 1 hour longer.

YIELD: 4 to 6 servings

NUTRITIONAL ANALYSIS: 440 calories; 22 g fat (48.7% calories from fat); 28 g protein; 26 g carbohydrate; 2 g dietary fiber; 90 mg cholesterol; 159 mg sodium.

Pork Chops Braised with Fennel

Fennel's licorice bite fades to a wonderful sweetness with slow cooking.

PREP TIME: 20 minutes   **COOKING TIME:** 5–6 hours
ADDITIONAL STEPS: Brown the pork chops before adding to the slow cooker

4 (8-ounce or 225-g) center-cut pork chops, bone-in

Salt and pepper to taste

Cooking oil

2 medium-size fennel bulbs

$\frac{1}{2}$ cup (120 ml) apple juice

Season the pork chops with salt and pepper. Heat a large sauté pan over medium-high heat and add a couple of tablespoons (30 ml) of oil. Add the pork chops and brown on both sides, about 5 minutes per side. Cut the top stalk off of the fennel bulbs and discard. Trim away any damaged outside layers from the fennel bulbs and trim the root ends. Cut each bulb into 6 to 8 wedges.

Put the fennel into the slow cooker and top with the pork chops. Pour the apple juice over. Cook for 5 to 6 hours on LOW. Serve each chop with some of the braised fennel and some of the pan juices spooned over the top.

YIELD: 4 servings

NUTRITIONAL ANALYSIS: 401 calories; 23 g fat (51.1 % calories from fat); 36 g protein; 12 g carbohydrate; 4 g dietary fiber; 112 mg cholesterol; 150 mg sodium.

🐏 Lamb Shanks with Lentils

Most folks tend to relegate lentils to the sproutsy crowd, and that's a shame. These cousins of beans and peas are packed with protein, are rich in iron, and contain folic acid. Moreover, they are a classic item in French cooking, as this delicious dish attests.

PREP TIME: 10 minutes   **COOKING TIME:** 8 hours
ADDITIONAL STEPS: Brown the lamb shanks before adding them to the slow cooker; deglaze the sauté pan; check after 4 hours

2 cups (400 g) lentils, picked over and rinsed

4 lamb shanks (about 3 pounds or 1365 g)

Salt and pepper to taste

Cooking oil

2 cups (470 ml) red wine

Put the lentils into the slow cooker. Season the lamb shanks with salt and pepper. Heat a sauté pan over medium-high heat and add a couple of tablespoons (30 ml) of oil. Sear the shanks, in batches if necessary, to brown on all sides. Put the shanks into the slow cooker. Deglaze the sauté pan with the red wine and add to the slow cooker. Add 1 cup (235 ml) water to the cooker. Cook for 8 hours on LOW. Check after 4 hours or so and add more water, if needed.

YIELD: 4 servings

NUTRITIONAL ANALYSIS: 957 calories; 38 g fat (38.6% calories from fat); 78 g protein; 57 g carbohydrate; 29 g dietary fiber; 182 mg cholesterol; 241 mg sodium.

ADD IT IN! Several peeled garlic cloves added to the slow cooker will give this dish a definite kick.

🐐Pomegranate Lamb

Pomegranate juice continues to be a culinary darling, and with good reason. This combination provides a piquant and delicious meal.

PREP TIME: 30 minutes   **COOKING TIME:** 6–7 hours

3 medium-size onions

1 boneless leg of lamb (about 3 pounds or 1365 g)

Salt and pepper to taste

1 cup (235 ml) pomegranate juice

Peel and slice the onions ¼ inch (6 mm) thick. Break up the onion rings into the slow cooker. Trim as much fat as possible from the lamb and cut the meat into 2-inch (5-cm) chunks. Add to the cooker. Season with salt and pepper to taste and pour the pomegranate juice over the meat. Cook for 6 to 7 hours on LOW.

YIELD: 6 servings

NUTRITIONAL ANALYSIS: 456 calories; 31 g fat (61.4% calories from fat); 33 g protein; 11 g carbohydrate; 1 g dietary fiber; 124 mg cholesterol; 107 mg sodium.

🐏 Rosemary Lamb Stew

The distinctive aroma of rosemary will scent the whole house. Great with garlic mashed potatoes and a green salad.

COOKING TIME: 6 to 8 hours on LOW, 4 to 5 hours on HIGH
ATTENTION: Minimal

1¹/₂ to 2 pounds (683 to 910 g) lean lamb or lamb shanks, cut into 1-inch (2.5-cm) cubes

One 14-ounce (398-g) can diced tomatoes with green pepper and onion, undrained

1¹/₂ teaspoons (9 g) salt

¹/₂ teaspoon freshly ground black pepper

1 sprig fresh rosemary

Spray the inside of the slow cooker with cooking spray.

Put the lamb cubes in the slow cooker and cover them with the diced tomatoes. Add the salt, pepper, and rosemary, and stir to combine. Cover and cook on LOW for 6 to 8 hours or on HIGH for 4 to 5 hours. (Cooking this stew on LOW, especially if using mutton, a less tender alternative to lamb, will bring out the best flavor.)

Before serving, remove the rosemary sprig.

YIELD: 6 servings

NUTRITIONAL ANALYSIS: One serving of the basic recipe (made with 1¹/₂ pounds lean lamb) contains 250 calories; 19 g fat; 16 g protein; 4 g carbohydrate; and 1.2 g dietary fiber.

ADD IT IN: Add 4 medium potatoes, peeled and cut into 1-inch (2.5-cm) cubes, and ¹/₂ cup (61 g) baby carrots along with the lamb. Arrange the vegetables around the sides of the slow cooker to help them cook faster.

ᚼ Venison Steak

Slow cooking makes venison moist and tender. Serve with wild rice and Ginger-Apricot-Cranberry Sauce (page 104).

COOKING TIME: 8 to 10 hours   **ATTENTION:** Minimal

3 pounds (1.4 kg) boneless shoulder-cut venison steaks

½ cup (170 g) frozen Seasoning-Blend Vegetables (page 29), thawed

One 10¾-ounce (305-g) can condensed cream of mushroom soup

1 soup can (306 ml) water

1 teaspoon (6 g) salt

In a large skillet over medium heat, brown the venison steaks on both sides to render the fat; do not discard the fat. Drain the venison, then place it in the slow cooker.

Add the Seasoning-Blend Vegetables to the skillet and sauté them in the venison fat until the onion is translucent and all the vegetables are tender. Stir in the condensed soup, water, and salt, then pour the mixture over the venison steaks. Cover and cook on LOW for 8 to 10 hours, or until the venison steaks are tender. (Do not cook this dish on HIGH.)

YIELD: 12 servings

NUTRITIONAL ANALYSIS: One serving of the basic recipe contains 170 calories; 5 g fat; 27 g protein; 3 g carbohydrate; and .5 g dietary fiber.

DID YOU KNOW? If you're having a hard time finding venison locally, or just want to learn more about it, go online to the Venison Forum, www.venison.com.

CHAPTER 11

MAIN DISHES: POULTRY

Chicken and turkey are so versatile and delicious! But nothing steals the fun from family dinners faster than sitting down to the same old poultry main dish night after night after night— except, perhaps, slaving over a hot stove. Get into a new groove! Explore the versatility of chicken and turkey, as well as Cornish game hen, using your slow cooker. Your family will enjoy the moist, delicious meals, and you'll appreciate the virtually care-free preparation

Baked Whole Chicken

A slow-baked chicken makes a nice presentation at the table. Not only does the chicken look festive on the platter, but its appetizing aroma announces that a special dinner is ready.

COOKING TIME: 6 to 8 hours   **ATTENTION:** Minimal

1 tablespoon (14 ml) olive oil

1 teaspoon adobo seasoning

One 3- to 3½-pound (1.4- to 1.6-kg) whole chicken, rinsed and dried inside and out

Put the olive oil and adobo seasoning in a small bowl and stir to combine. Spread the mixture evenly over the chicken, then place the chicken breast side up in the slow cooker. Cover and cook on LOW for 6 to 8 hours, or until the chicken is tender and the juices run clear.

Remove the chicken from the slow cooker using several spatulas or a meat fork, taking care to preserve the chicken's shape.

YIELD: 6 servings

NUTRITIONAL ANALYSIS: One serving of the basic recipe (made with a 3-pound whole chicken) contains 355 calories; 26 g fat; 29 g protein; .5 g carbohydrate; and trace dietary fiber.

TIP: To make a yummy gravy from the cooking liquid, dissolve 3 tablespoons (24 g) flour in ½ cup (120 ml) water and stir the mixture into the cooking liquid remaining in the slow cooker after the chicken has been removed. With the slow cooker on HIGH, cook and stir the mixture continuously until it thickens. Season the gravy with salt and freshly ground black pepper to taste.

ADD IT IN! Add ½ teaspoon Hungarian paprika to the olive oil along with the adobo seasoning. For a one-pot meal, put 4 potatoes, peeled and cubed, 1 cup (122 g) baby carrots, and ½ cup (120 ml) water in the bottom of the slow cooker, then place the prepared chicken on top of them. Increase the cooking time by about 1 hour, to ensure that the chicken is done and the vegetables are tender.

Sweet-and-Sour Roast Chicken

Carve up this sweet-and-sour taste treat. They'll think you spent an afternoon basting it to perfection. You won't need to mention that all you did was prepare the rice.

COOKING TIME: 6 to 8 hours
ATTENTION: Remove cooking juices and add another ingredient during final hour

1 teaspoon adobo seasoning

One 10-ounce (280-g) jar sweet-and-sour sauce

One 3- to 4-pound (1.4- to 1.8-kg) whole roasting chicken, rinsed and dried inside and out

Put the adobo seasoning and 2 tablespoons (28 g) of the sweet-and-sour sauce in a small bowl and stir to combine. Brush the mixture evenly over the chicken, then place the chicken in the slow cooker. Cover and cook on LOW for 6 to 8 hours.

An hour before the chicken is done, remove most of the accumulated broth from the slow cooker using a bulb baster, leaving only enough to cover the bottom of the slow cooker. Pour the remaining sweet-and-sour sauce over the chicken and cook for 1 more hour, or until the sauce is bubbly and the chicken is fully cooked.

YIELD: 4 servings

NUTRITIONAL ANALYSIS: One serving of the basic recipe (made with a 3-pound whole roasting chicken) contains 808 calories; 39 g fat; 43 g protein; 69 g carbohydrate; and 2 g dietary fiber.

TRY THIS! Serve this rich dish with a luscious, refreshing fruit tea: Make unsweetened iced tea. Fill a pitcher 3/4 full with the tea, then top off with half orange juice and half apricot, peach, or mango nectar. Add slices of lemon and lime and serve over ice.

Coq au Vin

What better way to prepare this traditional French dish than in the slow cooker? So simple, yet so full-flavored. Serve over egg noodles, with a slice of French bread.

COOKING TIME: 6 to 8 hours on LOW, 3 to 4 hours on HIGH
ATTENTION: Minimal

4 slices thickly cut bacon, cooked, drained, and crumbled

One 3-pound (1.4-kg) whole frying chicken, cut into pieces

2 cups (475 ml) wine-flavored marinara sauce

Salt and freshly ground black pepper

Put the crumbled bacon in the slow cooker. Place the chicken pieces on top of the bacon and pour the marinara sauce over the chicken. Cover and cook on LOW for 6 to 8 hours or on HIGH for 3 to 4 hours, or until the chicken is thoroughly cooked.

Before serving, stir the chicken and sauce, and season them with salt and pepper to taste.

YIELD: 10 servings

NUTRITIONAL ANALYSIS: One serving of the basic recipe contains 359 calories; 29 g fat; 19 g protein; 4 g carbohydrate; and .8 g dietary fiber.

ADD IT IN! In addition to the crumbled bacon, layer 1 cup (130 g) pearl onions, 1 cup (100 g) sliced mushrooms, and 1 clove garlic, minced, on the bottom of the slow cooker.

TRY THIS! Don't forget the vin with your Coq au Vin! Buy a nice French red like a Bordeaux to add the perfect touch to this famous dish.

Hearty Chicken Stew

This recipe is great served over biscuits, rice, or mashed potatoes.

PREP TIME: 20 minutes   **COOKING TIME:** 2–3 hours on HIGH, 5–6 hours on LOW

2 pounds (910 g) boneless, skinless chicken breasts

1 (16-ounce or 475-ml) jar chicken gravy

1 (16-ounce or 455-g) bag frozen mixed vegetables

Cut the chicken into 1- to 2-inch (2.5- to 5-cm) pieces. Put the chicken into the slow cooker and add the gravy and vegetables. Cook for 2 to 3 hours on HIGH or 5 to 6 hours on LOW. Stir well before serving.

YIELD: 4 to 6 servings

NUTRITIONAL ANALYSIS: 287 calories; 9 g fat (27.2% calories from fat); 38 g protein; 14 g carbohydrate; 4 g dietary fiber; 94 mg cholesterol; 552 mg sodium.

Chicken Vegetable Stuffing-Topped Casserole

In the great debate over whether outside stuffing is better than inside stuffing, we'd like to add this slow-cooker candidate for consideration.

PREP TIME: 45 minutes   **COOKING TIME:** 2–3 hours on HIGH, 5–6 hours on LOW
ADDITIONAL STEPS: Sear the chicken pieces before adding to the slow cooker; mix the stuffing before adding to the slow cooker

1 fryer chicken, cut up into 8 pieces, or 8 to 10 chicken pieces (about 4 pounds or 1820 g)

Salt and pepper to taste

Cooking oil

1 (1-pound or 455-g) bag Italian broccoli vegetable mix

1 (12-ounce or 340-g) package stuffing mix

4 tablespoons (½ stick or 55 g) butter or margarine

Season the chicken pieces with salt and pepper. Heat a large sauté pan over medium-high heat and add a couple of tablespoons (30 ml) of oil. Sear the chicken on all sides to brown well, cooking in batches, if needed, to avoid crowding the pieces.

Put the seared chicken into the slow cooker and add the vegetables. Put the stuffing mix into a large bowl. Melt the butter over LOW heat and stir in 1 cup (235 ml) warm water. Stir the liquid into the stuffing mix. Spoon the stuffing on top of the chicken and vegetables in the slow cooker. Cook for 2 to 3 hours on HIGH or 5 to 6 hours on LOW.

Serve some of the stuffing along with the chicken and vegetables.

YIELD: 4 to 6 servings

NUTRITIONAL ANALYSIS: 871 calories; 49 g fat (51.0% calories from fat); 52 g protein; 54 g carbohydrate; 5 g dietary fiber; 248 mg cholesterol; 1189 mg sodium.

ADD IT IN! Stir some Bell's Poultry Seasoning into the stuffing mix along with the butter and water.

Chicken and Dumplings

This home-style favorite adapts beautifully to the slow cooker.

PREP TIME: 40 minutes   **COOKING TIME:** 3 hours on HIGH, 5–6 hours on LOW
ADDITIONAL STEPS: Brown the chicken; mix and add the dumplings in the last hour of cooking

---

1 fryer chicken, cut up into 8 pieces, or 8 to 10 chicken pieces (about 4 pounds or 1820 g)

Salt and pepper to taste

Cooking oil

2 teaspoons (5 g) poultry seasoning mix

2 cups (250 g) self-rising flour

½ cup (100 g) shortening, such as Crisco

Season the chicken pieces with salt and pepper. Heat a large sauté pan over medium-high heat and add a couple of tablespoons (30 ml) of oil. Sear the chicken on all sides to brown well, cooking in batches, if needed, to avoid crowding the pieces. Put the seared chicken into the slow cooker. Add the poultry seasoning and 3 cups (705 ml) water. Cook for 2 hours on HIGH or 4 to 5 hours on LOW.

Put the self-rising flour and the shortening into a mixing bowl. Cut the shortening into the flour. Stir in enough water to form a dough, and drop the dough by spoonfuls into the slow cooker. Cook for another hour. Serve pieces of chicken with some of the broth and a few dumplings in bowls.

YIELD: 4 to 6 servings

NUTRITIONAL ANALYSIS: 835 calories; 56 g fat (61.8% calories from fat); 47 g protein; 31 g carbohydrate; 1 g dietary fiber; 226 mg cholesterol; 703 mg sodium.

ADD IT IN: Toss a couple of handfuls of baby carrots into the pot for a one-stop meal.

Chicken and Potatoes in Tomato Sauce

Here is a delicious and hearty meal to greet you on your return home.

PREP TIME: 30 minutes **COOKING TIME:** 3 hours on HIGH, 5–6 hours on LOW
ADDITIONAL STEPS: Brown the chicken pieces before adding to the slow cooker

1 fryer chicken, cut up into 8 pieces, or 8 to 10 chicken pieces (about 4 pounds or 1820 g)

Salt and pepper to taste

Cooking oil

3 pounds (1365 g) potatoes

1 (14-ounce or 395-g) can diced tomatoes with celery and onion

Season the chicken pieces with salt and pepper. Heat a large sauté pan over medium-high heat and add a couple of tablespoons (30 ml) of oil. Sear the chicken on all sides to brown well, cooking in batches, if needed, to avoid crowding the pieces.

Peel the potatoes and slice them about ½ inch (1 cm) thick. Add the potatoes to the cooker. Put the seared chicken into the slow cooker. Add the diced tomatoes. Cook for 3 hours on HIGH or 5 to 6 hours on LOW. Serve pieces of chicken with some of the potatoes and sauce.

YIELD: 4 to 6 servings

NUTRITIONAL ANALYSIS: 729 calories; 39 g fat (48.9% calories from fat); 48 g protein; 44 g carbohydrate; 4 g dietary fiber; 226 mg cholesterol; 193 mg sodium.

ADD IT IN! Sprinkle in a handful of chopped fresh oregano.

Chicken and Potatoes

What a wonderful one-pot meal you'll have with only a few moments of preparation. Serve with biscuits and real creamery butter.

COOKING TIME: 6 to 8 hours on LOW, 3 to 4 hours on HIGH
ATTENTION: Minimal

½ cup (175 ml) water

4 cups (480 g) frozen stew vegetables including potatoes, thawed

3 pounds (1.4 kg) bone-in chicken pieces with skin

1 teaspoon dried basil

½ teaspoon salt

½ teaspoon freshly ground black pepper

Pour the water into the slow cooker and add the stew vegetables. Place the chicken pieces on top of the stew vegetables, then sprinkle the chicken with the dried basil, salt, and pepper. Cover and cook on LOW for 6 to 8 hours or on HIGH for 3 to 4 hours.

YIELD: 6 servings

NUTRITIONAL ANALYSIS: One serving of the basic recipe contains 412 calories; 24 g fat; 33 g protein; 17 g carbohydrate; and 5 g dietary fiber.

TIP: To make a yummy gravy from the cooking liquid, dissolve 3 tablespoons (24 g) flour in ½ cup (120 ml) water and stir the mixture into the cooking liquid remaining in the slow cooker after the chicken and vegetables have been removed. With the slow cooker on HIGH, cook and stir the mixture continuously until it thickens. Season the gravy with salt and freshly ground black pepper to taste.

ADD IT IN! Substitute chicken broth for the water.

Chicken Breasts Italian

If you use your favorite bottled Italian dressing, you can't go wrong. And you won't waste any time either. Easy, quick, and delicioso!

COOKING TIME: 5 to 7 hours   **ATTENTION:** Minimal

½ cup (175 ml) fat-free Italian dressing

6 bone-in chicken breast halves

Pour the Italian dressing into the slow cooker. Add the chicken breast halves and turn them to coat them with the dressing. Cover and cook on LOW for 5 to 7 hours, or until done.

YIELD: 6 servings

NUTRITIONAL ANALYSIS: One serving of the basic recipe contains 261 calories; 13 g fat; 30 g protein; 3 g carbohydrate; and 0 g dietary fiber.

IT'S GOOD FOR YOU: Serve this simple, healthy entrée with steamed spinach or broccoli and a fresh mixed-green salad with plenty of veggies for a super low-calorie meal. Or enjoy your spinach sautéed in oil with minced garlic for a heart-healthy treat.

Chicken Cacciatore

You can add your own dimension to this dish with the sauce that you choose—there are several that feature peppers, if you really want to emphasize the pepper taste here.

PREP TIME: 45 minutes   **COOKING TIME:** 2–3 hours on HIGH, 5–6 hours on LOW
ADDITIONAL STEPS: Sear the chicken pieces before adding to the slow cooker; sauté the peppers before adding to the slow cooker

1 fryer chicken, cut up into 8 pieces, or 8 to 10 chicken pieces
   (about 2½ pounds or 1140 g)

Salt and pepper to taste

Cooking oil

1 (10-ounce or 280-g) bag frozen pepper stir-fry mix

2 cups (490 g) marinara sauce

Season the chicken pieces with salt and pepper. Heat a large sauté pan over medium-high heat and add a couple of tablespoons (30 ml) of oil. Sear the chicken on all sides to brown well, cooking in batches, if needed, to avoid crowding the pieces.

Put the seared chicken into the slow cooker. Sauté the pepper mix in the same sauté pan for 4 to 5 minutes, and then add to the slow cooker. Pour the marinara sauce over all. Cook for 2 to 3 hours on HIGH or 5 to 6 hours on LOW. Serve in shallow bowls so you can serve some of the pan juices with the chicken and vegetables.

YIELD: 4 to 6 servings

NUTRITIONAL ANALYSIS: 600 calories; 41 g fat (62.1% calories from fat); 45 g protein; 10 g carbohydrate; 2 g dietary fiber; 226 mg cholesterol; 525 mg sodium.

ADD IT IN: Toss 2 cups (140 g) quartered white (button) mushrooms into the pot along with the rest of the ingredients. Pitted black kalamata olives would also work nicely.

Chicken in Salsa Verde

Salsa verde, or green salsa, is made from tomatillos. The tomatillo is a bright green cousin to the tomato and is typically covered in a paperlike husk. These tangy veggies make a terrific salsa, and this dish works well as a taco or burrito filling, or just served over rice and beans.

PREP TIME: 15 minutes   **COOKING TIME:** 3 hours on HIGH, 5–6 hours on LOW
ADDITIONAL STEPS: Add cilantro in the last hour of cooking

3 pounds (1365 g) boneless, skinless chicken breasts

2 (10-ounce 285-ml) cans salsa verde

1 bunch fresh cilantro, divided

Cut the chicken into 1- to 2-inch (2.5- to 5-cm) pieces and put into the slow cooker. Add the salsa verde. Cook for 2 hours on HIGH or 4 to 5 hours on LOW. Rinse the cilantro and remove the leaves, discarding the stems. Chop coarsely. Add half the cilantro to the slow cooker and stir in. Cook for another hour and serve with the remaining fresh cilantro sprinkled over each serving.

YIELD: 4 to 6 servings

NUTRITIONAL ANALYSIS: 301 calories; 6 g fat (18.9% calories from fat); 51 g protein; 7 g carbohydrate; trace dietary fiber; 138 mg cholesterol; 430 mg sodium.

✎ Moroccan Chicken Tagine

A tagine is a Moroccan stew. There are as many variations as there are grains of sand in the Sahara. (Although we might be exaggerating slightly here, there really are a lot.) This simple version is a pleasure served with steamed couscous.

A note on ingredients: Preserved lemons are available at specialty stores and from several online vendors. You can also make your own, but plan on starting them a couple of months prior to making this dish. Do use good imported olives, not the canned American kind.

PREP TIME: 45 minutes **COOKING TIME:** 3 hours on HIGH, 5–6 hours on LOW
ADDITIONAL STEPS: Brown the chicken before adding to the slow cooker

**1 fryer chicken, cut up into 8 pieces, or 8 to 10 chicken pieces
(about 4 pounds or 1820 g)**

Salt and pepper to taste

Cooking oil

3 small preserved lemons

2 cups (200 g) mixed olives

Season the chicken pieces with salt and pepper. Heat a large sauté pan over medium-high heat and add a couple of tablespoons (30 ml) of oil. Sear the chicken on all sides to brown well, cooking in batches, if needed, to avoid crowding the pieces.

Put the chicken into the slow cooker. Chop the preserved lemons into small pieces and add to the cooker. Add the olives and 1/2 cup (120 ml) water. Cook for 3 hours on HIGH or 5 to 6 hours on LOW. Serve the chicken pieces with some of the olives, lemon pieces, and pan juices.

YIELD: 4 to 6 servings

NUTRITIONAL ANALYSIS: 606 calories; 44 g fat (63.9% calories from fat); 44 g protein; 12 g carbohydrate; 2 g dietary fiber; 226 mg cholesterol; 1274 mg sodium.

Chicken and Spinach Tikka Masala

This dish is a rich, flavorful Indian favorite. Serve with basmati rice and some fresh cilantro sprinkled over each serving.

PREP TIME: 20 minutes   **COOKING TIME:** 3 hours on HIGH, 5–6 hours on LOW
ADDITIONAL STEPS: Thaw and squeeze out the spinach before adding to the cooker

2 (10-ounce or 280-g) packages frozen spinach

3 pounds (1365 g) boneless, skinless chicken breasts

1 (16-ounce or 475-ml) jar tikka masala cooking sauce

Thaw the spinach and squeeze out as much water as possible. Put the spinach into the slow cooker. Cut the chicken into 1- to 2-inch (2.5- to 5-cm) pieces and add to the slow cooker. Pour the tikka masala sauce over all. Cook for 3 hours on HIGH or 5 to 6 hours on LOW. Stir to combine all the ingredients well.

YIELD: 6 to 8 servings

NUTRITIONAL ANALYSIS: 526 calories; 34 g fat (58.5% calories from fat); 44 g protein; 10 g carbohydrate; 6 g dietary fiber; 113 mg cholesterol; 1776 mg sodium.

Chicken Korma with Chickpeas

This is a much-beloved Indian curried chicken dish. Spice it up with some extra hot pepper, if you wish. It's perfect served over basmati rice with all of those great chutneys, raitas, and pickles that make Indian food so special. (Many of those are available prepared at specialty food stores.)

PREP TIME: 20 minutes   **COOKING TIME:** 2–3 hours on HIGH, 5–6 hours on LOW

2 pounds (910 g) boneless, skinless chicken breasts

1 (14-ounce or 395-g) can chickpeas

1 (11-ounce or 320-ml) jar korma sauce

Cut the chicken into 1- to 2-inch (2.5- to 5-cm) pieces and add to the slow cooker. Drain the chickpeas and add to the chicken. Add the korma sauce and stir to combine. Cook for 2 to 3 hours on HIGH or 5 to 6 hours on LOW.

YIELD: 4 servings

NUTRITIONAL ANALYSIS: 735 calories; 20 g fat (24.2% calories from fat); 72 g protein; 67 g carbohydrate; 19 g dietary fiber; 138 mg cholesterol; 534 mg sodium.

Chicken Curry

Perfect for a romantic dinner for two. Garnish with chopped green onion, and serve with brown rice and hot Indian bread.

COOKING TIME: 3 to 4¹/₂ hours   **ATTENTION:** Minimal

2 skinless, boneless chicken breast halves, cut into strips

1 cup (225 g) curry sauce

Put the chicken strips and curry sauce in the slow cooker and stir to combine. Cook on LOW for 3 to 4¹/₂ hours, or until the chicken strips are thoroughly cooked.

YIELD: 2 servings

NUTRITIONAL ANALYSIS: One serving of the basic recipe contains 191 calories; 5 g fat; 29 g protein; 7 g carbohydrate; and 0 g dietary fiber.

DID YOU KNOW? For an authentic accompaniment, serve an Indian flatbread such as chapati or naan. Supermarkets are starting to carry Indian bread, but if yours doesn't, you can find it at an Indian grocery store.

Gingered Pineapple Chicken

Fresh ginger provides a little zing. Spoon the pineapple-ginger sauce over the chicken and rice. Serve with steamed asparagus.

COOKING TIME: 5 to 7 hours   **ATTENTION:** Minimal

One 16-ounce (455-g) can sweet-and-sour sauce with pineapple

1 tablespoon (6 g) minced fresh ginger

¹/₂ teaspoon salt

¹/₄ teaspoon freshly ground black pepper

6 skinless, boneless chicken breast halves, cut into cubes

Put the sweet-and-sour sauce, minced ginger, salt, and pepper in the slow cooker and stir to combine. Add the chicken cubes and stir again. Cover and cook on LOW for 5 to 7 hours, or until the chicken is thoroughly cooked.

Serve the chicken and sauce over rice.

YIELD: 6 servings

NUTRITIONAL ANALYSIS: One serving of the basic recipe contains 425 calories; 2 g fat; 28 g protein; 73 g carbohydrate; and 2 g dietary fiber.

ADD IT IN! Add 2 cloves garlic, minced, to the sauce. Garnish the chicken with sliced green onion.

TRY THIS! Serve this dish with ginger ale, or a punch made from equal parts ginger ale, pineapple juice, and cranberry juice.

Drumsticks with Hoisin and Honey

Sweet, sassy, and sticky—that's good chicken, and this is a kid favorite. The charter members of our local Suspicious Food Patrol scarfed these down and yelled for more. We were happy to oblige!

PREP TIME: 45 minutes   **COOKING TIME:** 2–3 hours on HIGH, 4–5 hours on LOW
ADDITIONAL STEPS: Pre-broil the chicken

2 pounds (910 g) chicken drumsticks

1 cup (250 g) hoisin sauce

1/2 cup (170 g) honey

Preheat the broiler. Put the drumsticks on a broiler pan and cook for 10 to 12 minutes, until the skin is crisp and brown. Mix together the hoisin sauce and the honey in a large bowl. Add the drumsticks and stir gently to coat. Put the drumsticks in the slow cooker. Cook for 2 to 3 hours on HIGH or 4 to 5 hours on LOW.

YIELD: 4 servings

NUTRITIONAL ANALYSIS: 579 calories; 22 g fat (34.4% calories from fat); 32 g protein; 63 g carbohydrate; 2 g dietary fiber; 139 mg cholesterol; 1166 mg sodium.

Teriyaki Chicken

An Asian-style favorite. Serve over rice, topped with sauce, and accompanied by Asian-blend vegetables.

COOKING TIME: 6 to 8 hours on LOW, 3 to 4 hours on HIGH
ATTENTION: Minimal

6 bone-in chicken breast halves

Two 16-ounce (455-g) cans pineapple chunks, one can drained and one can undrained

1 cup (288 ml) teriyaki sauce

Put the chicken breast halves in the slow cooker. In a large bowl, combine the pineapple chunks, pineapple juice, and teriyaki sauce, then pour the mixture over the chicken. Cover and cook on LOW for 6 to 8 hours or on HIGH for 3 to 4 hours, or until done.

YIELD: 6 servings

NUTRITIONAL ANALYSIS: One serving of the basic recipe contains 316 calories; 14 g fat; 33 g protein; 15 g carbohydrate; and .5 g dietary fiber.

ADD IT IN! Substitute $1/2$ cup (120 ml) white wine for $1/2$ cup (120 ml) of the teriyaki sauce, and add 1 teaspoon minced garlic and $1/2$ teaspoon minced fresh ginger. You can also add 8 ounces (225 g) fully cooked shrimp during the last hour of cooking. Continue cooking just until the shrimp are thoroughly warmed.

IT'S GOOD FOR YOU: End your meal as they do in Chinese restaurants, with fresh fruit: orange slices, melon balls, and (of course) fresh pineapple. Refreshing and good for you!

Mandarin Chicken

The addition of mandarin orange segments at the end of cooking sweetens this dish and adds eye appeal. Serve the chicken and sauce over hot rice, and garnish it with chopped green onion.

COOKING TIME: 6 to 8½ hours on LOW, 3 to 4½ hours on HIGH
ATTENTION: Stir and add more ingredients during final 5 to 10 minutes

2 pounds (910 g) skinless, boneless chicken breast halves

One 11-ounce (310-g) can mandarin orange segments, undrained

¾ cup (175 ml) Iron Chef Orange Sauce Glaze with Ginger

Salt and freshly ground black pepper

Put the chicken breast halves in the slow cooker. In a small bowl, combine the liquid from the canned mandarin orange segments and the glaze, then pour the mixture over the chicken. Cover and cook on LOW for 6 to 8 hours or on HIGH for 3 to 4 hours, or until the chicken is thoroughly cooked.

Stir the chicken and sauce, and season them with salt and pepper to taste. Add the mandarin orange segments and stir again. Cover and cook on LOW for an additional 5 to 10 minutes, or until the orange segments are thoroughly warmed.

YIELD: 8 servings

NUTRITIONAL ANALYSIS: One serving of the basic recipe contains 144 calories; 2 g fat; 27 g protein; 5 g carbohydrate; and .3 g dietary fiber.

ADD IT IN! Add an 8-ounce (225-g) can water chestnuts, drained; an 8-ounce (225-g) can sliced mushrooms, drained; and 1 tablespoon (14 ml) soy sauce along with the liquid from the mandarin orange segments and the glaze.

Barbecued Chicken

Serve over rice or on toasted rolls. The picnic table is optional.

COOKING TIME: 6 to 8 hours on LOW; 3 to 4 hours on HIGH
ATTENTION: Minimal

3 pounds (1.4 kg) skinless, boneless chicken breast halves

2 cups (500 g) barbecue sauce

1 onion, chopped

Put the chicken breast halves in the slow cooker. In a medium-size bowl, combine the barbecue sauce and chopped onion, then pour the mixture over the chicken. Cover and cook on LOW for 6 to 8 hours or on HIGH for 3 to 4 hours, or until the chicken is thoroughly cooked.

YIELD: 10 generous servings

NUTRITIONAL ANALYSIS: One serving of the basic recipe contains 192 calories; 3 g fat; 33 g protein; 7 g carbohydrate; and .8 g dietary fiber.

TRY THIS! Serve up your barbecued chicken with traditional sides—hush puppies, cole slaw, and, for dessert, fresh peaches over vanilla ice cream. Don't forget the iced tea!

Orange Chicken Breasts

Sweet and tangy at the same time, these citrusy chicken breasts are great with a loaf of crusty bread and a crisp, tossed salad.

PREP TIME: 30 minutes   **COOKING TIME:** 3 hours on HIGH, 5–6 hours on LOW
ADDITIONAL STEPS: Sear the chicken before adding to the slow cooker; degrease the sauce; stir in the sour cream just before serving

4 chicken breasts, bone-in and skin on (about 2½ pounds or 1140 g)

Salt and pepper to taste

Cooking oil

½ cup (140 g) orange juice concentrate

1 cup (230 g) sour cream

Season the chicken breasts with salt and pepper. Heat a large sauté pan over medium-high heat and add a couple of tablespoons (30 ml) of oil. Sear the chicken, skin side down, until well browned. Turn and brown the other side. Put the chicken breasts into the slow cooker and add the orange juice concentrate. (Don't dilute it with water—we want the full-bore concentrate treatment here.) Cook for 3 hours on HIGH or 5 to 6 hours on LOW. Remove the chicken and keep it warm. Degrease the sauce with a ladle and stir the sour cream into the sauce. Serve each chicken breast with some of the sauce poured over the top.

YIELD: 4 servings

NUTRITIONAL ANALYSIS: 570 calories; 33 g fat (53.0% calories from fat); 50 g protein; 16 g carbohydrate; trace dietary fiber; 171 mg cholesterol; 175 mg sodium.

Apricot Chicken

A sweet-and-sour chicken recipe in which apricots make all the difference. Serve with a salad of mixed baby greens and lemon–poppy seed muffins.

COOKING TIME: 6 to 8 hours on LOW, 3 to 4 hours on HIGH
ATTENTION: Minimal

8 bone-in chicken thighs, skin removed

One 2-ounce (55-g) envelope onion soup mix

One to two 12-ounce (355-ml) cans apricot nectar

Put the chicken thighs in the slow cooker. Sprinkle the chicken thighs with the soup mix, then pour enough apricot nectar into the slow cooker to cover them. Cover and cook on LOW for 6 to 8 hours or on HIGH for 3 to 4 hours, or until the chicken is thoroughly cooked.

YIELD: 8 servings

NUTRITIONAL ANALYSIS: One serving of the basic recipe (made with 1 can apricot nectar) contains 127 calories; 3 g fat; 15 g protein; 10 g carbohydrate; and 1 g dietary fiber.

Peachy Chicken

This light, refreshing chicken dish is delicious over angel hair pasta. Serve with summer squash and a crusty baguette with herbed butter.

COOKING TIME: 5 to 7 hours on LOW, 2^1/$_2$ to 3^1/$_2$ hours on HIGH
ATTENTION: Minimal

4 skinless, boneless chicken thighs

^{1}/$_2$ cup (160 g) peach preserves

2 tablespoons (28 ml) water

^{1}/$_2$ teaspoon dried basil

Salt and freshly ground black pepper

Put the chicken thighs in the slow cooker. In a small bowl, combine the peach preserves, water, and dried basil, then pour the mixture over the chicken. Cover and cook on LOW for 5 to 7 hours or on HIGH for 2^1/$_2$ to 3^1/$_2$ hours, or until the chicken is thoroughly cooked.

Before serving, stir the chicken and sauce, and season them with salt and pepper to taste.

YIELD: 4 servings

NUTRITIONAL ANALYSIS: One serving of the basic recipe contains 180 calories; 3 g fat; 14 g protein; 26 g carbohydrate; and .5 g dietary fiber.

Chicken Breasts with Sour Cherries

Adding the sour cream at the end makes for a smooth and flavorful sauce.

PREP TIME: 30 minutes
COOKING TIME: 3 hours on HIGH, 5–6 hours on LOW
ADDITIONAL STEPS: Sear the chicken pieces before adding to the slow cooker; degrease the sauce; stir in sour cream just before serving

4 pieces chicken breasts, bone-in and skin on (about 2^1/$_2$ pounds or 1140 g)

Salt and pepper to taste

Cooking oil

1 cup (155 g) bottled drained sour cherries, with 1/2 cup (120 ml) of the
   juice reserved

1 cup (230 g) sour cream

Season the chicken breasts with salt and pepper. Heat a large sauté pan over medium-high heat and add about 2 tablespoons (30 ml) of oil. Sear the chicken, skin side down, until well browned. Turn and brown the other side. Put the chicken breasts into the slow cooker and add the cherries and the reserved juice. Cook for 3 hours on HIGH or 5 to 6 hours on LOW. Remove the chicken and keep it warm. Degrease the sauce with a ladle. Stir the sour cream into the sauce. Serve the chicken breasts with some of the sauce and cherries poured over the top.

YIELD: 4 servings

NUTRITIONAL ANALYSIS: 480 calories; 19 g fat (37.4% calories from fat); 65 g protein; 8 g carbohydrate; 1 g dietary fiber; 199 mg cholesterol; 185 mg sodium.

Cranberry Chicken

Cranberry Chicken is a refreshing twist on the usual weeknight fare. The sweet cranberry essence is enhanced by the tartness of the dressing.

COOKING TIME: 5 to 7 hours | **ATTENTION:** Minimal

1 1/2 pounds (683 g) skinless, boneless chicken breast halves

One 16-ounce (455-g) can whole-berry or jellied cranberry sauce

1 cup (250 g) French dressing

Put the chicken breast halves in the slow cooker. In a medium-size bowl, combine the cranberry sauce and French dressing, then pour the mixture over the chicken. Cover and cook on LOW for 5 to 7 hours, or until the chicken is thoroughly cooked.

YIELD: 6 servings

NUTRITIONAL ANALYSIS: One serving of the basic recipe contains 485 calories; 18 g fat; 44 g protein; 36 g carbohydrate; and .8 g dietary fiber.

ADD IT IN! Add a 2-ounce (55-g) envelope onion soup mix to the sauce-and-dressing mixture for a more complex flavor.

Chicken-Pizza Hot Dish

Chicken on pizza—what a tasty combination. Serve this simple version over pasta, with a slice of garlic bread.

COOKING TIME: 6 to 8½ hours on LOW, 3 to 4½ hours on HIGH
ATTENTION: Stir and add more ingredients during final 5 to 10 minutes

8 skinless, boneless chicken breast halves

2 cups (500 g) chunky-style pasta sauce

Salt and freshly ground black pepper

1½ cups (168 g) shredded pizza-blend cheese

Put the chicken breast halves in the slow cooker and pour the pasta sauce over them. Cover and cook on LOW for 6 to 8 hours or on HIGH for 3 to 4 hours, or until the chicken is thoroughly cooked.

Stir the chicken and sauce, season them with salt and pepper to taste, and sprinkle them evenly with the shredded cheese. Cover and cook on LOW for an additional 5 to 10 minutes, or until the cheese has melted.

YIELD: 8 servings

NUTRITIONAL ANALYSIS: One serving of the basic recipe contains 198 calories; 7 g fat; 32 g protein; .5 g carbohydrate; and 0 g dietary fiber.

TRY THIS! Crank up the flavor by adding fresh or dried basil, thyme, and oregano to the sauce. Pour in some red wine (like Chianti) in the last half-hour of cooking to deepen the flavor. Serve with a crisp green salad with lots of raw veggies and a glass of red wine.

Cheesy Chicken, Potato, and Broccoli Bake

This homey casserole-type dinner is an all-in-one meal that's great with a simple salad.

PREP TIME: 30 minutes   **COOKING TIME:** 2–3 hours on HIGH, 5–6 hours on LOW
ADDITIONAL STEPS: Stir after 2 hours

2 pounds (910 g) boneless, skinless chicken breasts

3 pounds (1365 g) small red potatoes

1 (16-ounce or 455-g) package broccoli with cheese sauce

Cut the chicken into 1- to 2-inch (2.5- to 5-cm) pieces. Put them into the slow cooker. Cut the potatoes in half and add to the chicken. Add the broccoli and cheese sauce. Cook for 2 to 3 hours on HIGH or 5 to 6 hours on LOW, stirring after 2 hours.

YIELD: 4 to 6 servings

NUTRITIONAL ANALYSIS: 384 calories; 5 g fat (12.1% calories from fat); 40 g protein; 44 g carbohydrate; 5 g dietary fiber; 95 mg cholesterol; 186 mg sodium.

ADD IT IN! Stir in some shredded fresh cheddar for an even cheesier tang.

Cheesy Easy Chicken

Chicken smothered in cheese sauce is a winning recipe, especially when it's so simple to fix. Serve with the cheese sauce ladled over steamed broccoli and cauliflower, and complement it with a basket of blueberry muffins.

COOKING TIME: 6 to 8 hours on LOW, 3 to 4 hours on HIGH
ATTENTION: Minimal

2 pounds (910 g) skinless, boneless chicken breast halves

One 10³/₄-ounce (305-g) can condensed cream of chicken soup

One 10³/₄-ounce (305-g) can condensed cheddar cheese soup

Salt and freshly ground black pepper

Put the chicken breast halves in the slow cooker. In a medium-size bowl, combine the condensed cream of chicken soup and condensed cheddar cheese soup, then pour the mixture over the chicken. Cover and cook on LOW for 6 to 8 hours or on HIGH for 3 to 4 hours, or until the chicken is thoroughly cooked.

Before serving, stir the chicken and sauce, and season them with salt and pepper to taste.

YIELD: 8 servings

NUTRITIONAL ANALYSIS: One serving of the basic recipe contains 193 calories; 6 g fat; 28 g protein; 5 g carbohydrate; and .4 g dietary fiber.

ADD IT IN! Add 1$\frac{1}{2}$ to 2 cups (150 to 200 g) cooked macaroni at the end of cooking and continue cooking until the macaroni is thoroughly heated.

TRY THIS! Substitute a can of cream of tomato soup for the cream of chicken for a different but equally delicious flavor.

Sort of Jambalaya

Any self-respecting Cajun cook would not approve of this recipe, and we do admit that this is a vastly simplified version of that complex dish. The bottom line is, though, that it tastes great and is really easy to make.

PREP TIME: 20 minutes   **COOKING TIME:** 3 hours on HIGH, 5–6 hours on LOW

2 pounds (910 g) boneless, skinless chicken breasts

1$\frac{1}{2}$ cups (290 g) converted rice

2 cups (500 g) marinara sauce with sausage

Salt and pepper to taste

Cut the chicken into 1- to 2-inch (2.5- to 5-cm) pieces. Put the chicken, the rice, and the marinara sauce into the slow cooker. Add 1 cup (235 ml) water. Season with salt and pepper to taste. Stir well to coat the rice. Cook for 3 hours on HIGH or 5 to 6 hours on LOW, until the rice is tender and all of the water is absorbed.

YIELD: 4 servings

NUTRITIONAL ANALYSIS: 712 calories; 20 g fat (25.7% calories from fat); 62 g protein; 68 g carbohydrate; 2 g dietary fiber; 158 mg cholesterol; 824 mg sodium.

ADD IT IN! Chopped onion and garlic, celery chunks, chopped green peppers, and chopped andouille sausage—all would make this dish even more delicious.

Szechuan Chicken Stew

Spice up a boring weekday with this fabulous stew.

PREP TIME: 20 minutes **COOKING TIME:** 2 hours on HIGH, 3–4 hours on LOW
ADDITIONAL STEPS: Precook the vegetables

1 (1-pound or 455-g) bag frozen Szechuan vegetable blend

2 pounds (910 g) boneless, skinless chicken breasts

1 (12-ounce or 355-ml) bottle Szechuan cooking sauce

Put the vegetables into a saucepan and add 1 cup (235 ml) water. Cook over high heat until boiling. Cook for 2 to 3 minutes and drain well. Put the vegetables into the slow cooker.

Cut the chicken into 1- to 2-inch (2.5- to 5-cm) pieces and add to the slow cooker. Add the Szechuan cooking sauce. Cook for 2 hours on HIGH or 3 to 4 hours on LOW.

YIELD: 4 to 6 servings

NUTRITIONAL ANALYSIS: 253 calories; 4 g fat (15.0% calories from fat); 35 g protein; 15 g carbohydrate; 2 g dietary fiber; 92 mg cholesterol; 1795 mg sodium.

Chicken with Red Beans and Rice

Nutritious and delicious, this easy meal is sure to be a family favorite.

PREP TIME: 20 minutes   **COOKING TIME:** 3 hours on HIGH, 5–6 hours on LOW

2 pounds (910 g) boneless, skinless chicken breasts

1 (12-ounce or 340-g) package red beans and rice mix

4 cups (940 ml) chicken broth

Cut the chicken breasts into 1- to 2-inch (2.5- to 5-cm) pieces and put into the slow cooker. Add the rice and beans and the flavoring package. Add the broth and stir. Cook on HIGH for 3 hours or on LOW for 5 to 6 hours. The dish is finished when the rice and beans are tender and the stock is fully absorbed.

YIELD: 4 servings

NUTRITIONAL ANALYSIS: 603 calories; 8 g fat (12.1 % calories from fat); 68 g protein; 60 g carbohydrate; 11 g dietary fiber; 138 mg cholesterol; 896 mg sodium.

Chicken with Navy Beans

For a change of pace, try this delightful combination of chicken, navy beans, and tomatoes. Serve with French bread and herbed butter.

COOKING TIME: 5 to 7 hours　　　　　　　　**ATTENTION:** Minimal

6 skinless, boneless chicken breast halves

One 15-ounce (417-g) can navy beans, drained and rinsed

One 14-ounce (398-g) can diced tomatoes with balsamic vinegar, basil, and olive oil, undrained

1/2 teaspoon salt

1/4 teaspoon freshly ground black pepper

Put the chicken breast halves in the slow cooker. In a large bowl, combine the navy beans, diced tomatoes, salt, and pepper, then pour the mixture over the chicken. Cover and cook on LOW for 5 to 7 hours, or until the chicken is thoroughly cooked.

Serve the chicken on a warm platter, topped with the beans and sauce.

YIELD: 6 servings

NUTRITIONAL ANALYSIS: One serving of the basic recipe contains 227 calories; 2 g fat; 34 g protein; 18 g carbohydrate; and 5 g dietary fiber.

DID YOU KNOW? Navy beans are about the size of peas. Notwithstanding their diminutive size, navy beans are interchangeable with other white beans, so feel free to substitute Great Northern or cannelloni beans for navy beans in any recipe.

Santa Fe Chicken

This simple version of a favorite southwestern dish goes well with Cuban bread, butter, and a green salad.

COOKING TIME: 5 to 7 hours on LOW, $2^{1}/_{2}$ to $3^{1}/_{2}$ hours on HIGH
ATTENTION: Minimal

Two 15-ounce (417-g) cans Mexican corn with red and green peppers
1 cup (225 g) chunky-style salsa
6 skinless, boneless chicken breast halves

Put the corn and $^{1}/_{2}$ cup (113 g) of the salsa in the slow cooker and stir to combine. Place the chicken breast halves on top of the corn-salsa mixture, then pour the remaining salsa over the chicken. Cover and cook on LOW for 5 to 7 hours or on HIGH for $2^{1}/_{2}$ to $3^{1}/_{2}$ hours, or until the chicken is tender.

Serve the chicken from the slow cooker for an easy cleanup.

YIELD: 6 servings

NUTRITIONAL ANALYSIS: One serving of the basic recipe contains 265 calories; 5 g fat; 31 g protein; 27 g carbohydrate; and 3 g dietary fiber.

ADD IT IN! Add a 15-ounce (417-g) can black beans, rinsed and drained, along with the corn. When the chicken is done, sprinkle it with 1 cup (115 g) shredded Mexican-blend cheese, cover, and cook on LOW for an additional 10 minutes, or until the cheese has melted.

TRY THIS! Serve this colorful dish in bright Fiestaware or earthenware dishes with colorful napkins and placemats. Add some margaritas or Mexican beer like Dos Equis. Ole!

Chicken Adobo

COOKING TIME: 6 to 8 hours   **ATTENTION:** Minimal

You can dress up this versatile main dish or keep it simple. Feel free to use chicken thighs, breasts, or mixed light and dark meat. Any way you fix it, Chicken Adobo tastes fabulous, and it couldn't be easier to prepare.

2 pounds (910 g) bone-in chicken thighs with skin, browned in 1 tablespoon (14 ml) vegetable oil, if desired

1 cup (235 ml) water

½ cup (120 ml) apple cider vinegar

¼ cup (60 ml) soy sauce

1 teaspoon freshly ground black pepper

Put the chicken thighs in the slow cooker. In a medium-size bowl, combine the water, apple cider vinegar, soy sauce, and pepper, then pour the mixture over the chicken. Turn the chicken thighs to coat them with the sauce. Cover and cook on LOW for 6 to 8 hours.

YIELD: 4 generous servings

NUTRITIONAL ANALYSIS: One serving of the basic recipe contains 424 calories; 31 g fat; 32 g protein; 4 g carbohydrate; and .3 g dietary fiber.

ADD IT IN! If you like the taste of garlic, substitute garlic-flavored soy sauce for the plain soy sauce. If you don't have this gourmet soy sauce on hand, add 2 cloves garlic, minced, to the marinade along with the plain soy sauce. For an authentic touch, substitute coconut milk for the water.

TRY THIS! Serve on soft flour tortillas with a side of refried beans.

Italian Chicken

Mama mia! Prepared pasta sauce makes this main dish a snap. Serve over whole-wheat pasta or on a toasted roll, and add a green salad for a healthful treat.

COOKING TIME: 6 to 8 hours on LOW, 3 to 4 hours on HIGH
ATTENTION: Minimal

1 to 1½ pounds (455 to 683 g) bone-in chicken thighs, skin removed

One 32-ounce (905-g) jar chunky-style pasta sauce with mushrooms

1 teaspoon (.8 g) Italian Seasoning (page 28)

¼ teaspoon freshly ground black pepper

Put the chicken thighs in the slow cooker. In a large bowl, combine the pasta sauce, Italian Seasoning, and pepper, then pour the mixture over the chicken. Cover and cook on LOW for 6 to 8 hours or on HIGH for 3 to 4 hours, or until the chicken is thoroughly cooked.

YIELD: 4 generous servings

NUTRITIONAL ANALYSIS: One serving of the basic recipe (made with 1 pound chicken thighs) contains 78 calories; 3 g fat; 13 g protein; .3 g carbohydrate; and trace dietary fiber.

Hot Barbecued Chicken Wings

Everybody loves barbecue hot wings. Who knew they could be this easy to make? Serve as an appetizer, with celery and blue cheese dressing, or add fried potatoes and a green salad for a full meal.

COOKING TIME: 6 to 8 hours on LOW, 3 to 4 hours on HIGH
ATTENTION: Minimal

5 pounds (2.3 kg) chicken wings, with or without the tips cut off

One 16-ounce (455-g) bottle barbecue sauce

¼ teaspoon hot pepper sauce

Put the chicken wings in the slow cooker. In a medium-size bowl, combine the barbecue sauce and hot pepper sauce, then pour the mixture over the chicken wings. Cover and cook on LOW for 6 to 8 hours or on HIGH for 3 to 4 hours.

YIELD: 8 servings

NUTRITIONAL ANALYSIS: One serving of the basic recipe contains 383 calories; 26 g fat; 29 g protein; 7 g carbohydrate; and .6 g dietary fiber.

Lemon, Rosemary, and Garlic Chicken

This scrumptious chicken dish gets its sparkle from a bit o' the bubbly. Serve over rice, with a crusty loaf of focaccia bread and olive-oil dipping sauce.

COOKING TIME: 5 to 7 hours on LOW, 2$\frac{1}{2}$ to 3$\frac{1}{2}$ hours on HIGH
ATTENTION: Minimal

2 pounds (910 g) skinless, boneless chicken breasts, cut into chunks of uniform size

$\frac{3}{4}$ cup (175 ml) Emeril Lemon, Rosemary, and Garlic Marinade

$\frac{3}{4}$ cup (175 ml) lemon-lime soda

Put the chicken chunks in the slow cooker. In a small bowl, combine the marinade and lemon-lime soda, then pour the mixture over the chicken. Cover and cook on LOW for 5 to 7 hours or on HIGH for 2$\frac{1}{2}$ to 3$\frac{1}{2}$ hours, or until the chicken is thoroughly cooked.

YIELD: 8 servings

NUTRITIONAL ANALYSIS: One serving of the basic recipe contains 138 calories; 1.9 g fat; 27 g protein; 1.9 g carbohydrate; and .4 g dietary fiber.

TIP: If you use frozen chicken breasts for this recipe, partially thaw them in the microwave. When they're a smidgeon away from being completely thawed, cut them into chunks using a sharp knife. You'll be pleasantly surprised by how much easier it is to cut chicken that's still slightly firm from being frozen. Don't forget to finish thawing the chunks in the microwave or in cold water, if necessary, before placing them in the slow cooker. If you use fresh chicken, place the breasts in the freezer for 10 to 15 minutes to enjoy the same cutting ease.

Chicken Breasts with Endive

Belgian endive is chiefly seen as a handy dip or mousse container, but that wastes its true talent. This is a vegetable that, in our humble opinion, is better cooked than raw, because it develops a much deeper and sweeter flavor. The slow cooker is a perfect vehicle to produce soft and buttery endive.

PREP TIME: 30 minutes   **COOKING TIME:** 3 hours on HIGH, 5–6 hours on LOW
ADDITIONAL STEPS: Sear the chicken breasts before adding to the slow cooker

4 pieces chicken breasts, bone-in and skin on (about 2½ pounds or 1140 g)

Salt and pepper to taste

Cooking oil

4 heads Belgian endive

1 cup (235 ml) chicken stock or broth

Season the chicken breasts with salt and pepper. Heat a large sauté pan over medium-high heat and add a couple of tablespoons (30 ml) of oil. Sear the chicken, skin side down, until well browned. Turn and brown the other side. While the chicken is cooking, split the endive lengthwise in half and add to the slow cooker. Put the chicken on top and pour the stock over all. Cook for 3 hours on HIGH or 5 to 6 hours on LOW.

Serve the chicken with some of the endive and pan juices.

YIELD: 4 servings

NUTRITIONAL ANALYSIS: 428 calories; 8 g fat (17.9% calories from fat); 70 g protein; 17 g carbohydrate; 16 g dietary fiber; 173 mg cholesterol; 800 mg sodium.

Chicken with Fennel

We like this dish because it's a step above the everyday meal, but it's still a snap to make. Slow-cooked fennel develops a sweet flavor and velvety texture that is divine.

PREP TIME: 30 minutes   **COOKING TIME:** 3 hours on HIGH, 5–6 hours on LOW
ADDITIONAL STEPS: Brown the chicken pieces before adding to the slow cooker

1 fryer chicken, cut up into 8 pieces, or 8 to 10 chicken pieces (about 4 pounds or 1820 g)

Salt and pepper to taste

Cooking oil

2 fennel bulbs

1 cup (235 ml) white wine

Season the chicken pieces with salt and pepper. Heat a large sauté pan over medium-high heat and add a couple of tablespoons (30 ml) of oil. Sear the chicken on all sides to brown well, cooking in batches, if needed, to avoid crowding the pieces.

Remove the tops from the fennel bulbs and discard. Trim away any brown or damaged outer parts of the fennel bulb and cut in half lengthwise. Cut out the core and slice the fennel about $1/2$ inch (1 cm) thick.

Put the fennel into the slow cooker. Add the seared chicken to the slow cooker. Add the white wine. Cook for 3 hours on HIGH or 5 to 6 hours on LOW. Serve pieces of chicken with some of the fennel and pan sauce.

YIELD: 4 to 6 servings

NUTRITIONAL ANALYSIS: 587 calories; 39 g fat (63.6% calories from fat); 44 g protein; 6 g carbohydrate; 2 g dietary fiber; 226 mg cholesterol; 216 mg sodium.

Chicken with Mushrooms and Tarragon

These classic flavors blend together into a harmonious whole. Tarragon is an essential herb in French cooking, and it is one of our favorites as well.

PREP TIME: 30 minutes   **COOKING TIME:** 3 hours on HIGH, 5–6 hours on LOW
ADDITIONAL STEPS: Sear the chicken breasts before adding to the slow cooker

4 chicken breasts, bone-in and skin on (about 2½ pounds or 1140 g)

Salt and pepper to taste

Cooking oil

8 ounces (225 g) small white (button) mushrooms

½ cup (32 g) fresh tarragon leaves

Season the chicken breasts with salt and pepper. Heat a large sauté pan over medium-high heat and add a couple of tablespoons (30 ml) of oil. Sear the chicken, skin side down, until well browned. Turn and brown the other side. Put the chicken into the slow cooker and add the mushrooms, the tarragon, and salt and pepper to taste. Add ½ cup (120 ml) water. Cook for 3 hours on HIGH or 5 to 6 hours on LOW. Serve the chicken with some of the mushrooms, tarragon leaves, and pan juices.

YIELD: 4 servings

NUTRITIONAL ANALYSIS: 402 calories; 21 g fat (48.6% calories from fat); 48 g protein; 2 g carbohydrate; 0 g dietary fiber; 145 mg cholesterol; 318 mg sodium.

ADD IT IN: Substitute white wine for the water.

Chicken and Artichoke Casserole

With artichokes firmly ensconced in the Hildebrand Pantheon of all-time favorite vegetables, small wonder that we love this—it's creamy, delicious, and easy to make. Serve with rice pilaf or over pasta.

PREP TIME: 15 minutes **COOKING TIME:** 2 hours on HIGH, 4–5 hours on LOW

2 pounds (910 g) boneless, skinless chicken breasts

1 (14-ounce or 395-g) can artichoke hearts, drained

1 (12-ounce or 355-ml) can condensed cream of mushroom soup

Cut the chicken breasts into 2-inch (5-cm) pieces and put them into the slow cooker. Cut the artichoke hearts in half and add them to the chicken. Add the cream of mushroom soup. Cook for 2 hours on HIGH or 4 to 5 hours on LOW. Stir and serve.

YIELD: 4 servings

NUTRITIONAL ANALYSIS: 363 calories; 9 g fat (23.0% calories from fat); 55 g protein; 14 g carbohydrate; 6 g dietary fiber; 139 mg cholesterol; 574 mg sodium.

ADD IT IN: Quarter a handful of white (button) mushrooms and stir them into the mix.

Broccoli Chicken

A perennial favorite, this creamy broccoli-and-chicken meal tastes especially yummy served over rice and with homemade biscuits and honey.

COOKING TIME: 3 to 4 hours
ATTENTION: Add more ingredients during final hour

---

2 pounds (910 g) fully cooked skinless, boneless chicken breasts, cut into bite-size pieces

One 10³/₄-ounce (305-g) can condensed cream of broccoli soup

³/₄ cup (175 ml) milk

Salt and freshly ground black pepper

Put the chicken pieces and condensed soup in the slow cooker and mix well. Cover and cook on LOW for 2 to 3 hours.

Add the milk and stir. Season the mixture with salt and pepper to taste and stir again. Cover and cook for 1 more hour, or until the mixture is thoroughly heated.

YIELD: 8 servings

NUTRITIONAL ANALYSIS: One serving of the basic recipe contains 217 calories; 9 g fat; 29 g protein; 4 g carbohydrate; and .1 g dietary fiber.

ADD IT IN! Add 2 cups (140 g) broccoli florets, steamed, during the last half hour of cooking.

Cornish Game Hens and Wild Rice

These small hens are succulent and tender, and the wild rice is the perfect complement. Serve with Marmalade-Glazed Carrots (page 267) and crusty bread.

COOKING TIME: 6 to 8 hours   **ATTENTION:** Minimal

One 6-ounce (168-g) envelope wild rice and long-grain converted rice mix

1¹/₂ cups (355 ml) water

2 Cornish game hens

¹/₂ teaspoon salt

¹/₄ teaspoon freshly ground black pepper

Put the rice mix and water in the slow cooker and stir to combine. Place the Cornish game hens on top of the rice mixture and sprinkle them with the salt and pepper. Cover and cook on LOW for 6 to 8 hours, or until the hens are thoroughly cooked and the rice is tender.

YIELD: 2 generous servings

NUTRITIONAL ANALYSIS: One serving of the basic recipe contains 977 calories; 48 g fat; 70 g protein; 64 g carbohydrate; and 6 g dietary fiber.

Cornish Game Hens in Wine Sauce

For a change of pace, try Cornish game hen in place of chicken. Serve this elegant dish over rice or noodles and accompanied by Italian bread. Yummy!

COOKING TIME: 6 to 8 hours on LOW, 3 to 4 hours on HIGH
ATTENTION: Minimal

3 Cornish game hens, cut in half lengthwise

$\frac{1}{2}$ cup (120 ml) dry sherry

1 teaspoon Italian Seasoning (page 28)

Salt and freshly ground black pepper

Put the Cornish game hen halves in the slow cooker. Pour the dry sherry over the hens, then sprinkle the hens with the Italian Seasoning and salt and pepper to taste. Cover and cook on LOW for 6 to 8 hours or on HIGH for 3 to 4 hours, or until the hens are thoroughly cooked and the juices run clear.

YIELD: 6 servings

NUTRITIONAL ANALYSIS: One serving of the basic recipe contains 359 calories; 24 g fat; 29 g protein; 1 g carbohydrate; and trace dietary fiber.

ADD IT IN! Place the hens on top of 1 medium onion, chopped. Add $\frac{1}{2}$ cup (50 g) sliced fresh mushrooms along with the sherry.

Turkey Breast with Gravy

Slow cooking a turkey breast will provide the wonderful aroma you've come to expect from a holiday meal. Enjoy this moist and tender turkey with gravy, mashed potatoes, and a green vegetable.

COOKING TIME: 8 to 10 hours | **ATTENTION:** Minimal

One 2-pound (910-g) turkey breast, or a size that fits inside your covered slow cooker

One 12-ounce (340-g) jar turkey gravy

2 cloves garlic, minced

Put the turkey breast in the slow cooker. In a small bowl, combine the turkey gravy and minced garlic, then pour the mixture over the turkey. Cover and cook on LOW for 8 to 10 hours, or until the turkey is thoroughly cooked.

Remove the turkey from the slow cooker, place it on a platter, and let it rest for 10 minutes. Serve it with the extra gravy on the side.

YIELD: 8 servings

NUTRITIONAL ANALYSIS: One serving of the basic recipe contains 149 calories; 2 g fat; 29 g protein; 2 g carbohydrate; and .1 g dietary fiber.

ADD IT IN: Substitute 1$\frac{1}{2}$ cups (285 ml) dry white wine mixed with two .9-ounce (25-g) envelopes chicken-and-herb gravy mix for the jar of turkey gravy.

Turkey Dinner

It's so simple and quick to make a one-pot turkey meal. Thicken the gravy, if you wish, and enjoy it with the turkey, vegetables, and biscuits.

COOKING TIME: 8 to 10 hours on LOW, 4 to 5 hours on HIGH
ATTENTION: Minimal

4 cups (480 g) frozen stew vegetables, thawed

2 pounds (910 g) bone-in turkey thighs, skin removed

One 10³/₄-ounce can (305-g) condensed cream of mushroom soup

¹/₄ cup (60 ml) water

Put the stew vegetables in the bottom of the slow cooker and place the turkey thighs on top of them. In a small bowl, combine the condensed soup and water, then pour the mixture over the turkey and vegetables. Cover and cook on LOW for 8 to 10 hours or on HIGH for 4 to 5 hours, or until the turkey is thoroughly cooked and the vegetables are tender.

YIELD: 8 generous servings

NUTRITIONAL ANALYSIS: One serving of the basic recipe contains 332 calories; 14 g fat; 35 g protein; 15 g carbohydrate; and 4 g dietary fiber.

ADD IT IN: Add 1 medium onion, chopped, and 2 cloves garlic, minced, to the soup mixture, and substitute sherry for the water.

Broccoli, Rice, and Turkey

This flavorful one-pot meal pleases with so little effort. A perfect follow-up meal after a holiday stint in the kitchen. Serve with steamed broccoli and dinner rolls.

COOKING TIME: 6 to 8 hours   **ATTENTION:** Minimal

1¼ cups (231 g) raw converted rice

¼ teaspoon freshly ground black pepper

2 pounds (910 g) skinless, boneless turkey breast, cut into strips

1½ cups (355 ml) hot water

One 3-ounce (85-g) envelope cream of broccoli soup mix

Spray the inside of the slow cooker with cooking spray.

Put the raw rice in the slow cooker, sprinkle it with the pepper, and top it with the turkey strips. In a medium-size bowl, combine the hot water and soup mix, then pour the mixture over the rice and turkey strips. Cover and cook on LOW for 6 to 8 hours, or until the turkey strips are thoroughly cooked and the rice is tender.

YIELD: 8 servings

NUTRITIONAL ANALYSIS: One serving of the basic recipe contains 243 calories; 1 g fat; 30 g protein; 25 g carbohydrate; and .5 g dietary fiber.

TIP: If you're using fresh turkey breast for this recipe, use this trick to make slicing it quick and easy. Place the turkey breast in the freezer for 10 to 15 minutes, until ice crystals just start to form on the surface of the meat. Remove the meat from the freezer and cut it into strips using a sharp knife. Don't forget to thaw the strips in cold water, if necessary, before placing them in the slow cooker.

Cheesy Scalloped Turkey

Another holiday-meal follow-up dish. Cheesy potatoes make this one a welcome reprise.

COOKING TIME: 5 to 7 hours on LOW, 2$\frac{1}{2}$ to 3$\frac{1}{2}$ hours on HIGH
ATTENTION: Minimal

2 cups (475 ml) water

One 5-ounce (140-g) package cheesy scalloped potatoes and seasoning mix

**One 1-pound (455-g) fully cooked skinless, boneless turkey breast,
cut into strips**

One 10-ounce (280-g) package frozen peas

Put the water and the contents of the scalloped potatoes kit, including the seasoning mix, in the slow cooker and stir to combine. Add the turkey strips and frozen peas, and stir again. Cover and cook on LOW for 5 to 7 hours or on HIGH for 2$\frac{1}{2}$ to 3$\frac{1}{2}$ hours.

YIELD: 4 servings

NUTRITIONAL ANALYSIS: One serving of the basic recipe contains 391 calories; 10 g fat; 39 g protein; 36 g carbohydrate; and 8 g dietary fiber.

Savory Turkey and Rice

One-pot dishes are fabulous for those days when you're pushed for time. A basket of flaky biscuits or crusty bread is all you need for a lovely meal.

COOKING TIME: 6 to 8 hours on LOW, 3 to 4 hours on HIGH
ATTENTION: Minimal

2 cups (350 g) chopped cooked turkey

One 14-ounce (398-g) can diced tomatoes with garlic, oregano, and basil, undrained

1 cup (235 ml) water

³/₄ cup (139 g) raw converted rice

Salt and freshly ground black pepper

Put the chopped cooked turkey, diced tomatoes, water, and raw rice in the slow cooker and stir to combine. Cover and cook on LOW for 6 to 8 hours or on HIGH for 3 to 4 hours.

Before serving, stir the turkey mixture and season it with salt and pepper to taste.

YIELD: 8 servings

NUTRITIONAL ANALYSIS: One serving of the basic recipe contains 135 calories; 2 g fat; 12 g protein; 16 g carbohydrate; and 1 g dietary fiber.

ADD IT IN: Add 1¹/₂ cups (340 g) frozen Seasoning-Blend Vegetables (page 29), ¹/₂ cup (120 ml) sherry, and 2 cloves garlic, minced.

Turkey Tortilla Pie

This is a great way to use up leftovers from a holiday meal. It can also be made with cooked chicken meat, so why wait for a holiday?

PREP TIME: 30 minutes   **COOKING TIME:** 2 hours on HIGH, 4 hours on LOW

4 cups (560 g) cooked, cubed, boneless turkey meat, divided

4 cups (900 g) salsa, divided

12 (8-inch or 20-cm) corn tortillas, divided

Spread 1 cup (140 g) of turkey in the slow cooker. Top with 1 cup (225 g) of salsa, then top that with 4 tortillas, arranged to fill the circumference of the slow cooker. Repeat the layers twice more, finishing with the remaining 1 cup (140 g) of turkey and 1 cup (225 g) of salsa. Cook for 2 hours on HIGH or 4 hours on LOW.

YIELD: 4 servings

NUTRITIONAL ANALYSIS: 504 calories; 13 g fat (22.6% calories from fat); 48 g protein; 51 g carbohydrate; 8 g dietary fiber; 104 mg cholesterol; 1333 mg sodium.

ADD IT IN! Add 2 cups (230 g) shredded Monterey Jack or cheddar cheese, divided among the layers.

CHAPTER 12

MAIN DISHES: FISH AND SHELLFISH

Fish and shellfish are naturally tender and flavorful. They are a fabulous source of lean protein and other important nutrients, so two servings a week are recommended. Zesty Citrus Catfish (page 209), Wine-Poached Salmon (page 214), and Shrimp and Mushroom Marinara (page 229) are just some of the tasty slow-cooker recipes you can use to tempt your taste buds to eat right. Employ your slow cooker in the pursuit of exceptional health!

Zesty Citrus Catfish

Lime is the twist in this zesty dish. Serve with parsleyed new potatoes and a salad of spring-mix greens.

COOKING TIME: 2 to 3 hours   **ATTENTION:** Minimal

1 cup (235 ml) chicken broth

½ cup (120 ml) Lawry's Tequila Lime Marinade

1½ pounds (683 g) catfish fillets of uniform thickness

Salt and freshly ground black pepper

Spray the inside of the slow cooker with cooking spray.

Put the chicken broth and marinade in the slow cooker and stir to combine. Arrange the catfish fillets skin sides down in the broth-marinade mixture. Cover and cook on LOW for 2 to 3 hours, or until the fish can easily be flaked with a fork.

Before serving, season the catfish with salt and pepper to taste.

YIELD: 6 servings

NUTRITIONAL ANALYSIS: One serving of the basic recipe contains 177 calories; 10 g fat; 20 g protein; 1 g carbohydrate; and trace dietary fiber.

IT'S GOOD FOR YOU: Spring mix, also called field greens or mesclun, is becoming all the rage for the health-conscious. Originating in France, spring mix consists of tender young leaves from a variety of plants, as well as edible flowers upon occasion. The bags of prewashed spring mix found at your local grocer are likely to include endive, radicchio, sorrel, frissee, chervil, and other highly nutritious greens, but probably not the edible flowers.

Catfish and Beans

Here's a slow-cooker twist on a classic Southern taste combo.

PREP TIME: 10 minutes   **COOKING TIME:** 1 hour on HIGH, 2 hours on LOW

2 pounds (910 g) catfish fillets

Salt and pepper to taste

1 (14-ounce or 395-g) can pinto beans, drained and rinsed

1 (12-ounce or 340-g) can diced tomatoes with onions and peppers

Put the catfish into the slow cooker and season with salt and pepper. Pour the beans over the fish and add the tomatoes. Cook for 1 hour on HIGH or 2 hours on LOW, until the fish is firm and cooked through. Serve the catfish with some of the beans and sauce.

YIELD: 4 servings

NUTRITIONAL ANALYSIS: 311 calories; 7 g fat (20.5% calories from fat); 42 g protein; 18 g carbohydrate; 4 g dietary fiber; 132 mg cholesterol; 518 mg sodium.

SERVING SUGGESTION: This dish tastes great with hush puppies.

Poached Salmon in Creamy Lemon Sauce

Delicate salmon with a piquant sauce. This is a classy and classic dish that's great for your next dinner party.

PREP TIME: 10 minutes   **COOKING TIME:** 1 hour
ADDITIONAL STEPS: Stir in the crème fraîche just before serving

4 pieces salmon fillet (about 1½ pounds or 685 g)

Salt and pepper to taste

2 tablespoons (30 ml) lemon juice

½ cup (115 g) crème fraîche

Put the salmon into the slow cooker and season with salt and pepper. Pour the lemon juice over the fish and cook for 1 hour on LOW. Carefully remove the fish from the slow cooker and whisk the crème fraîche into the pan juices. Pour some of the sauce over each piece of fish.

YIELD: 4 servings

NUTRITIONAL ANALYSIS: 282 calories; 14 g fat (47.1 % calories from fat); 35 g protein; 2 g carbohydrate; trace dietary fiber; 115 mg cholesterol; 127 mg sodium.

ADD IT IN: Sprinkle fresh chopped chives or chervil over each serving.

Lemon-Poached Salmon

Slow cooking brings out the flavor in Lemon-Poached Salmon. Serve with garlic mashed potatoes and a green vegetable.

COOKING TIME: 3 to 4 hours on LOW, 1¹/₂ to 2 hours on HIGH
ATTENTION: Minimal

1 cup (235 ml) chicken broth

1¹/₄ pounds (569 g) salmon fillets of uniform thickness

¹/₂ teaspoon salt

¹/₄ teaspoon freshly ground black pepper

¹/₂ lemon, cut into thin slices

Spray the inside of the slow cooker with cooking spray.

Pour the chicken broth into the slow cooker, then arrange the salmon fillets skin sides down in one layer in the broth. Season the fillets with the salt and pepper, and place the lemon slices on top of them. Cover and cook on LOW for 3 to 4 hours or on HIGH for 1¹/₂ to 2 hours, or until the salmon can easily be flaked with a fork.

YIELD: 4 servings

NUTRITIONAL ANALYSIS: One serving of the basic recipe contains 175 calories; 5 g fat; 30 g protein; .3 g carbohydrate; and trace dietary fiber.

ADD IT IN: Substitute white wine for half the chicken broth, and sprinkle a mixture of ¹/₂ cup (65 g) chopped onion, ¹/₂ cup (60 g) chopped celery, and 1 clove garlic, minced, around the fillets.

Orange Salmon

The subtle infusion of orange and ginger gives this salmon dish a fresh flavor that's perfect for company. Garnish with chopped green onion, and serve with fluffy rice and steamed snow peas.

COOKING TIME: 3 to 4 hours on LOW, 1½ to 2 hours on HIGH
ATTENTION: Minimal

1 pound (455 g) salmon fillets of uniform thickness

¾ cup (175 ml) Iron Chef Orange Sauce Glaze with Ginger

¼ cup (60 ml) vegetable or chicken broth

Spray the inside of the slow cooker with cooking spray.

Arrange the salmon fillets skin sides down in one layer in the bottom of the slow cooker. In a small bowl, combine the glaze and broth, then pour the mixture over the fillets. Cover and cook on LOW for 3 to 4 hours or on HIGH for 1½ to 2 hours, or until the salmon can easily be flaked with a fork.

YIELD: 4 servings

NUTRITIONAL ANALYSIS: One serving of the basic recipe (made with vegetable broth) contains 172 calories; 4 g fat; 24 g protein; 8 g carbohydrate; and .3 g dietary fiber.

ADD IT IN! For salmon with a zing, add ½ teaspoon grated fresh ginger to the glaze-broth mixture.

Teriyaki Salmon

The tasty teriyaki sauce made with this dish is also good over hot, buttered rice. Add a salad of baby greens, and you're all set for dinner.

COOKING TIME: 3 to 4 hours on LOW, 1$\frac{1}{2}$ to 2 hours on HIGH
ATTENTION: Minimal

$\frac{3}{4}$ cup (175 ml) apple cider

$\frac{1}{4}$ cup (60 ml) teriyaki sauce

1$\frac{1}{4}$ pounds (569 g) salmon fillets of uniform thickness

$\frac{1}{2}$ teaspoon salt

Spray the inside of the slow cooker with cooking spray.

Put the apple cider and teriyaki sauce in the slow cooker and stir to combine. Arrange the salmon fillets skin sides down in one layer in the apple cider–teriyaki sauce mixture, then sprinkle the fillets with the salt. Cover and cook on LOW for 3 to 4 hours or on HIGH for 1$\frac{1}{2}$ to 2 hours, or until the salmon can easily be flaked with a fork.

YIELD: 4 servings

NUTRITIONAL ANALYSIS: One serving of the basic recipe contains 202 calories; 5 g fat; 29 g protein; 8 g carbohydrate; and trace dietary fiber.

ADD IT IN! Add 1 to 2 teaspoons (3 to 7 g) minced garlic to the sauce mixture. Garnish the salmon with chopped green onion.

Wine-Poached Salmon

This classic salmon preparation is as delicious as it's healthful. Serve with Hollandaise sauce, if desired, and add Maple-Glazed Baby Carrots (page 266) and potato sourdough rolls to round out the menu.

COOKING TIME: 3 to 4 hours on LOW, 1½ to 2 hours on HIGH
ATTENTION: Minimal

1 pound (455 g) salmon fillets of uniform size and thickness

½ teaspoon salt

¼ teaspoon freshly ground black pepper

6 ounces (175 ml) white wine

6 ounces (175 ml) water

1 teaspoon dried bouquet garni, bundled in cheesecloth

Spray the inside of the slow cooker with cooking spray.

Arrange the salmon fillets in one layer in the bottom of the slow cooker and sprinkle them with the salt and pepper. In a small bowl, combine the white wine and water, then pour the mixture over the fillets. Add the bouquet garni, allowing it to float in the wine mixture. Cover and cook on LOW for 3 to 4 hours or on HIGH for 1½ to 2 hours, or until the salmon can easily be flaked with a fork.

Before serving, remove the bouquet garni.

YIELD: 4 servings

NUTRITIONAL ANALYSIS: One serving of the basic recipe contains 161 calories; 4 g fat; 23 g protein; .5 g carbohydrate; and trace dietary fiber.

IT'S GOOD FOR YOU: Bouquet garni is a mixture of herbs, either fresh or dried. It's used to enhance the flavor of soups, stews, and sauces. You can find dried bouquet garni in the spice aisle of your supermarket, or you can make your own fresh bouquet garni by tying together 3 sprigs of fresh parsley, 1 sprig of fresh thyme, and 1 bay leaf. Use clean kitchen string to bundle them so that you can easily remove them before serving your meal.

Au Gratin Salmon and Potato Bake

The marriage of salmon and potatoes is comfort food at its best. Serve with corn-on-the-cob and whole-wheat rolls.

COOKING TIME: $4^1/2$ to $5^1/2$ hours   **ATTENTION:** Minimal

One 19-ounce (540-g) bag frozen Green Giant Au Gratin Potatoes

One $14^1/2$-ounce (419-g) can Alaskan salmon, drained and flaked

One $10^3/4$-ounce (305-g) can condensed cream of celery soup

Spray the inside of the slow cooker with cooking spray.

Put the frozen potatoes in the slow cooker and spread them out evenly. Top the potatoes with the salmon, then pour the condensed soup over the potatoes. Cover and cook on HIGH for $4^1/2$ to $5^1/2$ hours, or until the potatoes are fork-tender.

YIELD: 5 servings

NUTRITIONAL ANALYSIS: One serving of the basic recipe contains 245 calories; 11 g fat; 20 g protein; 15 g carbohydrate; and 2 g dietary fiber.

IT'S GOOD FOR YOU: Always choose wild Alaskan salmon over farmed salmon. Wild salmon is an important source of heart-healthy omega-3 fats and vitamin E. More important, it's harvested from the pristine waters of Alaska, where it matured untouched by antibiotics, pesticides, growth hormones, and synthetic coloring agents.

White Beans with Tuna

Traditionally served cold, this summer favorite can be just as yummy hot from the slow cooker. Serve with crusty French bread slathered with melted basil-garlic butter (see "Try This," below).

COOKING TIME: $5^1/2$ to $7^1/2$ hours on LOW, 3 to 4 hours on HIGH
ATTENTION: Change heat setting and add another ingredient during final 30 minutes

2 cups (500 g) olive oil, garlic, and tomato–flavored pasta sauce

One 16-ounce (455-g) can white beans, rinsed and drained

Two 12-ounce (340-g) cans tuna, drained and flaked

Salt and freshly ground black pepper

Put the pasta sauce and white beans in the slow cooker and stir to combine. Cover and cook on LOW for 5 to 7 hours or on HIGH for $2^1/2$ to $3^1/2$ hours.

Add the flaked tuna and stir. Cover and cook on HIGH for an additional 30 minutes.

Before serving, stir the mixture again and season it with salt and pepper to taste.

YIELD: 8 servings

NUTRITIONAL ANALYSIS: One serving of the basic recipe contains 165 calories; .9 g fat; 26 g protein; 13 g carbohydrate; and 3 g dietary fiber.

TRY THIS! To make basil-garlic butter, combine 8 tablespoons (1 stick, or 112 g) butter, softened, 3 tablespoons (7.5 g) finely chopped fresh basil or 1 teaspoon dried basil, 2 teaspoons (7 g) finely minced garlic, and 1 teaspoon lemon juice.

Olive-Oil-Poached Tuna

This one may not fall under the category of comfort food classics, but it sure is good! The oil infuses the flavors of the pesto into the fish, and the texture is like butter.

PREP TIME: 10 minutes   **COOKING TIME:** 1 hour
ADDITIONAL STEPS: Add the pesto and tuna for the last 10–15 minutes

3 cups (705 ml) extra-virgin olive oil

½ cup (130 g) basil pesto

4 tuna steaks (about 2 pounds or 910 g)

Salt and pepper to taste

Put the olive oil into the slow cooker and heat on LOW for about 40 minutes. Stir in the pesto and heat for another 5 minutes. Season the tuna with salt and pepper and add to the slow cooker. Cook for 10 to 12 minutes for medium fish, less for rare, more for well done. Carefully remove the tuna from the slow cooker using a slotted spoon.

YIELD: 4 servings

NUTRITIONAL ANALYSIS: 1911 calories; 187 g fat (87.5% calories from fat); 58 g protein; 2 g carbohydrate; trace dietary fiber; 95 mg cholesterol; 295 mg sodium.

Tuna Casserole

A perennial favorite, Tuna Casserole is ready for the table after a scant few minutes of preparation in the morning. Serve over egg noodles or rice—and don't forget the basket of flaky buttermilk biscuits.

COOKING TIME: 5 to 6 hours on LOW, 2$\frac{1}{2}$ to 3 hours on HIGH
ATTENTION: Minimal

Two 10$\frac{3}{4}$-ounce (305-g) cans condensed cream of chicken soup

One 10-ounce (280-g) bag frozen peas and carrots, thawed

Three 6$\frac{1}{2}$-ounce (183-g) cans tuna, drained and flaked

Salt and freshly ground black pepper

Put the condensed soup and thawed peas and carrots in the slow cooker and stir to combine. Add the flaked tuna and stir again gently. Cover and cook on LOW for 5 to 6 hours or on HIGH for 2$\frac{1}{2}$ to 3 hours.

Before serving, stir the casserole and season it with salt and pepper to taste.

YIELD: 6 generous servings

NUTRITIONAL ANALYSIS: One serving of the basic recipe contains 210 calories; 6 g fat; 27 g protein; 12 g carbohydrate; and 2 g dietary fiber.

ADD IT IN: Add 1 cup (235 ml) evaporated milk to the soup mixture. An hour before the casserole is done, stir in 8 ounces (225 g) uncooked egg noodles and 3 hard-boiled eggs, chopped; cook until the egg noodles are tender.

Seafood Chowder

Straight from the slow cooker to the table—serve this classic Seafood Chowder with your favorite soup crackers.

COOKING TIME: 6 to 8 hours   **ATTENTION:** Minimal

One 14-ounce (398-g) can diced tomatoes with sweet onion, undrained

One 13-ounce (390-ml) can evaporated milk

½ teaspoon salt

¼ teaspoon freshly ground black pepper

1½ pounds (683 g) firm fish fillets, such as haddock or cod

Put the diced tomatoes, evaporated milk, salt, and pepper in the slow cooker and stir to combine. Add the fish fillets and stir to moisten them. Cover and cook on LOW for 6 to 8 hours, or until the fish can easily be flaked with a fork.

To serve, break the fish fillets into bite-size chunks. Stir the chowder and season it with additional salt and pepper, if desired.

YIELD: 6 servings

NUTRITIONAL ANALYSIS: One serving of the basic recipe (made with haddock fillets) contains 198 calories; 6 g fat; 27 g protein; 10 g carbohydrate; and 1 g dietary fiber.

ADD IT IN! Add 4 medium potatoes, peeled and cubed.

Salt Cod with Onions and Tomatoes

Salt cod is the ultimate comfort food for many of Italian and Portuguese ancestry. One must never overcook salt cod, or it will be tough. The slow cooker is great for the gentle cooking required.

PREP TIME: 20 minutes   **COOKING TIME:** 2 hours on HIGH, 3–4 hours on LOW
ADDITIONAL STEPS: Refresh the cod before cooking; add the cod to the slow cooker for the last ½ or 1 hour of the cooking time

1 pound (455 g) salt cod, refreshed

2 pounds (910 g) onions

1 (14-ounce or 395-g) can diced tomatoes with herbs and garlic

To refresh the salt cod, soak the cod in cold water for 3 days in the refrigerator, changing the water daily.

Peel the onions and slice them thin. Put the onions into the slow cooker and add the tomatoes. Cook for 1½ hours on HIGH or 3 hours on LOW. Add the cod, nestling it into the onions and sauce. Continue cooking for ½ hour on HIGH or 1 hour on LOW, until the cod is tender and flakes. Serve the cod with some of the sauce and onions.

YIELD: 4 servings

NUTRITIONAL ANALYSIS: 428 calories; 3 g fat (7.2% calories from fat); 74 g protein; 22 g carbohydrate; 5 g dietary fiber; 173 mg cholesterol; 7991 mg sodium.

SERVING SUGGESTION: Simple boiled potatoes are a great accompaniment.

Cod and Broccoli Casserole

Any white fish, such as haddock, pollock, or sole, will work well in this yummy casserole.

PREP TIME: 15 minutes   **COOKING TIME:** 1 hour on HIGH, 2 hours on LOW
ADDITIONAL STEPS: Add the fish and cracker crumbs after ½ hour

1 (16-ounce or 455-g) package frozen broccoli in cheese sauce

1-pound (455-g) cod fillet

Salt and pepper to taste

1 cup (100 g) buttery cracker crumbs, such as Ritz

Put the broccoli and cheese sauce into the slow cooker and cook on HIGH for ½ hour or on LOW for 1 hour. Lay the cod on top of the broccoli and season with salt and pepper. Sprinkle the cracker crumbs over the fish, and continue cooking for ½ hour on HIGH or 1 hour on LOW, until the fish is firm, opaque, and flakes when cut.

YIELD: 4 servings

NUTRITIONAL ANALYSIS: 278 calories; 7 g fat (21.7% calories from fat); 25 g protein; 28 g carbohydrate; 1 g dietary fiber; 49 mg cholesterol; 931 mg sodium.

Crab Hot Pot

You can use Dungeness crab, snow crab claws, king crab, or, of course, blue crab for this dish.

PREP TIME: 10 minutes   **COOKING TIME:** 1–2 hours

4 pounds (1820 g) whole crabs or cut-up pieces of king crabs

¼ cup (25 g) crab boil, such as Old Bay

1 cup (235 ml) white wine

Put the crabs into the slow cooker. Sprinkle the seasoning over them and add the wine. Cook for 1 to 2 hours on HIGH, until the crabs are red. Serve with melted butter for dipping.

YIELD: 4 servings

NUTRITIONAL ANALYSIS: 421 calories; 3 g fat (6.8% calories from fat); 83 g protein; trace carbohydrate; 0 g dietary fiber; 191 mg cholesterol; 3996 mg sodium.

Creamed Lobster

Creamed lobster is something that our grandmother would have ordered for lunch at the yacht club, where she regularly terrorized the daytime waitstaff. While this may be a bit old school, it does make for an elegant and sinfully rich meal.

PREP TIME: 10 minutes   **COOKING TIME:** 1 hour

1 pound (455 g) cooked lobster meat

1 (12-ounce or 355-ml) can condensed cream of celery soup

1 cup (115 g) shredded Monterey Jack cheese

Put the lobster meat into the slow cooker. Add the soup and sprinkle the cheese over the top. Cook for 1/2 hour on LOW, then stir and cook for another 1/2 hour, until the cheese is melted and the lobster is heated through.

YIELD: 4 servings

NUTRITIONAL ANALYSIS: 248 calories; 11 g fat (41.5% calories from fat); 31 g protein; 5 g carbohydrate; trace dietary fiber; 112 mg cholesterol; 914 mg sodium.

SERVING SUGGESTION: Serve over rice or toast points, or in pastry shells (you can find them in the freezer section of the grocery store; prepare them according to the package directions).

Garlic Clams

Use fresh garlic if at all possible, rather than the bottled minced product. This makes an absolutely fabulous, although messy, snack-type food for a casual get-together.

PREP TIME: 10 minutes   **COOKING TIME:** 1 hour

1 cup (235 ml) white wine

2 pounds (910 g) littleneck clams

1/4 cup (38 g) minced garlic

Salt and pepper to taste

Put the wine into the slow cooker and turn it on HIGH. Rinse the clams and discard any that are open and do not close when tapped. Add the clams to the slow cooker. Add the garlic and salt and pepper to taste. Cook for about

1 hour, until the clams are open and tender. Serve in bowls with some of the cooking juices.

YIELD: 4 servings

NUTRITIONAL ANALYSIS: 221 calories; 2 g fat (11.5% calories from fat); 30 g protein; 9 g carbohydrate; trace dietary fiber; 77 mg cholesterol; 131 mg sodium.

SERVING SUGGESTION: Get a loaf of crusty French bread and tear off chunks to sop up the broth. Good stuff!

Lemon Pepper Clams

These clams have a zesty citrus tang to them that is sure to delight.

PREP TIME: 10 minutes   **COOKING TIME:** 1 hour

1 cup (235 ml) white wine

2 pounds (910 g) littleneck clams

½ cup (120 ml) lemon pepper marinade

Put the wine into the slow cooker and turn it on HIGH. Rinse the clams and discard any that are open and do not close when tapped. Add the clams to the slow cooker. Add the lemon pepper marinade. Cook for about 1 hour on HIGH, until the clams are open and tender. Serve in bowls with some of the cooking juices.

YIELD: 4 servings

NUTRITIONAL ANALYSIS: 244 calories; 3 g fat (12.3% calories from fat); 30 g protein; 13 g carbohydrate; 1 g dietary fiber; 77 mg cholesterol; 2170 mg sodium.

Manhattan Braised Halibut

The firm texture of halibut makes it a natural for braising in the slow cooker.

PREP TIME: 10 minutes   **COOKING TIME:** 2 hours

4 halibut steaks (about 2 pounds or 910 g)

1 (14-ounce or 355-ml) can Manhattan-style clam chowder

1 tablespoon (8 g) cornstarch

Put the halibut into the slow cooker and pour the clam chowder over it. Cook on LOW for 1½ hours, until the halibut is firm and cooked through. Remove the halibut from the cooker and keep warm. Turn the cooker up to HIGH. Mix the cornstarch with enough water to make a slurry, then stir it into the pan juices. Stir until the sauce clears and thickens a little. Serve with sauce.

YIELD: 4 servings

NUTRITIONAL ANALYSIS: 289 calories; 6 g fat (20.0% calories from fat); 48 g protein; 7 g carbohydrate; 1 g dietary fiber; 74 mg cholesterol; 358 mg sodium.

Swordfish Braised with Thai Green Curry

Swordfish is a firm fish that's flavorful enough to take the warmth of a curry.

PREP TIME: 10 minutes   **COOKING TIME:** 2 hours

4 swordfish steaks (about 2 pounds or 910 g)

1 tablespoon (15 g) Thai green curry paste

1 (12-ounce or 355-ml) can coconut milk

Put the swordfish into the slow cooker. In a small bowl, mix together the green curry paste and the coconut milk. Pour over the swordfish and cook for about 2 hours on LOW, until the fish is cooked through but still tender. Serve the fish with some of the sauce.

YIELD: 4 servings

NUTRITIONAL ANALYSIS: 491 calories; 31 g fat (57.4% calories from fat); 47 g protein; 5 g carbohydrate; 2 g dietary fiber; 89 mg cholesterol; 329 mg sodium.

Swordfish with Ginger and Soy

The clean taste of ginger makes a terrific foil for soy—great flavor buddies, as you'll see in this delicious dish.

PREP TIME: 10 minutes   **COOKING TIME:** 1 hour on HIGH, 2 hours on LOW

4 swordfish steaks (about 2 pounds or 910 g)

Salt and pepper to taste

2 tablespoons (12 g) peeled, minced fresh ginger root

1/4 cup (60 ml) soy sauce

Put the swordfish into the slow cooker. Season with salt and pepper. Sprinkle with the ginger and pour the soy sauce over all. Cook for about 1 hour on HIGH or 2 hours on LOW, until the fish is cooked through but still tender. Serve the fish with some of the sauce.

YIELD: 4 servings

NUTRITIONAL ANALYSIS: 286 calories; 9 g fat (30.0% calories from fat); 46 g protein; 2 g carbohydrate; trace dietary fiber; 89 mg cholesterol; 1233 mg sodium.

Mexican Braised Mahi Mahi

The firm texture and succulence of mahi mahi is perfect for this braised dish. You can also substitute wahoo or swordfish.

PREP TIME: 10 minutes   **COOKING TIME:** 1 hour on HIGH, 2 hours on LOW
ADDITIONAL STEPS: Add the pineapple in the last few minutes of cooking

4 pieces mahi mahi (about 1 1/2 pounds or 685 g)

Salt and pepper to taste

1 (14-ounce or 395-g) can diced Mexican tomatoes with chiles and cilantro

1 (8-ounce or 225-g) can pineapple chunks

Put the mahi mahi into the slow cooker and season with salt and pepper. Add the diced tomatoes and cook for 45 to 50 minutes on HIGH or 1 hour 45 minutes on LOW, until the fish is cooked through. Drain the pineapple and add it to the slow cooker. Cook for another 10 to 15 minutes. Serve the fish with some of the sauce and pineapple over it.

YIELD: 4 servings

NUTRITIONAL ANALYSIS: 55 calories; trace fat (5.4% calories from fat); 1 g protein; 14 g carbohydrate; 1 g dietary fiber; 0 mg cholesterol; 9 mg sodium.

ADD IT IN! Sprinkle fresh chopped cilantro and squeeze a wedge of lime over each serving. You can also add more chopped chiles to the pot if you want a spicier dish.

Mussels with Marinara

This is a classic dish for good reason—it's delicious!

PREP TIME: 10 minutes   **COOKING TIME:** 1 hour

1 cup (235 ml) white wine

2 pounds (910 g) mussels

1 cup (245 g) marinara sauce

Put the wine into the slow cooker and turn it on HIGH. Rinse the mussels and discard any that are open and do not close when tapped. Add the mussels to the slow cooker. Add the marinara sauce. Cook for about 1 hour on HIGH, until the mussels are open and tender. Serve in bowls with some of the sauce.

YIELD: 4 servings

NUTRITIONAL ANALYSIS: 271 calories; 6 g fat (25.2% calories from fat); 28 g protein; 14 g carbohydrate; 1 g dietary fiber; 64 mg cholesterol; 91 mg sodium.

ADD IT IN! The Brotherhood of Garlic-Lovin' Fools would like to point out that a couple of cloves of chopped garlic would spice this up nicely.

Mussels with Wine and Pesto

Tender mussels steamed in wine fragrant with basil and garlic. Oh yeah!

PREP TIME: 10 minutes   **COOKING TIME:** 1 hour

1 cup (235 ml) white wine

2 pounds (910 g) mussels

½ cup (130 g) basil pesto

Put the wine into the slow cooker and turn it on HIGH. Rinse the mussels and discard any that are open and do not close when tapped. Add the mussels and pesto to the slow cooker. Cook for about 1 hour on HIGH, until the mussels are open and tender.

YIELD: 4 servings

NUTRITIONAL ANALYSIS: 387 calories; 19 g fat (50.0% calories from fat); 32 g protein; 11 g carbohydrate; trace dietary fiber; 72 mg cholesterol; 858 mg sodium.

Scallops with Spinach and Cheese Sauce

Quick and easy and oh, so good. Buy fresh-pack (also known as natural) scallops.

PREP TIME: 20 minutes   **COOKING TIME:** 1 hour
ADDITIONAL STEPS: Precook the spinach

1 pound (455 g) fresh spinach

1 pound (455 g) sea scallops, side muscles removed

1 (12-ounce or 355-ml) can cheddar cheese soup

Put the spinach into a large pot with 2 cups (470 ml) water. Cook over high heat only until the spinach wilts. Remove and drain well.

Put the scallops into the slow cooker, then top with the cooked spinach. Pour the cheddar soup over all. Cook for 1 hour on HIGH.

YIELD: 4 servings

NUTRITIONAL ANALYSIS: 178 calories; 5 g fat (23.9% calories from fat); 24 g protein; 10 g carbohydrate; 3 g dietary fiber; 48 mg cholesterol; 602 mg sodium.

Simple Shrimp Jambalaya

This is a vastly simplified version of a very complex dish, but it's still quite tasty.

PREP TIME: 10 minutes
COOKING TIME: 1 1/2 hours on HIGH, 3 hours on LOW
ADDITIONAL STEPS: Add the shrimp toward the end of cooking

2 cups (390 g) uncooked white rice

1 (14-ounce 395-g) can diced tomatoes with peppers and onions

Salt and pepper to taste

1 pound (455 g) shelled shrimp

Put the rice into the slow cooker. Add the tomatoes, salt and pepper to taste, and 3 cups (705 ml) water. Stir. Cook for 1 hour on HIGH or 2 hours on LOW, until the rice is tender and most of the water is absorbed. Stir in the shrimp and continue to cook for another 1/2 hour on HIGH or 1 hour on LOW, until all the water is absorbed and the shrimp are tender and pink.

YIELD: 4 servings

NUTRITIONAL ANALYSIS: 479 calories; 3 g fat (5.5% calories from fat); 30 g protein; 79 g carbohydrate; 2 g dietary fiber; 173 mg cholesterol; 182mg sodium.

ADD IT IN! Slice up 1 pound (455 g) chorizo sausage and add it with the rice.

Spicy Shrimp with Peppers

Use a spicy marinara sauce, usually called fra diavolo, to give this recipe its kick.

PREP TIME: 20 minutes   **COOKING TIME:** 1 1/2 hours on HIGH, hours on LOW

2 pounds (910 g) sweet bell peppers (about 3 or 4), whichever color you prefer

3 cups (735 g) fra diavolo or other spicy marinara sauce

2 pounds (910 g) shelled shrimp (20 to 24 count per pound or larger)

Remove the tops from the peppers, cut out the seeds, and core. Cut the peppers into 1/2 -inch (1-cm) rings and add to the slow cooker. Add the sauce and cook for 1 hour on HIGH or 2 hours on LOW. Add the shrimp and continue to cook for 1/2 hour on HIGH or 1 hour on LOW, until the shrimp are pink.

YIELD: 4 to 6 servings

NUTRITIONAL ANALYSIS: 265 calories; 5 g fat (18.5% calories from fat); 33 g protein; 20 g carbohydrate; 4 g dietary fiber; 230 mg cholesterol; 741 mg sodium.

SERVING SUGGESTION: Serve over pasta or rice.

Shrimp and Mushroom Marinara

Shrimp and mushrooms in red sauce is a perennial favorite. Serve over angel hair pasta, linguine, or penne pasta, topped with shredded mozzarella or Parmesan cheese. For a change of pace, serve bread and olive oil for dipping as a healthful alternative to garlic bread.

COOKING TIME: 2$\frac{1}{2}$ to 3$\frac{1}{2}$ hours
ATTENTION: Add another ingredient during final 15 to 30 minutes; watch to prevent overcooking

One 26-ounce (735-g) jar marinara sauce

1 cup (100 g) sliced mushrooms

$\frac{3}{4}$ teaspoon salt

$\frac{1}{4}$ teaspoon freshly ground black pepper

1 pound (455 g) frozen cooked shrimp, thawed and deveined

Put the marinara sauce, sliced mushrooms, salt, and pepper in the slow cooker and stir to combine. Cover and cook on LOW for 2 to 3 hours, or until the mushrooms are thoroughly cooked and the flavors have melded.

Add the thawed shrimp and stir. Cover and cook for another 15 to 30 minutes, or just until the shrimp are thoroughly warmed; do not overcook or the shrimp will become tough.

YIELD: 5 generous servings

NUTRITIONAL ANALYSIS: One serving of the basic recipe contains 178 calories; 4 g fat; 21 g protein; 13 g carbohydrate; and 3 g dietary fiber.

Shrimp Creole

This is a traditional Creole favorite made simple using your slow cooker. Enjoy today with dirty rice, fried okra, and cornbread. Tomorrow, enjoy the leftovers, which taste even better.

COOKING TIME: 6½ to 8½ hours on LOW, 3½ to 4½ hours on HIGH
ATTENTION: Add another ingredient during final 15 to 30 minutes; watch to prevent overcooking

One 32-ounce (905-g) jar onion-and-garlic-flavored pasta sauce

1½ cups (340 g) frozen Seasoning-Blend Vegetables (page 29), thawed

¾ teaspoon salt

¼ teaspoon freshly ground black pepper

1½ pounds (683 g) frozen cooked shrimp, thawed, shelled, and deveined

Put the pasta sauce, thawed vegetables, salt, and pepper in the slow cooker and stir to combine. Cook on LOW for 6 to 8 hours or on HIGH for 3 to 4 hours.

Add the thawed shrimp to the sauce mixture and stir again. Cover and cook for another 15 to 30 minutes, or until the shrimp are thoroughly warmed; do not overcook or the shrimp will become tough.

YIELD: 8 generous servings

ADD IT IN: Add 2 to 6 drops hot sauce along with the shrimp to kick up the heat.

Sweet-and-Sour Shrimp

Who can resist Sweet-and-Sour Shrimp with Asian-blend vegetables over fluffy white rice? Pick your favorite Asian or stir-fry blend of vegetables for this recipe, and enjoy!

COOKING TIME: 2½ to 3 hours
ATTENTION: Add another ingredient during final 15 to 30 minutes; watch to prevent overcooking

One 12-ounce (340-g) bag frozen Asian-blend vegetables

¾ cup (188 g) sweet-and-sour sauce

1 pound (455 g) frozen cooked shrimp, thawed, shelled, and deveined

Salt and freshly ground black pepper

Put the frozen vegetables and sweet-and-sour sauce in the slow cooker and stir to combine. Cover and cook on LOW for 2 to 2 1/2 hours, or until the vegetables are tender but not mushy.

Add the thawed shrimp to the slow cooker and stir. Cover and cook for another 15 to 30 minutes, or until the shrimp are thoroughly warmed; do not overcook or the shrimp will become tough.

Before serving, stir the mixture and season with salt and pepper to taste.

YIELD: 4 servings

NUTRITIONAL ANALYSIS: One serving of the basic recipe contains 222 calories; 2 g fat; 27 g protein; 25 g carbohydrate; and 4 g dietary fiber.

DID YOU KNOW? Asian-blend, or stir-fry, vegetables can consist of any combination of these vegetables: broccoli, mushrooms, green beans, onion, water chestnuts, red peppers, sugar snap peas, baby cob corn, carrots, celery, bamboo shoots, edamame.

Szechwan Shrimp

Enjoy this hot-and-spicy shrimp dish over hot white rice.

COOKING TIME: 1 to 1 1/2 hours   **ATTENTION:** Minimal

1/2 cup (120 ml) water

1/4 cup (60 ml) soy sauce

2 tablespoons (31 g) Szechwan hot-and-spicy sauce

1 pound (455 g) frozen cooked shrimp, thawed, shelled, and deveined

Salt and freshly ground black pepper

Put the water, soy sauce, and Szechwan sauce in the slow cooker and stir to combine. Add the thawed shrimp and stir to coat them. Cover and cook on HIGH for 1 to 1 1/2 hours, or until the sauce and shrimp are thoroughly heated.

Before serving, stir the mixture and season with salt and pepper to taste.

YIELD: 4 servings

NUTRITIONAL ANALYSIS: One serving of the basic recipe contains 123 calories; 1 g fat; 25 g protein; 2 g carbohydrate; and .3 g dietary fiber.

ADD IT IN! Substitute chicken broth for the water, and add 2 teaspoons (7 g) minced garlic to the sauce mixture. Thicken the sauce with 1 tablespoon (8 g) cornstarch, and garnish the dish with chopped green onion.

NOTE: The secret to this delicious dish is the rich, spicy flavor of the Szechwan peppercorn in the Szechwan hot-and-spicy sauce.

Shrimp Newburg

For a change of pace, enjoy Shrimp Newburg over toast points or pasta instead of white rice. Sautéed spinach (see "Try This," below) and potato rolls round out this special but simple-to-prepare meal.

COOKING TIME: 1 to 1½ hours   **ATTENTION:** Minimal

10¾-ounce (305-g) can condensed cream of shrimp soup

⅔ cup (157 ml) evaporated milk

1 pound (455 g) frozen cooked shrimp, thawed, shelled, and deveined

Salt and freshly ground black pepper

Put the condensed soup and evaporated milk in the slow cooker and stir to combine. Add the thawed shrimp and stir again. Cover and cook on HIGH for 1 to 1½ hours, or until the sauce and shrimp are thoroughly heated.

Before serving, stir the mixture and season with salt and pepper to taste.

YIELD: 4 servings

NUTRITIONAL ANALYSIS: One serving of the basic recipe contains 214 calories; 7 g fat; 28 g protein; 8 g carbohydrate; and .3 g dietary fiber.

ADD IT IN! Add 1 cup (100 g) sliced fresh mushrooms and 1 tablespoon (14 ml) cooking sherry along with the shrimp.

TRY THIS! It's simple to prepare sautéed spinach. Sauté minced garlic in equal parts butter and olive oil. Add fresh spinach leaves to the skillet, and sauté the spinach just until it's wilted.

Calamari Fra Diavolo

Fra diavolo, which means "brother devil," is a traditional spicy red sauce, and here it gives a lovely kick to calamari. Calamari must either be cooked very fast at high heat or very slowly at low heat to be tender. We are using a slow cooker, so of course we opt for the latter. Ratchet up the pepper heat to your own taste.

PREP TIME: 15 minutes   **COOKING TIME:** 2 hours

2 pounds (910 g) calamari rings and tentacles

2 cups (490 g) marinara sauce

2 tablespoons (7 g) red pepper flakes

Salt and pepper to taste

Put the calamari into the slow cooker. Add the marinara sauce and red pepper flakes, along with salt and pepper to taste. Cook on LOW for 2 hours.

YIELD: 4 servings

NUTRITIONAL ANALYSIS: 281 calories; 6 g fat (19.0% calories from fat); 37 g protein; 17 g carbohydrate; 2 g dietary fiber; 529 mg cholesterol; 615 mg sodium.

SERVING SUGGESTION: This is terrific served over linguine.

CHAPTER 13

MAIN DISHES: PASTA

Slow cookers can do the casserole thing, too, with a few modifications. Those homey baked pasta dishes so popular at many dinner tables translate well to the slow cooker. From Baked Ziti (page 242) to Penne with Broccoli (page 238), these pasta dishes can stand duty as either a hearty side dish or a main meal by themselves. (Of course, many of the other recipes in this book use pasta as an ingredient; check the index to find them. But in the recipes in this chapter, pasta plays the starring role.)

Chicken and Vegetable Lasagna

A white lasagna is an intriguing take on the traditional red sauce version, and it's just as delicious.

PREP TIME: 30 minutes   **COOKING TIME:** 3 hours on HIGH, 6–7 hours on LOW
ADDITIONAL STEPS: Precook the lasagna for 8 minutes

1 pound (455 g) dry lasagna pasta

2 (16-ounce or 485-ml) jars four-cheese Alfredo sauce

1 (16-ounce or 910-g) package frozen chicken and vegetable mix

Bring a large pot of salted water to a boil. Add the lasagna and cook at a low boil for 8 minutes. Drain the pasta and rinse with cold water to cool.

Spray the crock with nonstick cooking spray. Coat the bottom of the slow cooker with 1 cup (235 ml) Alfredo sauce, and then layer with lasagna. You may have to cut the pieces of lasagna to get them to fit into the round pot. Spread the pasta with one-fourth of the chicken and vegetables, and top with 1 cup (235 ml) Alfredo sauce. Repeat the layering process, finishing with Alfredo sauce. Cook for 3 hours on HIGH or 6 to 7 hours on LOW. Allow to sit for 10 to 15 minutes before serving.

YIELD: 6 to 8 servings

NUTRITIONAL ANALYSIS: 492 calories; 24 g fat (44.3% calories from fat); 17 g protein; 52 g carbohydrate; 2 g dietary fiber; 83 mg cholesterol; 635 mg sodium.

Creamy Spinach Lasagna

This creamy, cheesy take on lasagna looks as good as it tastes.

PREP TIME: 30 minutes   **COOKING TIME:** 2 hours on HIGH, 4–5 hours on LOW
ADDITIONAL STEPS: Precook the lasagna for 8 minutes; soften the creamed spinach

1 pound (455 g) dry lasagna pasta

2 (12-ounce or 340-g) packages frozen creamed spinach

2 cups (160 g) shredded Parmesan cheese

Bring a large pot of salted water to a boil. Add the lasagna and cook at a low boil for 8 minutes. Drain the pasta and rinse with cold water to cool. While the pasta is cooking, heat the spinach in a saucepan over medium heat until softened.

Spray the crock with nonstick cooking spray. Coat the bottom of the slow cooker with 1 cup (225 g) spinach, and then layer with lasagna. You may have to cut the pieces of lasagna to get them to fit into the round pot. Spread the pasta with more spinach, then sprinkle 1/2 cup (40 g) cheese over. Repeat the layering process, finishing with spinach and cheese. Cook for 2 hours on HIGH or 4 to 5 hours on LOW. Allow to sit for 10 to 15 minutes before serving.

YIELD: 6 to 8 servings

NUTRITIONAL ANALYSIS: 408 calories; 15 g fat (34.1% calories from fat); 17 g protein; 49 g carbohydrate; 3 g dietary fiber; 25 mg cholesterol; 571 mg sodium.

ADD IT IN: Dot the spinach layer with small spoonfuls of ricotta cheese.

🥣 Lasagna Casserole

Hungry for some classic lasagna with red sauce? Simple and satisfying anytime, lasagna is always a family favorite. Pair it with a salad and some crusty garlic bread, and you're in dinner heaven.

PREP TIME: 30 minutes **COOKING TIME:** 2 hours on HIGH, 4–5 hours on LOW
ADDITIONAL STEPS: Precook the lasagna for 8 minutes

1 pound (455 g) dry lasagna pasta

1 (32-ounce or 905-g) jar pasta sauce with meatballs

4 cups (460 g) shredded mozzarella

Bring a large pot of salted water to a boil. Add the lasagna and cook at a low boil for 8 minutes. Drain the pasta and rinse with cold water to cool.

Spray the crock with nonstick cooking spray. Coat the bottom of the slow cooker with pasta sauce, and then layer with lasagna. You may have to cut the pieces of lasagna to get them to fit into the round pot. Spread the pasta with more pasta sauce, then sprinkle 1 cup (115 g) cheese over the top. Repeat the layering process, finishing with sauce and cheese. Cook for 2 hours on HIGH or 4 to 5 hours on LOW. Allow to sit for 10 to 15 minutes before serving.

YIELD: 6 to 8 servings

NUTRITIONAL ANALYSIS: 479 calories; 22 g fat (42.6% calories from fat); 24 g protein; 44 g carbohydrate; 1 g dietary fiber; 75 mg cholesterol; 259 mg sodium.

ADD IT IN! Shake some dried or chopped fresh oregano over each meat sauce layer, and dot a few spoonfuls of ricotta cheese on top as well.

🥣 Macaroni and Cheese Bake

Mom liked to add chunks of hot dog to this dish back in our childhood days, but we prefer to add ham these days.

PREP TIME: 30 minutes   **COOKING TIME:** 1¹/₂ hours on HIGH, 3–4 hours on LOW
ADDITIONAL STEPS: Precook the macaroni for 6 minutes

1 pound (455 g) elbow macaroni

1 (16-ounce or 475-ml) jar Alfredo sauce

3 cups (345 g) shredded cheddar cheese, divided

Bring a large pot of salted water to a boil. Add the macaroni and cook at a low boil for 6 minutes. Drain the pasta.

Spray the crock with nonstick cooking spray such. Add the macaroni, the Alfredo sauce, and 2 cups (230 g) cheese. Stir to combine well. Top with the remaining 1 cup (115 g) cheese. Cook for 1¹/₂ hours on HIGH or 3 to 4 hours on LOW.

YIELD: 6 to 8 servings

NUTRITIONAL ANALYSIS: 491 calories; 25 g fat (45.9% calories from fat); 21 g protein; 46 g carbohydrate; 1 g dietary fiber; 76 mg cholesterol; 569 mg sodium.

ADD IT IN! Stir in 1 cup (150 g) chopped, cooked ham and with Alfredo sauce and cheese.

🍲 Penne with Broccoli

This creamy and delicious recipe works wonderfully as both a side and a main dish.

PREP TIME: 30 minutes   **COOKING TIME:** 1 hour on HIGH, 3–4 hours on LOW
ADDITIONAL STEPS: Precook the penne for 8 minutes; add the penne and cheese after 45 minutes

---

1 (16-ounce or 455-g) package frozen broccoli with cheese sauce

½ pound (230 g) penne pasta

1 cup (80 g) shredded Parmesan cheese

Spray the crock with nonstick cooking spray. Put the frozen broccoli with cheese sauce into the slow cooker. Cook on HIGH for 45 minutes. While the broccoli is cooking, bring a large pot of salted water to a boil. Add the penne and cook at a low boil for 8 minutes. Drain the pasta and add it to the slow cooker. Stir to combine the pasta and the broccoli and sauce, then top with the Parmesan cheese. Continue to cook on HIGH for 1 hour or on LOW for 2 to 3 hours.

YIELD: 4 servings

NUTRITIONAL ANALYSIS: 362 calories; 8 g fat (21.1 % calories from fat); 17 g protein; 52 g carbohydrate; 2 g dietary fiber; 14 mg cholesterol; 884 mg sodium.

ADD IT IN: You can spice up this dish with a few shakes of red pepper flakes, or add a couple of cloves of minced garlic for a pungent kick.

🥣 Sausage and Pasta Bake

Gemelli is a good pasta to use for this hearty dish, but you can substitute other sturdy shapes, such as penne.

PREP TIME: 30 minutes   **COOKING TIME:** 1½ to 2 hours, HIGH, 3–4 hours on LOW
ADDITIONAL STEPS: Precook the gemelli for 8 minutes

1 pound (455 g) gemelli pasta

1 (32-ounce or 905-g) jar marinara sauce with sausage chunks

2 cups (500 g) ricotta cheese

Bring a large pot of salted water to a boil. Add the gemelli and cook at a low boil for 8 minutes. Drain the pasta.

Spray the crock with nonstick cooking spray. Add the gemelli and the marinara sauce, along with the ricotta cheese. Stir to combine well. Cook for 1½ to 2 hours on HIGH or 3 to 4 hours on LOW.

YIELD: 6 to 8 servings

NUTRITIONAL ANALYSIS: 484 calories; 22 g fat (41.4% calories from fat); 19 g protein; 52 g carbohydrate; 3 g dietary fiber; 50 mg cholesterol; 595 mg sodium.

ADD IT IN: Add 1 cup (115 g) shredded mozzarella cheese to the gemelli for more cheesy goodness. A handful of chopped fresh basil is also delicious.

🍲 Zesty Baked Bowties

Bowtie, or farfalle, pasta is a great pasta to bake, and the novel shape provides eating entertainment for the small-fry.

PREP TIME: 30 minutes   **COOKING TIME:** 1½ hours on HIGH, 3–4 hours on LOW
ADDITIONAL STEPS: Precook the farfalle for 8 minutes

1 pound (455 g) farfalle (bowtie) pasta

1 (20-ounce or 570-ml) jar puttanesca sauce

3 cups (345 g) shredded mozzarella, divided

Bring a large pot of salted water to a boil. Add the farfalle and cook at a low boil for 6 minutes. Drain the pasta.

Spray the crock with nonstick cooking spray. Add the farfalle and the puttanesca sauce. Add 2 cups (230 g) mozzarella. Stir to combine well. Add ½ cup (115 ml) water. Top with the remaining 1 cup (115 g) cheese. Cook for 1½ hours on HIGH or 3 to 4 hours on LOW.

YIELD: 6 to 8 servings

NUTRITIONAL ANALYSIS: 374 calories; 13 g fat (30.4% calories from fat); 18 g protein; 47 g carbohydrate; 2 g dietary fiber; 38 mg cholesterol; 605 mg sodium.

ADD IT IN: Olive lovers might want to stir even more chopped black olives into the casserole. (There are already some olives in the puttanesca sauce.)

🍲 Ziti with Creamy Sun-Dried Tomato Sauce

Sun-dried tomato pesto adds rich flavor to this dish. Pestos come in a variety of flavors and packages, from fresh to bottled. This recipe will adapt to fit many different flavors of pesto, so feel free to experiment.

PREP TIME: 30 minutes   **COOKING TIME:** 1½ hours on HIGH, 3–4 hours on LOW
ADDITIONAL STEPS: Precook the ziti for 8 minutes

1 pound (455 g) ziti

1 cup (260 g) sun-dried tomato pesto

1 (16-ounce or 475-ml) jar Alfredo sauce

Bring a large pot of salted water to a boil. Add the ziti and cook at a low boil for 8 minutes. Drain the pasta.

Spray the crock with nonstick cooking spray. Add the ziti, pesto, and Alfredo sauce. Stir gently. Cook for 1¹/₂ to 2 hours on HIGH or 3 to 4 hours on LOW.

YIELD: 6 to 8 servings

NUTRITIONAL ANALYSIS: 445 calories; 19 g fat (38.6% calories from fat); 13 g protein; 56 g carbohydrate; 3 g dietary fiber; 32 mg cholesterol; 701 mg sodium.

ADD IT IN! Stir a handful of fresh chopped basil into the casserole before cooking. You can garnish each plate with more of the same for a visual exclamation point.

Mushroom Marinara

This tasty, versatile sauce also goes great over cooked pasta, meat, or chicken. For a distinctive vegetarian treat, serve over spinach-and-cheese-stuffed manicotti, served with rustic Italian bread.

COOKING TIME: 6 to 7 hours   **ATTENTION:** Minimal

One 32-ounce (905-g) jar marinara sauce

1¹/₂ cups (340 g) frozen Seasoning-Blend Vegetables (page 29), thawed

One 12-ounce (340-g) bag frozen sliced mushrooms, thawed

Salt and freshly ground black pepper

Put the marinara sauce, thawed vegetables, and thawed mushrooms in the slow cooker and stir to combine. Cover and cook on LOW for 6 to 7 hours.

Before serving, stir the mixture again and season it with salt and pepper to taste.

YIELD: 8 servings

NUTRITIONAL ANALYSIS: One serving of the basic recipe contains 97 calories; 3 g fat; 4 g protein; 16 g carbohydrate; and 4 g dietary fiber.

IT'S GOOD FOR YOU: Trade mushrooms for meat? Not such a novel idea. The vitamin content of mushrooms resembles that of meat, yet mushrooms are very low in calories, are fat-free, and contain fiber. What a deal!

Ravioli Stew

"Quick and easy" best describes this ravioli dish. But the taste—now, that's indescribable. Ladle into shallow bowls, top with your favorite grated cheese, and enjoy with garlic breadsticks fresh from the oven.

COOKING TIME: 45 to 60 minutes
ATTENTION: Add another ingredient after 30 minutes

One 32-ounce (905-g) jar chunky garden-style pasta sauce

2 teaspoons (1.6 g) dried basil

One 9-ounce (255-g) package refrigerated cheese ravioli

Put the pasta sauce and dried basil in the slow cooker and stir to combine. Cover and cook on HIGH for 30 minutes, or until the sauce is hot and bubbly.

Add the ravioli and stir. Cover and cook for another 15 to 30 minutes, or until the ravioli are tender but not mushy.

YIELD: 4 servings

NUTRITIONAL ANALYSIS: One serving of the basic recipe contains 116 calories; 5 g fat; 6 g protein; 13 g carbohydrate; and .8 g dietary fiber.

ADD IT IN! Add a 15-ounce (417-g) can cannelloni beans, rinsed and drained, to the pasta sauce, and cook the mixture on HIGH for 1 hour instead of 30 minutes. Add 1/8 teaspoon crushed red pepper along with the ravioli, and cook for another 15 to 30 minutes.

Baked Ziti

This is another of those comforting and homey casseroles that migrates well to slow-cooker land.

PREP TIME: 30 minutes   **COOKING TIME:** 1½ hours on HIGH, 3–4 hours on LOW
ADDITIONAL STEPS: Precook the ziti for 8 minutes

1 pound (455 g) ziti

1 (20-ounce or 570-ml) jar four-cheese marinara sauce

1 cup (260 g) basil pesto

Bring a large pot of salted water to a boil. Add the ziti and cook at a low boil for 8 minutes. Drain the pasta and rinse with cold water to cool.

Spray the crock with nonstick cooking spray. Add the ziti and the marinara and pesto sauces. Stir to combine well. Cook for 1½ hours on HIGH or 3 to 4 hours on LOW.

YIELD: 6 to 8 servings

NUTRITIONAL ANALYSIS: 403 calories; 16 g fat (36.8% calories from fat); 13 g protein; 50 g carbohydrate; 3 g dietary fiber; 9 mg cholesterol; 502 mg sodium.

ADD IT IN: You can add a top layer of grated Parmesan cheese to this dish if you like lots of cheese.

Three-Cheese Vegetarian Spaghetti

Preparing a delicious, home-cooked spaghetti dinner for your family is a labor of love—or it used to be. This delicious one-pot spaghetti dish gives you some labor-free time away from the kitchen.

COOKING TIME: 6 to 8 hours on LOW, 3 to 4 hours on HIGH
ATTENTION: Change heat setting and add another ingredient during final hour

One 28-ounce (795-g) jar three-cheese-flavored pasta sauce

12 ounces (340 g) imitation ground burger

6 ounces (168 g) dry spaghetti, broken into 4-inch (10-cm) pieces

Put the pasta sauce and imitation ground burger in the slow cooker and stir to combine. Cover and cook on LOW for 6 to 8 hours or on HIGH for 3 to 4 hours.

An hour before the dish is done, add the dry spaghetti and stir. Cook on HIGH for 1 more hour, or until the spaghetti is tender but not mushy.

YIELD: 4 servings

NUTRITIONAL ANALYSIS: One serving of the basic recipe contains 411 calories; 1 g fat; 61 g protein; 49 g carbohydrate; and 17 g dietary fiber.

Mock Meaty Pasta Sauce

The supermarket shelves are crowded with good pasta sauces. Grab your favorite, and with a little help from your slow cooker, you can get a wonderful, full-bodied, meaty sauce. You'll know it's vegetarian, but will anyone else?

COOKING TIME: 6 to 8 hours on LOW, 3 to 4 hours on HIGH
ATTENTION: Minimal

One 28-ounce (795-g) jar vegetarian pasta sauce

12 ounces (340 g) imitation ground burger

1½ cups (340 g) frozen Seasoning-Blend Vegetables (page 29)

Salt and freshly ground black pepper

Put the pasta sauce, imitation ground burger, and frozen vegetables in the slow cooker and stir to combine. Cover and cook on LOW for 6 to 8 hours or on HIGH for 3 to 4 hours.

Just before serving, stir the sauce again and season it with salt and pepper to taste.

YIELD: 10 servings

NUTRITIONAL ANALYSIS: One serving of the basic recipe contains 119 calories; 4 g fat; 23 g protein; 11 g carbohydrate; and 7.3 g dietary fiber.

ADD IT IN! Add 2 cloves garlic, minced.

Cheesy Italian Casserole

This easy meal is made irresistible by the yummy goodness of mozzarella cheese. Serve over pasta, with grated Parmesan and garlic toast.

COOKING TIME: $6^1/_2$ to $7^1/_2$ hours
ATTENTION: Add another ingredient during final 10 to 15 minutes

One 32-ounce (905-g) jar chunky-style pasta sauce with mushrooms

12 ounces (340 g) imitation ground burger

$^1/_4$ teaspoon freshly ground black pepper

1 cup (112 g) shredded Italian or mozzarella cheese

Put the pasta sauce, imitation ground burger, and pepper in the slow cooker and stir to combine. Cover and cook on LOW for 6 to 7 hours.

Stir the casserole again and sprinkle it with the cheese. Cover and cook for another 10 to 15 minutes, or until the cheese has melted.

YIELD: 8 servings

NUTRITIONAL ANALYSIS: One serving of the basic recipe (made with shredded mozzarella cheese) contains 172 calories; 4 g fat; 31 g protein; 9 g carbohydrate; and 8 g dietary fiber.

ADD IT IN! About 30 minutes before the casserole is done, stir in 2 cups total of any or all of these veggies, all lightly steamed: broccoli, cauliflower, zucchini, carrots.

CHAPTER 14

MAIN DISHES:VEGETARIAN

Vegetarian fare is fast becoming a centerpiece meal for the mainstream. Many people are starting to promote health by substituting one or more meatless meals a week. A vegetarian diet is associated with major health benefits because of the vitamins, the minerals, and the cancer-fighting phytochemicals and dietary fiber that beans, legumes, and vegetables supply. But you know all that! You're turning to this chapter because vegetarian meals are a natural for the slow cooker—easy to prepare and serve, with a surefire, delicious result. You know just how rich and satisfying dinner can be when the main dish is a steaming bowl of Santa Fe Black Beans and Corn (page 248), or even Vegetarian Sloppy Joes (page 259) for the kids. Your family won't even know the meat's missing—because it's all about great taste!

● No-Frill Beans

You might want to cook up batches of dried beans in your slow cooker, some to use right away and some to freeze for later. That way, you'll always have a nice assortment of beans in the freezer, ready to pop into a recipe. A scant 1¼ cups of cooked beans is approximately equivalent to a 14-ounce (398-g) can of beans.

COOKING TIME: 8 to 10 hours on LOW, 4 to 5 hours on HIGH
ATTENTION: Minimal

1 pound (455 g) dried beans

1½ quarts (1.4 L) water

2 onions, chopped

2 to 3 cloves garlic, minced

Put the beans in a large colander, pick through them to remove any debris, and rinse them under running water. Put them in a large bowl, cover them with water, and let them soak for 6 to 8 hours, or overnight.

Pour the beans back into the colander, discarding the used water, and rinse the beans again under running water. Place the beans in the slow cooker and add the 1½ quarts (1.4 L) water, chopped onions, and minced garlic. Cover and cook on LOW for 8 to 10 hours or on HIGH for 4 to 5 hours.

Return the beans to the colander, drain them, and rinse them under running water once more. Use them in a recipe, or allow them to cool and then freeze them for later use.

YIELD: 10 servings

NUTRITIONAL ANALYSIS: One serving of the basic recipe contains 161 calories; .6 g fat; 10 g protein; 30 g carbohydrate; and 12 g dietary fiber.

● Special Baked Beans

There are almost as many ways to make baked beans as there are cooks. Bring this special recipe to the picnic or to that important family get-together. Or make it the centerpiece of a vegetarian meal, served with 7-grain rolls or wheat-berry bread.

COOKING TIME: 4 to 6 hours   **ATTENTION:** Minimal

One 28-ounce (795-g) can vegetarian baked beans

½ cup (120 g) vegetarian ketchup

¼ cup (56 g) brown sugar, packed

Salt and freshly ground black pepper

Put the canned baked beans, ketchup, and brown sugar in the slow cooker and stir to combine. Cover and cook on LOW for 4 to 6 hours.

Before serving, stir the mixture again and season it with salt and pepper to taste.

YIELD: 6 servings

NUTRITIONAL ANALYSIS: One serving of the basic recipe contains 178 calories; .7 g fat; 7 g protein; 42 g carbohydrate; and 7 g dietary fiber.

ADD IT IN: Add 1 pound (455 g) meatless sausage, ground-style or chopped into small pieces, ½ cup (65 g) chopped onion, and 1 teaspoon (3 g) minced garlic, and increase the cooking time to 6 to 9 hours.

● Santa Fe Black Beans and Corn

Serve this deceptively simple main dish rolled in corn tortillas or spooned over Yellow Rice (page 307). For a change of pace, serve it as a nacho topping or as a dip accompanied by blue tortilla chips for scoops.

COOKING TIME: 3 to 4 hours   **ATTENTION:** Minimal

Two 15-ounce (417-g) cans Mexican corn with red and green peppers

One 15-ounce (417-g) can black beans, rinsed and drained

1 cup (225 g) chunky-style salsa

Put the Mexican corn, black beans, and salsa in the slow cooker and stir to combine. Cover and cook on LOW for 3 to 4 hours.

YIELD: 6 servings

NUTRITIONAL ANALYSIS: One serving of the basic recipe contains 195 calories; 4 g fat; 8 g protein; 36 g carbohydrate; and 7 g dietary fiber.

ADD IT IN! Sprinkle 1 cup (115 g) shredded Mexican-blend cheese over the mixture 15 minutes before it's done and continue cooking until the cheese has melted.

● Black Bean Chili

Nothing's better on a cold, blustery day than a big steaming bowl of chili. Serve with a slab of cornbread smothered in butter.

COOKING TIME: 8 to 10 hours on LOW, 4 to 5 hours on HIGH
ATTENTION: Minimal

Two 14¹/₂-ounce (413-g) cans Mexican-flavored stewed tomatoes

One 15-ounce (417-g) can vegetarian chili, with or without beans

One 15-ounce (417-g) can ready-to-eat black bean soup

Salt and freshly ground black pepper

Put the stewed tomatoes, chili, and black bean soup in the slow cooker and stir to combine. Cover and cook on LOW for 8 to 10 hours or on HIGH for 4 to 5 hours.

Before serving, stir the mixture again and season it with salt and pepper to taste.

YIELD: 6 servings

NUTRITIONAL ANALYSIS: One serving of the basic recipe (made with vegetarian chili without beans) contains 165 calories; 2 g fat; 16 g protein; 25 g carbohydrate; and 5 g dietary fiber.

ADD IT IN! Add an undrained 17-ounce (483-g) can Mexican-style whole-kernel corn with peppers, 1¹/₂ cups (340 g) frozen Seasoning-Blend Vegetables (page 29), a 1.25-ounce (35-g) envelope chili seasoning mix, and 2 cloves garlic, minced.

Vegetarian Hoppin' John

Hoppin' John is served on New Year's Day for good luck in the coming year. Make today your lucky day. Enjoy an overflowing bowl of black-eyed peas and rice, with Collard Greens (page 271) and cornbread on the side.

COOKING TIME: 6 to 8 hours on LOW, 3 to 5 hours on HIGH
ATTENTION: Minimal

¾ cup (175 ml) hot water

1 vegetable bouillon cube

One 14-ounce (398-g) can diced tomatoes with green chilies, undrained

One 7-ounce (197-g) package black-eyed peas and rice mix

Salt and freshly ground black pepper

Put the hot water and bouillon cube in the slow cooker and stir until the bouillon cube has dissolved. Add the diced tomatoes and black-eyed peas and rice mix, and stir again. Cover and cook on LOW for 6 to 8 hours or on HIGH for 3 to 5 hours.

Before serving, stir the mixture and season it with salt and pepper to taste.

YIELD: 8 servings

NUTRITIONAL ANALYSIS: One serving of the basic recipe contains 97 calories; .4 g fat; .7 g protein; 18 g carbohydrate; and 7 g dietary fiber.

ADD IT IN! Add 1 medium onion, chopped, and 3 cloves garlic, minced, along with the diced tomatoes and black-eyed peas and rice mix.

● Saucy Italian Chick Peas

This is a super simple dish to throw together for a light but healthful dinner.
Serve it over pasta shells, topped with Parmesan cheese, or eat it all by itself.

COOKING TIME: 6 to 8 hours on LOW, 3 to 4 hours on HIGH
ATTENTION: Minimal

Two 14-ounce (398-g) cans diced tomatoes with garlic, oregano, and basil, undrained

One 19-ounce (540-g) can chick peas, rinsed and drained

1 teaspoon Italian Seasoning (page 28)

Salt and freshly ground black pepper

Put the diced tomatoes, chick peas, and Italian Seasoning in the slow cooker and stir to combine. Cover and cook on LOW for 6 to 8 hours or on HIGH for 3 to 4 hours.

Before serving, stir the mixture again and season it with salt and pepper to taste.

YIELD: 6 servings

NUTRITIONAL ANALYSIS: One serving of the basic recipe contains 140 calories; 1 g fat; 7 g protein; 27 g carbohydrate; and 6 g dietary fiber.

ADD IT IN! Add 2 large cloves garlic, minced, and ⅛ teaspoon chili flakes.

Field Peas with Snaps and Rice

Enjoy this Southern specialty with the traditional accompaniment, cornbread, or with flaky biscuits slathered with Apricot Preserves (page 111).

COOKING TIME: 4 to 5 hours | **ATTENTION:** Minimal

---

2 vegetable bouillon cubes

2 cups (475 ml) hot water

One 15-ounce (417-g) can field peas with snaps

¾ cup (139 g) raw long-grain white rice

Salt and freshly ground black pepper

Put the hot water and bouillon cubes in the slow cooker and stir until the bouillon cubes have dissolved. Add the field peas with snaps and dry rice, and stir again. Cover and cook on LOW for 4 to 5 hours, or until the rice is tender.

Before serving, stir the mixture and season it with salt and pepper to taste. This dish tastes especially good with lots of pepper.

YIELD: 6 servings

NUTRITIONAL ANALYSIS: One serving of the basic recipe contains 143 calories; .8 g fat; 5 g protein; 28 g carbohydrate; and 3 g dietary fiber.

DID YOU KNOW? Field peas with snaps are actually the beans known worldwide as cowpeas. Immature pods—only the youngest and most tender—are typically broken into a batch of field peas, and these are called snaps.

● Northern Bean Soup

This vegetarian soup is healthful and delicious. Enjoy with hot buttered cornbread on cold winter days.

COOKING TIME: 8 to 10 hours on LOW, 4 to 6 hours on HIGH
ATTENTION: Mash beans during final 1 to 2 hours; add another ingredient during final 30 minutes

Two 15-ounce (417-g) cans Great Northern beans or navy beans, rinsed and drained

Two 10¾-ounce (305-g) cans condensed vegetarian vegetable soup

¾ cup (175 ml) water

3 tablespoons (45 ml) olive oil

Salt and freshly ground black pepper

Put the beans, condensed soup, and water in the slow cooker and stir to combine. Cover and cook on LOW for 8 to 10 hours or on HIGH for 4 to 6 hours.

Between 1 and 2 hours before the soup is done, thicken the soup by mashing the beans with a potato masher. About 30 minutes before the soup is done, add the olive oil and mix well. Just before serving, stir the soup again and season it with salt and pepper to taste.

YIELD: 6 servings

NUTRITIONAL ANALYSIS: One serving of the basic recipe (made with Great Northern beans) contains 270 calories; 9 g fat; 12 g protein; 38 g carbohydrate; and 7 g dietary fiber.

ADD IT IN! Add 10 ounces (280 g) meatless sausage cut into bite-size pieces and 2 teaspoons (10 ml) vegetarian Worcestershire sauce along with the beans and condensed soup.

● Garlic-Barbecue Baked Beans

Baked beans are a staple of the vegetarian diet. Enjoy this garlicky version with a tossed salad and crusty bread.

COOKING TIME: 8 to 10 hours   **ATTENTION:** Minimal

Two 15-ounce (417-g) cans Great Northern beans, rinsed and drained

1¹/₂ cups (375 g) garlic-flavored barbecue sauce

1 onion, chopped

Salt and freshly ground black pepper

Put the Great Northern beans, barbecue sauce, and chopped onion in the slow cooker and stir to combine. Cover and cook on LOW for 8 to 10 hours.

Before serving, stir the mixture again and season it with salt and pepper to taste.

YIELD: 6 servings

NUTRITIONAL ANALYSIS: One serving of the basic recipe contains 216 calories; 2 g fat; 12 g protein; 39 g carbohydrate; and 8 g dietary fiber.

● Gussied-Up Baked Beans

Give those canned baked beans some personality, and give this recipe your own twist by choosing your favorite barbecue sauce.

PREP TIME: 10 minutes   **COOKING TIME:** 1 hour on HIGH, 3–4 hours on LOW

2 (16-ounce or 455-g) cans baked beans

¹/₂ cup (125 g) barbecue sauce

¹/₄ cup (60 g) Dijon mustard

Combine all the ingredients in the slow cooker. Cook for 1 hour on HIGH or 3 to 4 hours on LOW.

YIELD: 8 to 10 servings

NUTRITIONAL ANALYSIS: 98 calories; 1 g fat (7.3% calories from fat); 5 g protein; 21 g carbohydrate; 5 g dietary fiber; 0 mg cholesterol; 537 mg sodium.

Chili Beans

These are nice in a burrito or as a side with any Tex-Mex feast.

PREP TIME: 10 minutes   **COOKING TIME:** 1¹/₂ hours on HIGH, 3–4 hours on LOW

1 medium-size onion

2 (16-ounce or 455-g) cans pinto beans

3 or 4 ancho chiles or other favorite dried chile

Salt and pepper to taste

Peel the onion and chop into small dice. Add the onion to the slow cooker. Drain the beans and add them to the cooker. Remove the stems and seeds from the chiles and break them up into the slow cooker. Add ¹/₂ cup (120 ml) water, season with salt and pepper to taste, and stir. Cook for 1¹/₂ hours on HIGH or 3 to 4 hours on LOW.

YIELD: 6 to 8 servings

NUTRITIONAL ANALYSIS: 103 calories; trace fat (3.6% calories from fat); 6 g protein; 20 g carbohydrate; 5 g dietary fiber; 0 mg cholesterol; 474 mg sodium.

Bean, Barley, and Mock-Sausage Stew

Don't you love the smell of slow-cooking stew on a cold winter's day? Serve this aromatic and full-flavored stew with Maple-Glazed Baby Carrots (page 266) and sourdough bread.

COOKING TIME: 8 to 10 hours   **ATTENTION:** Minimal

Two 15-ounce (417-g) cans light red kidney beans, rinsed and drained

3¹/₂ cups (823 ml) water

1 pound (455 g) meatless Italian sausage, cut into chunks

1 cup (200 g) uncooked pearl barley

Salt

Put the kidney beans, water, mock sausage, and pearl barley in the slow cooker and stir to combine. Cover and cook on LOW for 8 to 10 hours.

Before serving, stir the stew again and season it with salt to taste.

YIELD: 8 servings

NUTRITIONAL ANALYSIS: One serving of the basic recipe contains 324 calories; 11 g fat; 19 g protein; 42 g carbohydrate; and 12 g dietary fiber.

ADD IT IN! Substitute vegetable broth for the water, and add ¹/₂ cup (65 g) chopped onion and 2 cloves garlic, minced.

● Barley Casserole

The mildly nutty flavor of barley combines superbly with mixed vegetables in a tomato-based broth. Serve with cornbread or hush puppies for a delicious meal.

COOKING TIME: 6 to 10 hours | **ATTENTION:** Minimal

Two 19-ounce (540-g) cans ready-to-eat vegetarian vegetable soup

1 cup (200 g) uncooked pearl barley

1 tablespoon (14 ml) Worcestershire sauce

Salt and freshly ground black pepper

Put the vegetable soup, pearl barley, and Worcestershire sauce in the slow cooker and stir to combine. Cover and cook on LOW for 6 to 10 hours, or until the barley is tender.

Before serving, stir the casserole again and season it with salt and pepper to taste.

YIELD: 6 servings

NUTRITIONAL ANALYSIS: One serving of the basic recipe contains 173 calories; 2 g fat; 5 g protein; 35 g carbohydrate; and 6 g dietary fiber.

ADD IT IN! Add a drained 15-ounce (417-g) can garbanzo beans and 2 to 10 drops hot sauce.

Barley with Porcini Mushrooms

Dried porcini mushrooms taste wonderful, and their soaking liquid is used as a flavorful stock, letting us double down on flavor by doubling the effectiveness of one ingredient.

PREP TIME: 30 minutes **COOKING TIME:** 2 hours on HIGH, 4–5 hours on LOW
ADDITIONAL STEPS: Steep the porcini before adding to the slow cooker

2 ounces (about 2 cups or 55 g) dried porcini mushrooms

1 medium-size onion

1 pound (455 g) pearl barley

Salt and pepper to taste

Bring 4 cups (940 ml) water to a boil. Put the porcini into a large bowl and pour the boiling water over them. Allow to steep for 20 minutes.

Peel the onion and chop it into small dice. Put the onion, the barley, and the porcini, along with the soaking liquid, into the slow cooker. Season with salt and pepper. Cook for 2 hours on HIGH or 4 to 5 hours on LOW, until the water is absorbed and the barley is tender.

YIELD: 6 to 8 servings

NUTRITIONAL ANALYSIS: 226 calories; 1 g fat (2.8% calories from fat); 6 g protein; 51 g carbohydrate; 10 g dietary fiber; 0 mg cholesterol; 6 mg sodium.

ADD IT IN! Add some chopped fresh oregano to the mixture.

Kasha

Kasha, or buckwheat, has an unforgettable flavor that is quite addictive.

PREP TIME: 30 minutes **COOKING TIME:** 2 hours on HIGH, 3–4 hours on LOW

1 (1-pound or 455-g) box medium kasha

2 eggs

3 cups (705 ml) chicken stock or broth

Put the kasha into the slow cooker. Turn on the cooker to HIGH. Break the eggs into a bowl and whisk lightly. Add to the kasha and stir until the grains are coated. Cook for 15 to 20 minutes on HIGH, stirring every few minutes, then add the stock. Cover and cook for another 1½ hours on HIGH or turn to LOW and cook for 3 to 4 hours. The kasha is done when it is tender and the liquid is absorbed.

YIELD: 4 to 6 servings

NUTRITIONAL ANALYSIS: 292 calories; 4 g fat (12.2% calories from fat); 12 g protein; 55 g carbohydrate; 8 g dietary fiber; 62 mg cholesterol; 1093 mg sodium.

● Stewed Lentils with Red Wine

Because lentils are seldom used in mainstream American cuisine, this dish may be the road less taken for many people. But it's a fabulous side to lamb and beef. Try it and see for yourself!

PREP TIME: 15 minutes   **COOKING TIME:** 2 hours on HIGH, 6–7 hours on LOW
ADDITIONAL STEPS: Wash and pick over the lentils

1 pound (455 g) lentils

1 medium-size onion

2 cups (470 ml) red wine

Salt and pepper to taste

Pick over the lentils, removing any shriveled or discolored ones and any grit or stones, and rinse them in a colander. Put the lentils into the slow cooker.

Chop the onion into small dice and add to the slow cooker. Add the red wine and 1 cup (235 ml) water, and season with salt and pepper to taste. Cook for 2 hours on HIGH or 6 to 7 hours on LOW, until the lentils are tender and the liquid is mostly absorbed.

YIELD: 4 to 6 servings

NUTRITIONAL ANALYSIS: 319 calories; 1 g fat (2.4% calories from fat); 22 g protein; 46 g carbohydrate; 23 g dietary fiber; 0 mg cholesterol; 59 mg sodium.

ADD IT IN: Finely chop a couple of carrots and mix them in when you add the onion.

Vegetarian Sloppy Joes

Kids—from 3 to 103—love Sloppy Joes.

COOKING TIME: 5 to 9 hours on LOW, 2½ to 4 hours on HIGH
ATTENTION: Minimal

12 ounces (340 g) imitation ground burger, browned and drained

One 15-ounce (417-g) can vegetarian chili with beans

½ cup (125 g) barbecue sauce

Salt and freshly ground black pepper

In a large skillet over medium heat, brown the imitation ground burger. Drain it well, then place it in the slow cooker.

Add the chili and barbecue sauce to the browned imitation meat and stir to combine. Cover and cook on LOW for 5 to 9 hours or on HIGH for 2½ to 3 hours.

Stir the mixture again and season it with salt and pepper to taste. Serve it on hamburger buns.

YIELD: 8 servings

NUTRITIONAL ANALYSIS: One serving of the basic recipe contains 208 calories; 2 g fat; 37 g protein; 18 g carbohydrate; and 10 g dietary fiber.

ADD IT IN! Add 1 cup (227 g) frozen Seasoning-Blend Vegetables (page 29), 2 teaspoons (10 ml) Worcestershire sauce, and 2 cloves garlic, minced.

◉ Chili Hot Dogs

Hot dog fanatics will love being able to dip into the slow cooker for the makings for a chili dog. Serve on toasted rolls, and top with cheddar cheese and green onion.

COOKING TIME: 4 to 5 hours on LOW, 2 to 2¹/₂ hours on HIGH
ATTENTION: Minimal

8 vegetarian hot dogs

One 15-ounce (417-g) can vegetarian chili with beans

1 large onion, chopped

Salt and freshly ground black pepper

Put the hot dogs, chili, and chopped onion in the slow cooker and stir to combine. Cover and cook on LOW for 4 to 5 hours or on HIGH for 2 to 2¹/₂ hours.

Just before serving, stir the mixture again and season it with salt and pepper to taste.

YIELD: 8 servings

NUTRITIONAL ANALYSIS: One serving of the basic recipe contains 194 calories; 8 g fat; 22 g protein; 10 g carbohydrate; and 4 g dietary fiber.

ADD IT IN! Add 1 teaspoon chili powder.

CHAPTER 15
VEGETABLES AND OTHER SIDE DISHES

Side dishes are designed to round out the nutrition of a meal, as well as to set off the entrée by adding interest, variety, and color. Many slow-cooker side dishes, such as our White Beans with Sun-Dried Tomatoes (page 285), are hearty enough to function as a main dish as well. Some side dishes go exceptionally well with certain main dishes; a good example is Candied Sweet Potatoes (page 302), which is great with any holiday meal. Others—say, Fabulous Foil Potatoes (page 288)—can be paired with just about any main dish. So, when you want to try a little color next to your main course, check out our Cheesy California Vegetables (page 262), Rustic Mashed Potatoes (page 296), or Maple-Apple Sweet Potatoes (page 301). And when you just want to make it easier to get everything on the table at the same time, pick any slow-cooker side dish you wish!

Easiest Vegetable-Surprise Dish

The surprise is that this dish is so quick and easy. While you run to the gym, you can be cooking a healthful veggie side dish.

COOKING TIME: 1¹/₂ to 2¹/₂ hours on LOW, 45 to 75 minutes on HIGH
ATTENTION: Minimal

Two 16-ounce (455-g) bags frozen mixed vegetables, partially thawed

One 10³/₄-ounce (305-g) can condensed cream of mushroom or cream of celery soup

1 small onion, chopped

¹/₂ teaspoon salt

Put the partially thawed vegetables, condensed soup, chopped onion, and salt in the slow cooker and stir to combine. Cover and cook on LOW for 1¹/₂ to 2¹/₂ hours or on HIGH for 45 to 75 minutes.

YIELD: 8 servings

NUTRITIONAL ANALYSIS: One serving of the basic recipe (made with condensed cream of mushroom soup) contains 117 calories; 4 g fat; 5 g protein; 19 g carbohydrate; and 5 g dietary fiber.

Cheesy California Vegetables

You'll enjoy the cheesy taste of these sweet California vegetables even more because fixing them was so quick and easy. Broccoli, cauliflower, carrots—you never had them so good.

COOKING TIME: 1¹/₂ to 2¹/₂ hours on LOW, 45 to 75 minutes on HIGH
ATTENTION: Minimal

Two 16-ounce (455-g) bags frozen California-blend vegetables, partially thawed

One 10³/₄-ounce (305-g) can condensed cheddar cheese soup

2 cloves garlic, minced

¹/₂ teaspoon salt

Put the partially thawed vegetables, condensed soup, minced garlic, and salt in the slow cooker and stir to combine. Cover and cook on LOW for 1$\frac{1}{2}$ to 2$\frac{1}{2}$ hours or on HIGH for 45 to 75 minutes.

YIELD: 8 servings

NUTRITIONAL ANALYSIS: One serving of the basic recipe contains 113 calories; 3 g fat; 5 g protein; 18 g carbohydrate; and 5 g dietary fiber.

Creamy Veggie Casserole

Super simple and super delicious. Enjoy this side dish with virtually any meal.

COOKING TIME: 8 to 10 hours on LOW, 4 to 5 hours on HIGH
ATTENTION: Minimal

2$\frac{1}{2}$ cups (588 ml) hot water

3 chicken bouillon cubes

6 cups (720 g) frozen stew vegetables, partially thawed

Two 10$\frac{3}{4}$-ounce (305-g) cans condensed cream of chicken soup

Put the hot water and bouillon cubes in the slow cooker and stir until the bouillon cubes have dissolved. Add the partially thawed vegetables and condensed soup, and stir again. Cover and cook on LOW for 8 to 10 hours or on HIGH for 4 to 5 hours, or until the vegetables are tender.

YIELD: 12 servings

NUTRITIONAL ANALYSIS: One serving of the basic recipe contains 100 calories; 3 g fat; 4 g protein; 16 g carbohydrate; and 4 g dietary fiber.

ADD IT IN! For a richer taste, add 5$\frac{1}{2}$ tablespoons ($\frac{1}{3}$ cup, or 75 g) butter, melted, and 2 tablespoons (8 g) chopped fresh parsley.

Acorn Squash

This is just too simple! Pair Acorn Squash with Chunky Applesauce (page 331) and your favorite entrée.

COOKING TIME: 8 to 10 hours **ATTENTION:** Minimal

1¹/₂- to 2-pound (683- to 910-g) whole acorn squash, rinsed well

2 teaspoons (12 g) salt

¹/₂ teaspoon freshly ground black pepper

6 tablespoons (84 g) butter, melted

2 tablespoons (28 g) brown sugar, packed

Pierce the acorn squash in several places with a fork and place it in the slow cooker. Cover and cook on LOW for 8 to 10 hours, or until the squash is fork-tender.

Remove the squash from the slow cooker and allow it to cool enough to be handled safely. Cut the squash in half, then cut each half in half. Scoop out and discard the seeds, place each squash quarter pulp side up on a plate, and season each squash quarter with one-fourth of the salt and pepper. In a small bowl, combine the melted butter and brown sugar, then pour one-fourth of the mixture over each squash quarter.

YIELD: 4 servings

NUTRITIONAL ANALYSIS: One serving of the basic recipe (made with a 1¹/₂-pound acorn squash) contains 231 calories; 18 g fat; 1 g protein; 20 g carbohydrate; and 2 g dietary fiber.

TIP: Place the cooked, seasoned squash quarters on a baking sheet, then fill them with the butter–brown sugar mixture. Warm the squash quarters in a 350°F (180°C) oven for 10 minutes, or until the brown sugar has melted.

Asparagus Side Dish

A delicious side dish without comparison. Serve this tempting fare with any Italian entrée for a real treat.

COOKING TIME: 4 to 6 hours **ATTENTION:** Minimal

1½ pounds (683 g) asparagus, sliced diagonally into 1-inch (2.5-cm) pieces

One 10¾-ounce (305-g) can condensed cream of celery soup

¾ cup (86 g) coarsely crushed saltine crackers

Spray the inside of the slow cooker with cooking spray.

Place the asparagus pieces in the slow cooker, pour the condensed soup over them, and sprinkle them with the cracker crumbs. Cover and cook on LOW for 4 to 6 hours.

YIELD: 6 servings

NUTRITIONAL ANALYSIS: One serving of the basic recipe contains 89 calories; 3 g fat; 3 g protein; 13 g carbohydrate; and 2 g dietary fiber.

ADD IT IN! Add 1 cup (120 g) grated cheddar when the asparagus has finished cooking. Cover and heat on LOW for another 15 to 30 minutes, or until the cheese has melted. Stir the mixture before serving it.

Candied Carrots and Pecans

Flavored syrup gives this carrot dish a nutty taste. Delicious with pork and wild rice.

COOKING TIME: 6 to 8 hours on LOW, 3 to 4 hours on HIGH
ATTENTION: Minimal

Two 16-ounce (455-g) packages frozen sliced carrots

¾ cup (242 g) butter pecan–flavored syrup

½ cup (113 g) brown sugar, packed

Put the sliced carrots, syrup, and brown sugar in the slow cooker and stir to combine. Cover and cook on LOW for 6 to 8 hours or on HIGH for 3 to 4 hours.

YIELD: 8 servings

NUTRITIONAL ANALYSIS: One serving of the basic recipe contains 95 calories; .1 g fat; 1 g protein; 24 g carbohydrate; and 3 g dietary fiber.

ADD IT IN! Add 1 cup (109 g) chopped pecans, and cook the dish on HIGH for 5½ to 6½ hours. Do not cook this dish on LOW if you add the nuts.

Glazed Crinkle Carrots

For a change of pace, cash in on the fabulous sweet-and-sour taste of these glazed carrot coins.

COOKING TIME: 4 to 6 hours on LOW, 2 to 3 hours on HIGH
ATTENTION: Stir every hour

8 large carrots, sliced into crinkle-cut coins

½ cup (113 g) brown sugar, packed

¼ cup (60 g) Dijon mustard

Put the crinkle-cut carrots, brown sugar, and mustard in the slow cooker and stir to combine. Cover and cook on LOW for 4 to 6 hours or on HIGH for 2 to 3 hours, or until the carrot slices are tender, stirring once an hour.

YIELD: 8 servings

NUTRITIONAL ANALYSIS: One serving of the basic recipe contains 88 calories; .5 g fat; 1 g protein; 21 g carbohydrate; and 2 g dietary fiber.

ADD IT IN! Add 1 teaspoon minced fresh ginger.

TRY THIS! Replace the brown sugar with honey for a different flavor. You can also experiment with the many flavored mustards on the market to find your family's favorite.

Maple-Glazed Baby Carrots

Maple flavoring gives these babies a sweet, delicate flavor, making them a perfect accompaniment to chicken, pork, or beef.

COOKING TIME: 6 to 8 hours on LOW, 3 to 4 hours on HIGH
ATTENTION: Stir every hour

2 pounds (910 g) baby carrots

¼ cup (81 g) pure maple syrup

2 tablespoons (28 g) butter

¼ teaspoon salt

⅛ teaspoon freshly ground black pepper

Put the baby carrots, maple syrup, butter, salt, and pepper in the slow cooker and stir to combine. Cover and cook on LOW for 6 to 8 hours or on HIGH for 3 to 4 hours, or until the carrots are tender and glazed, stirring once an hour.

YIELD: 10 servings

NUTRITIONAL ANALYSIS: One serving of the basic recipe contains 76 calories; 3 g fat; .8 g protein; 13 g carbohydrate; and 2 g dietary fiber.

IT'S GOOD FOR YOU: Carrots are a superb source of antioxidants including beta-carotene (vitamin A) as well as vitamin C, the B vitamins, potassium, and calcium pectate, which has been shown to lower cholesterol.

Marmalade-Glazed Carrots

This medley of tangy-sweet orange marmalade and inherently sweet carrots is divine. You can almost eat this one for dessert.

COOKING TIME: $2^1/_2$ to $4^1/_2$ hours
ATTENTION: Drain juices and add more ingredients during final 20 to 30 minutes

4 cups (488 g) diagonally sliced carrots

$2^1/_2$ cups (588 ml) water

$^1/_2$ teaspoon salt

4 tablespoons (55 g) butter or margarine

$^1/_2$ cup (75 g) orange marmalade

Put the sliced carrots, water, and salt in the slow cooker and stir to combine. Cover and cook on HIGH for 2 to 4 hours, or until the carrot slices are tender.

Turn the heat OFF and allow the slow cooker to cool enough so that you can handle the ceramic pot safely. Drain the carrots well, add the butter and orange marmalade, and stir the mixture. Cover and cook on HIGH for 20 to 30 minutes.

YIELD: 8 servings

NUTRITIONAL ANALYSIS: One serving of the basic recipe (made with butter) contains 102 calories; 6 g fat; .8 g protein; 13 g carbohydrate; and 2 g dietary fiber.

ADD IT IN! Add $^1/_2$ cup (30 g) chopped walnuts along with the butter and marmalade.

TRY THIS! Try this dish with lime or lemon marmalade instead of orange marmalade, or substitute currant jelly or apricot preserves.

Maple Walnut Carrots

Sweet and earthy with the added crunch of the walnuts, these carrots make a delightful side dish for a holiday meal, or any day.

PREP TIME: 30 minutes **COOKING TIME:** 3 hours on HIGH, 5–6 hours on LOW

2 pounds (910 g) carrots

1 cup (340 g) maple syrup

3 tablespoons (42 g) unsalted butter

Salt and pepper to taste

1 cup (125 g) walnut pieces

Peel the carrots and cut them into 2- or 3-inch (5- or 7.5-cm) pieces. Put the carrots into the slow cooker along with the maple syrup, the butter, 1/2 cup (120 ml) water, and salt and pepper to taste. Sprinkle the walnuts over all and cook for 3 hours on HIGH or 5 to 6 hours on LOW, until the carrots are tender. Stir.

YIELD: 4 to 6 servings

NUTRITIONAL ANALYSIS: 373 calories; 18 g fat (41.0% calories from fat); 7 g protein; 51 g carbohydrate; 5 g dietary fiber; 16 mg cholesterol; 111 mg sodium.

ADD IT IN! Toss the carrots with a little orange zest before serving.

Parsnip and Carrot Medley

If you've ever had parsnips that have stayed in the ground beyond the first frost, you know how sweet this delightful root can be. Here we capitalize on that sweetness, to the delight of parsnip fans everywhere.

PREP TIME: 30 minutes **COOKING TIME:** 2 hours on HIGH, 5–6 hours on LOW

1 pound (455 g) carrots

1 pound (455 g) parsnips

1 teaspoon (2.2 g) nutmeg

Salt and pepper to taste

3 tablespoons (42 g) unsalted butter

Peel the carrots and the parsnips and cut them into 1-inch-long (2.5-cm) pieces. Put the vegetables into the slow cooker. Stir in the nutmeg and season with salt and pepper to taste. Add ½ cup (120 ml) water and dot with the butter. Cook for 2 hours on HIGH or 5 to 6 hours on LOW, until the vegetables are tender.

YIELD: 4 to 6 servings

NUTRITIONAL ANALYSIS: 130 calories; 6 g fat (40.9% calories from fat); 2 g protein; 19 g carbohydrate; 5 g dietary fiber; 16 mg cholesterol; 89 mg sodium.

Beets with Ginger and Orange

The sweet earthiness of beets is one of our favorites, and here it sparkles with the infusion of ginger and orange.

PREP TIME: 30 minutes **COOKING TIME:** 3 hours on HIGH, 6–7 hours on LOW

3 pounds (1365 g) beets

Salt and pepper to taste

1 tablespoon (6 g) minced fresh ginger

1 cup (235 ml) orange juice

2 to 3 tablespoons (28 to 42 g) unsalted butter

Wash and peel the beets and slice them ½ inch (1 cm) thick. Put the beets into the slow cooker and season with salt and pepper to taste. Sprinkle the ginger over the beets and pour the orange juice on top. Top with the butter cut into small pieces. Cook for 3 hours on HIGH or 6 to 7 hours on LOW, until the beets are tender.

YIELD: 6 to 8 servings

NUTRITIONAL ANALYSIS: 102 calories; 5 g fat (38.6% calories from fat); 2 g protein; 14 g carbohydrate; 3 g dietary fiber; 12 mg cholesterol; 133 mg sodium.

● Black-Eyed Peas

Serve these delicious peas with some tender stewed greens and cornbread for a simple Southern feast.

PREP TIME: 15 minutes   **COOKING TIME:** 5–6 hours
ADDITIONAL STEPS: Pick over and wash the peas; soak the peas overnight in cold water

1 pound (455 g) black-eyed peas

1/2 pound (225 g) smoked ham hock

1 medium-size onion

Salt and pepper to taste

Pick over the black-eyed peas, discarding discolored peas and any grit or stones. Put the rest of the peas into a bowl and cover with water 3 to 4 inches (7.5 to 10 cm) above the top of the peas. Soak overnight.

Drain the peas. Put the ham hock and the black-eyed peas into the slow cooker. Peel the onion and chop into small dice. Add the onion to the slow cooker with enough water to just cover the peas and season with salt and pepper to taste. Cook for 5 to 6 hours on LOW, until the water is almost gone and the peas are tender.

YIELD: 4 to 6 servings

NUTRITIONAL ANALYSIS: 361 calories; 8 g fat (19.9% calories from fat); 26 g protein; 47 g carbohydrate; 8 g dietary fiber; 40 mg cholesterol; 36 mg sodium.

ADD IT IN! Add a bay leaf to the recipe to heighten the play of flavors.

● Stewed Greens

This Southern staple is perfect for the slow cooker. The liquid, known as the "pot likker," makes a great dip for your cornbread.

PREP TIME: 20 minutes   **COOKING TIME:** 3 hours on HIGH, 6–7 hours on LOW

1 bunch greens, such as collards, mustard greens, or kale

3 strips bacon

1/4 cup (60 ml) apple cider vinegar

Salt and pepper to taste

Strip out the large stems from the greens and wash them thoroughly. Chop the greens and put them into the slow cooker. Chop the bacon into small pieces and add it to the greens. Add the vinegar, salt and pepper to taste, and 2 cups (470 ml) water. Cook on HIGH for 3 hours or on LOW for 6 to 7 hours. Serve in bowls with some of the cooking liquid.

YIELD: 4 servings

NUTRITIONAL ANALYSIS: 32 calories; 2 g fat (63.4% calories from fat); 2 g protein; 1 g carbohydrate; trace dietary fiber; 4 mg cholesterol; 78 mg sodium.

SERVING SUGGESTION: This is traditionally served with a square of cornbread.

Collard Greens

Enjoy this Southern favorite with a cabbage-like flavor that pairs so well with ham. Simple, yet hearty and delicious.

COOKING TIME: 8 to 10 hours   **ATTENTION:** Minimal

4 ounces (115 g) seasoned ham, sliced

2 to 3 pounds (.9 to 1.4 kg) collard greens, washed, dried, and stems removed

2 cups (475 ml) water

⅛ cup (28 ml) white vinegar

Put the sliced seasoned ham in the bottom of the slow cooker and place the collard greens on top of it. In a small bowl, combine the water and white vinegar, then pour the mixture over the collard greens. Cover and cook on LOW for 8 to 10 hours.

YIELD: 8 servings

NUTRITIONAL ANALYSIS: One serving of the basic recipe (made with 2 pounds collard greens) contains 60 calories; 2 g fat; 5 g protein; 7 g carbohydrate; and 4 g dietary fiber.

ADD IT IN: Add 6 red potatoes, quartered, and 1 onion, sliced, along with the collard greens.

IT'S GOOD FOR YOU: Collards are an excellent source of vitamin A, vitamin C, manganese, and folate, and are also a good source of calcium and fiber.

Creamy Corn

Corn-on-the-cob goodness plus cheese in your slow cooker—without the cob. Enjoy!

COOKING TIME: 1$\frac{1}{2}$ to 3$\frac{1}{2}$ hours   **ATTENTION:** Minimal

One 16-ounce (455-g) bag frozen corn, partially thawed

One 3-ounce (85-g) package cream cheese, softened

2 tablespoons (28 g) butter

$\frac{1}{2}$ teaspoon salt

Spray the inside of the slow cooker with cooking spray.

Put the partially thawed corn, softened cream cheese, butter, and salt in the slow cooker and stir to combine. Cook on LOW for 1$\frac{1}{2}$ to 3$\frac{1}{2}$ hours, or until the corn is thoroughly heated and the cream cheese has melted.

YIELD: 4 servings

NUTRITIONAL ANALYSIS: One serving of the basic recipe contains 200 calories; 12 g fat; 5 g protein; 24 g carbohydrate; and 3 g dietary fiber.

TRY THIS! Mmm, mmm, good! Try this dish with sliced frozen carrots or frozen lima beans instead of the corn.

Corn with Peppers and Onion

The colors in this dish are pretty and the taste delights.

PREP TIME: 15 minutes   **COOKING TIME:** 1$\frac{1}{2}$ hours on HIGH, 3–4 hours on LOW

1 pound (455 g) frozen corn

1 medium-size onion

1 bell pepper (red or orange)

2 to 3 tablespoons (28 to 42 g) unsalted butter

Salt and pepper to taste

Put the corn into the slow cooker. Peel and dice the onion into small pieces. Core the pepper and dice into $\frac{1}{2}$-inch (1-cm) pieces. Add the onion and pepper to the corn and stir. Top with the butter and season with salt and pepper to taste. Cook for 1½ hours on HIGH or 3 to 4 hours on LOW.

YIELD: 4 to 6 servings

NUTRITIONAL ANALYSIS: 130 calories; 6 g fat (40.3% calories from fat); 3 g protein; 19 g carbohydrate; 2 g dietary fiber; 16 mg cholesterol; 62 mg sodium.

ADD IT IN! Sprinkle a handful of chopped fresh cilantro over the corn before serving to create a bright trifecta of color.

Polenta

This is a sophisticated dish that's a welcome change from the usual starches. Serve this soft straight from the slow cooker, or cool, slice, and fry or grill.

PREP TIME: 20 minutes **COOKING TIME:** 2 hours on HIGH, 3–4 hours on LOW
ADDITIONAL STEPS: Boil the liquids before adding to the slow cooker; stir in the cheese at the end.

2 cups (275 g) cornmeal (medium to coarse is best)

Salt and pepper to taste

2 cups (470 ml) milk

1 cup (100 g) grated Parmesan cheese

Put the cornmeal into the slow cooker and stir in salt and pepper to taste. Turn on the slow cooker to HIGH or LOW, as you prefer.

Put the milk and 2 cups (470 ml) water into a saucepan and bring to a boil.

Stir the liquid into the cornmeal. Cook for 2 hours on HIGH or 3 to 4 hours on LOW, until the liquid is absorbed and the polenta is creamy. Stir in the cheese and serve.

YIELD: 4 to 6 servings

NUTRITIONAL ANALYSIS: 279 calories; 7 g fat (24.4% calories from fat); 12 g protein; 40 g carbohydrate; 3 g dietary fiber; 22 mg cholesterol; 289 mg sodium.

Cheese Grits

Grits have pretty much been relegated to the breakfast table, but these are crowd-pleasers any time of day. Try them as a side at dinner—they taste great with so many partners.

PREP TIME: 20 minutes **COOKING TIME:** 2 hours on HIGH, 3–4 hours on LOW
ADDITIONAL STEPS: Boil the water before adding to the slow cooker; stir in the cheese at the end

Butter or nonstick cooking spray

2 cups (275 g) grits (not instant)

Salt and pepper to taste

1 teaspoon (5 g) hot sauce

2 cups (225 g) shredded cheddar cheese

Butter the sides of the slow cooker. Put the grits into the slow cooker and stir in salt and pepper to taste. Turn on the slow cooker to HIGH or LOW, as your prefer.

Put 4 cups (940 ml) water into a saucepan and bring to a boil. Stir the boiling water into the grits in the slow cooker, along with the hot sauce. Cook for 2 hours on HIGH or 3 to 4 hours on LOW, until the liquid is absorbed and the grits are creamy. Stir in the cheese.

YIELD: 4 to 6 servings

NUTRITIONAL ANALYSIS: 345 calories; 13 g fat (34.6% calories from fat); 14 g protein; 42 g carbohydrate; trace dietary fiber; 40 mg cholesterol; 255 mg sodium.

Summer Stewed Tomatoes

This recipe is another great way to use the bounty of your (or your local farmer's) harvest. We always run amok when the tomatoes come in, as our New England winter is so very long, and grocery store tomatoes—although much improved—still aren't the same as garden-fresh.

PREP TIME: 20 minutes **COOKING TIME:** 3 hours on HIGH, 6–7 hours on LOW

3 pounds (1365 g) ripe tomatoes

2 tablespoons (20 g) minced garlic

¹/₂ cup (20 g) shredded fresh basil

Salt and pepper to taste

Core the tomatoes and cut them into wedges. Put the tomatoes into the slow cooker and add the garlic and basil, along with salt and pepper to taste. Stir gently. Cook for 3 hours on HIGH or 6 to 7 hours on LOW.

YIELD: 4 to 6 servings

NUTRITIONAL ANALYSIS: 49 calories; 1 g fat (11.1 % calories from fat); 2 g protein; 11 g carbohydrate; 2 g dietary fiber; 0 mg cholesterol; 19 mg sodium.

SERVING SUGGESTION: Cook up a pot of pasta and toss this on as a delicious summer sauce.

Braised Red Cabbage

This savory dish is great with sausages, pot roast, and roast pork.

PREP TIME: 20 minutes **COOKING TIME:** 3 hours on HIGH, 6–7 hours on LOW

---

1 head red cabbage (about 2 pounds or 910 g)

¹/₂ cup (120 ml) red wine vinegar

2 tablespoons (13 g) caraway seeds

Salt and pepper to taste

Core the cabbage and shred it. Add the cabbage to the slow cooker. Pour the vinegar over the cabbage and sprinkle with the caraway seeds. Season with salt and pepper to taste. Cook for 3 hours on HIGH or 6 to 7 hours on LOW, until the cabbage is soft. Stir and serve.

YIELD: 6 to 8 servings

NUTRITIONAL ANALYSIS: 38 calories; 1 g fat (10.3% calories from fat); 2 g protein; 9 g carbohydrate; 3 g dietary fiber; 0 mg cholesterol; 13 mg sodium.

Braised Artichoke Hearts

We would happily eat these as a main dish, not a side, but then again we are helpless in the grip of our deep and abiding love for all things artichoke. (Kind of strange when you realize it's a member of the thistle family.)

PREP TIME: 10 minutes **COOKING TIME:** 2 hours on HIGH, 4–5 hours on LOW

2 (12-ounce or 340-g) packages frozen artichoke hearts

1 cup (180 g) canned diced tomatoes

½ cup (120 ml) light cream

Salt and pepper to taste

Put the artichoke hearts into the slow cooker. Add the tomatoes and the cream and stir gently. Season with salt and pepper to taste. Cook for 2 hours on HIGH or 4 to 5 hours on LOW. Stir and serve.

YIELD: 4 to 6 servings

NUTRITIONAL ANALYSIS: 99 calories; 5 g fat (41.0% calories from fat); 3 g protein; 12 g carbohydrate; 7 g dietary fiber; 13 mg cholesterol; 85 mg sodium.

ADD IT IN! Sprinkle ½ cup (50 g) grated Parmesan cheese into the mixture.

Braised Leeks with Vinaigrette

Hailing originally from the Mediterranean region, leeks have been prized for centuries—sometimes for the belief that they gave strength (sixth-century Wales) and sometimes just because their subtle, mild flavor is delicious (rest of the world). This dish can be served hot or cold, and is sure to delight either way. As always, make sure you thoroughly wash these buggers, as they hide bits of dirt with great enthusiasm.

PREP TIME: 20 minutes **COOKING TIME:** 2 hours on HIGH, 5–6 hours on LOW

1 bunch leeks (usually 3 per bunch)

Salt and pepper to taste

¹/₂ cup (120 ml) Italian vinaigrette

¹/₄ cup (30 g) chopped flat-leaf parsley

Trim the root ends of the leeks and cut off the tough upper dark green parts. You can shave away some of the dark green to get to the tender light green part underneath. Split the leeks in half, lengthwise, and soak in lots of cold water for several minutes. It is important to soak leeks well to get out the grit between the layers of the vegetable.

Put the leeks into the slow cooker and add ¹/₂ cup (120 ml) water, along with salt and pepper to taste. Cook for 2 hours on HIGH or 5 to 6 hours on LOW, until the leeks are very tender. Remove the leeks carefully from the cooker and put them on a serving plate to serve hot, or refrigerate if serving cold. Either way, when ready to serve, drizzle the leeks with the vinaigrette and top with the parsley.

YIELD: 4 servings

NUTRITIONAL ANALYSIS: 182 calories; 16 g fat (75.5% calories from fat); 1 g protein; 10 g carbohydrate; 1 g dietary fiber; 0 mg cholesterol; 16 mg sodium.

Crumb-Topped Broccoli Bake

A wonderful side dish for fish or chicken, broccoli is generally a favorite with the small-fry, too.

PREP TIME: 15 minutes   **COOKING TIME:** 1½ hours on HIGH, 3–4 hours on LOW

1 bunch broccoli

2 cups (490 g) Alfredo sauce

1 cup (115 g) seasoned bread crumbs

Cut up the broccoli, discarding the last 2 to 3 inches (5 to 7.5 cm) of the stem. Put the broccoli into the slow cooker and pour the Alfredo sauce over it. Sprinkle the crumbs on top and cook for 1½ hours on HIGH or 3 to 4 hours on LOW.

YIELD: 4 servings

NUTRITIONAL ANALYSIS: 393 calories; 23 g fat (51.2% calories from fat); 15 g protein; 35 g carbohydrate; 6 g dietary fiber; 71 mg cholesterol; 1496 mg sodium.

Cumin-Scented Spinach with Chickpeas

Cumin, an aromatic spice that is a favorite in Middle Eastern, Asian, and Mediterranean cooking, is a foundation spice with curries. Here, we use it to add kick to spinach.

PREP TIME: 20 minutes   **COOKING TIME:** 2 hours on HIGH, 3–4 hours on LOW

1 pound (455 g) fresh spinach

1 (12-ounce or 340-g) can chickpeas (garbanzo beans)

1 tablespoon (7 g) ground cumin

Salt and pepper to taste

2 tablespoons (28 g) unsalted butter

Wash the spinach and pick through it, removing grit, large stems, and any rotten leaves. Put the spinach into the slow cooker. Drain the chickpeas and add them to the slow cooker. Add the cumin and salt and pepper to taste. Stir to combine and dot with the butter. Cook for 2 hours on HIGH or 3 to 4 hours on LOW. Stir and serve.

YIELD: 4 to 6 servings

NUTRITIONAL ANALYSIS: 261 calories; 8 g fat (25.5% calories from fat); 13 g protein; 37 g carbohydrate; 12 g dietary fiber; 10 mg cholesterol; 114 mg sodium.

Curried Cauliflower

Use a good-quality curry powder to make this dish sing.

PREP TIME: 15 minutes　　**COOKING TIME:** 2 hours on HIGH, 5–6 hours on LOW

1 head cauliflower

Salt and pepper to taste

1 medium-size onion

1 tablespoon (7 g) curry powder

Remove the outer leaves and the core from the cauliflower and cut it into florets. Put the florets into the slow cooker with salt and pepper to taste and 1/2 cup (120 ml) water. Peel the onion and chop it into small dice. Add the onion and the curry powder to the slow cooker and stir. Cook on HIGH for 2 hours or on LOW for 5 to 6 hours, until the cauliflower is tender.

YIELD: 4 to 6 servings

NUTRITIONAL ANALYSIS: 15 calories; trace fat (11.2% calories from fat); 1 g protein; 3 g carbohydrate; 1 g dietary fiber; 0 mg cholesterol; 6 mg sodium.

Eggplant, Zucchini, and Tomato Layered Casserole

This casserole answers the annual late-summer question of what the heck to do with all those zucchinis and tomatoes once the neighbors start locking their doors when you knock.

PREP TIME: 30 minutes **COOKING TIME:** 3 hours on HIGH, 6–7 hours on LOW

2 medium-size eggplants (about 2 pounds or 910 g)

2 pounds (910 g) zucchini squash

3 pounds (1365 g) tomatoes

Salt and pepper to taste

Peel the eggplants and slice them ½ inch (1 cm) thick across. Trim the ends from the squash and slice them ½ inch (1 cm) thick. Remove the core from the tomatoes and slice them ½ inch (1 cm) thick across. Layer tomatoes on the bottom of the slow cooker, and top with a layer of eggplant, then zucchini. Season with salt and pepper, then repeat layers until the vegetables are used up, finishing with a layer of tomato. Cook for 3 hours on HIGH or 6 to 7 hours on LOW. Serve right out of the slow cooker insert.

YIELD: 6 to 8 servings

NUTRITIONAL ANALYSIS: 77 calories; 1 g fat (8.4% calories from fat); 4 g protein; 17 g carbohydrate; 6 g dietary fiber; 0 mg cholesterol; 21 mg sodium.

ADD IT IN! Sliced onion and minced garlic are flavor-enhancing additions.

Eggplant, Basil, and Ricotta Bake

This hearty dish works nicely as a vegetarian entrée.

PREP TIME: 20 minutes **COOKING TIME:** 3 hours on HIGH, 6–7 hours on LOW

2 large eggplants (about 3 pounds or 1365 g)

1 cup (260 g) basil pesto

2 cups (500 g) ricotta cheese

Salt and pepper to taste

Peel the eggplants and cut them into slices about ½ inch (1 cm) thick. Layer the bottom of the slow cooker with eggplant. Mix the pesto and ricotta together in a bowl with salt and pepper to taste. Spread some of the ricotta mixture on the eggplant in the slow cooker. Repeat layers, finishing with a layer of eggplant. Cook for 3 hours on HIGH or 6 to 7 hours on LOW.

YIELD: 6 to 8 servings

NUTRITIONAL ANALYSIS: 289 calories; 22 g fat (67.6% calories from fat); 13 g protein; 11 g carbohydrate; 3 g dietary fiber; 40 mg cholesterol; 261 mg sodium.

ADD IT IN! Mix chopped fresh tomatoes in the pesto and ricotta to add another flavor layer.

Endive Baked with Gruyère

We aren't sure whether this fits into the category of classics, but it sure is good. Endive yields a mild and deliciously nutty flavor that far outstrips its sharp, raw taste.

PREP TIME: 15 minutes **COOKING TIME:** 2 hours on HIGH, 5–6 hours on LOW

4 heads Belgian endive

1 cup (110 g) shredded Gruyère or other Swiss-type cheese

2 tablespoons (5 g) minced fresh thyme

Salt and pepper to taste

Trim the root ends of the endive and split them lengthwise. Put the endive into the slow cooker and top with the cheese and thyme, along with salt and pepper to taste. Cook for 2 hours on HIGH or 5 to 6 hours on LOW, until the endive is very soft and a little caramelized.

YIELD: 4 servings

NUTRITIONAL ANALYSIS: 202 calories; 10 g fat (40.9% calories from fat); 15 g protein; 18 g carbohydrate; 16 g dietary fiber; 30 mg cholesterol; 205 mg sodium.

Slow-Baked Fennel and Onions

Fennel and onions are two vegetables that are sharp when raw but become mellow and sweet when cooked slowly, as they are in this scrumptious dish.

PREP TIME: 20 minutes **COOKING TIME:** 3 hours on HIGH, 6–7 hours on LOW

2 bulbs fennel

1 pound (455 g) onions (3 or 4 medium-size)

¼ cup (60 ml) extra-virgin olive oil

Salt and pepper to taste

1 cup (80 g) shredded Parmesan cheese

Remove the stalks from the fennel and discard them. Trim away any discolored outer layers from the bulbs. Split the bulbs in half, lengthwise, and remove the core. Slice the fennel thin and put it into a mixing bowl. Peel the onions and slice them thin. Add the onions to the fennel and toss with the extra-virgin olive oil and salt and pepper to taste.

Put the fennel and onion mixture into the slow cooker and smooth out the top of the mixed veggies. Sprinkle the Parmesan cheese over the top. Cook on HIGH for 3 hours or on LOW for 6 to 7 hours.

YIELD: 4 to 6 servings

NUTRITIONAL ANALYSIS: 185 calories; 13 g fat (60.7% calories from fat); 7 g protein; 12 g carbohydrate; 4 g dietary fiber; 10 mg cholesterol; 269 mg sodium.

Southern Slow-Cooked Green Beans

A simple recipe for fresh green beans that you'll enjoy again and again. Serve in a big bowl with the cooking juices and accompanied by a side of cornbread to sop up the "pot liquor."

COOKING TIME: $3^1/_2$ to $4^1/_2$ hours   **ATTENTION:** Minimal

1 cup (235 ml) hot water

2 vegetable or chicken bouillon cubes

1 quart (440 g) green beans, tips removed and beans snapped in half

1 large onion, chopped

Salt and freshly ground black pepper

Put the hot water and bouillon cubes in the slow cooker and stir until the bouillon cubes have dissolved. Add the snapped green beans and chopped onion, and stir again. Cover and cook on HIGH for 30 minutes, or until the mixture begins to simmer. Reduce the heat to LOW and simmer the green beans for another 3 to 4 hours.

Stir the green beans and season them with salt and pepper to taste. Serve them in their cooking juices.

YIELD: 6 servings

NUTRITIONAL ANALYSIS: One serving of the basic recipe (made with vegetable bouillon cubes) contains 33 calories; .3 g fat; 2 g protein; 7 g carbohydrate; and 3 g dietary fiber.

TRY THIS! For authentic Southern flavor, add 2 tablespoons of bacon grease to the pot.

Mushrooms Italian

Are you mad about mushrooms? This dish has a wonderful Italian essence that doesn't overpower the rich portobello flavor.

COOKING TIME: 3 to 4 hours on LOW, 1½ to 2 hours on HIGH
ATTENTION: Minimal

3 pounds (1.4 kg) whole baby portobello mushrooms

One 10¾-ounce (305-g) can condensed cream of mushroom soup

½ teaspoon Italian Seasoning (page 28)

Put the baby portobello mushrooms, condensed soup, and Italian Seasoning in the slow cooker and mix well. Cover and cook on LOW for 3 to 4 hours or on HIGH for 1½ to 2 hours.

YIELD: 10 servings

NUTRITIONAL ANALYSIS: One serving of the basic recipe contains 65 calories; 3 g fat; 3 g protein; 8 g carbohydrate; and 2 g dietary fiber.

ADD IT IN! Add 1 large sweet onion, very thinly sliced, and ¼ teaspoon crushed red pepper.

TRY THIS! Serve these mushrooms over toast or rice with a crisp green salad and sliced tomatoes. The perfect lunch!

Ranch Mushrooms

At first glance, mushrooms and ranch dressing seem like an unlikely pairing. But the finished dish reveals the combo to be wonderful!

COOKING TIME: 3 to 4 hours on LOW, 1½ to 2 hours on HIGH
ATTENTION: Minimal

2 pounds (910 g) whole button mushrooms

½ cup (120 ml) garlic-flavored olive oil

Two 1-ounce (28-g) envelopes ranch salad dressing mix

Put the button mushrooms, olive oil, and dressing mix in the slow cooker and stir well. Cover and cook on LOW for 3 to 4 hours or on HIGH for 1½ to 2 hours.

YIELD: 6 servings

NUTRITIONAL ANALYSIS: One serving of the basic recipe contains 222 calories; 19 g fat; 3 g protein; 12 g carbohydrate; and 2 g dietary fiber.

TRY THIS! Toss these mushrooms with cooked pasta for a delicious side dish or a quick lunch.

White Beans with Sun-Dried Tomatoes

This rich, satisfying dish is redolent with pungent garlic, sweet vine-ripened toma-toes, and lightly herbed olive oil. Enjoy with a Caesar salad and focaccia bread.

COOKING TIME: $2^1/_2$ to $4^1/_2$ hours on LOW, $1^1/_2$ to $2^1/_2$ hours on HIGH
ATTENTION: Mash beans and add another ingredient during final 10 minutes

Two 15-ounce (417-g) cans lightly seasoned white beans, undrained

$^1/_2$ cup (60 ml) water

2 to 4 cloves garlic, minced

3 ounces (85 g) Bella Sun Luci Sun Dried Tomatoes in Olive Oil and Spices, undrained, tomatoes chopped

Salt and freshly ground black pepper

Put the undrained white beans, water, and minced garlic in the slow cooker and stir to combine. Cover and cook on LOW for 2 to 4 hours or on HIGH for 1 to 2 hours.

Mash some of the beans using a potato masher to thicken the mixture. Add the chopped tomatoes with seasoned olive oil, and cook for another 10 minutes, or until the mixture is thoroughly warmed.

Before serving, season the mixture with salt and pepper to taste.

YIELD: 5 servings

NUTRITIONAL ANALYSIS: One serving of the basic recipe contains 24 calories; 3 g fat; 13 g protein; 42 g carbohydrate; and 9 g dietary fiber.

TRY THIS! Substitute vegetable bouillon for the water, and add 1 tablespoon (2.5 g) chopped fresh basil.

 Stewed Butterbeans

Also known as lima beans, these big, meaty beans deserve a better reputation than they have. (Our sister still refers to them as "little sandbags" and creates bean barricades on her plate when they appear—setting a bad example for her children, we might add.) Try this dish and we know you'll be on our side!

PREP TIME: 10 minutes **COOKING TIME:** 2 hours on HIGH, 4–5 hours on LOW

---

1 pound (455 g) frozen butter beans or large lima beans

1 medium-size onion

1 cup (180 g) diced fresh tomato

Salt and pepper to taste

Put the butter beans into the slow cooker. Peel the onion and cut it into small dice. Add the onion and the diced tomato and season with salt and pepper to taste. Stir and cover. Cook on HIGH for 2 hours or on LOW for 4 to 5 hours.

YIELD: 4 servings

NUTRITIONAL ANALYSIS: 170 calories; 1 g fat (3.5% calories from fat); 9 g protein; 33 g carbohydrate; 6 g dietary fiber; 0 mg cholesterol; 64 mg sodium.

ADD IT IN: Spice it up with a couple of cloves of minced garlic.

Baked Potatoes

If you had known that baking potatoes in your slow cooker was so easy, wouldn't you have tried it before?

COOKING TIME: 6 to 8 hours on LOW, 3 to 4 hours on HIGH
ATTENTION: Minimal

---

6 baking potatoes, unpeeled, scrubbed

Olive oil

Salt

Rub each potato with olive oil and sprinkle it with salt. Wrap each potato in aluminum foil and place all the potatoes in the slow cooker. Cover and cook on LOW for 6 to 8 hours or on HIGH for 3 to 4 hours, or until the potatoes are fork-tender.

YIELD: 6 servings

NUTRITIONAL ANALYSIS: One serving of the basic recipe (made with 1 tablespoon olive oil per potato) contains 265 calories; 14 g fat; 4 g protein; 33 g carbohydrate; and 3 g dietary fiber.

DID YOU KNOW? You can cook as few or as many potatoes as you wish in the slow cooker. Just make sure the potatoes fit in one layer on the bottom of the slow cooker, and adjust the cooking time accordingly.

🥔 Pizza Potatoes

Here are two favorite flavors slow-cooked to perfection. Serve to your favorite teenager for rave reviews.

COOKING TIME: 8 to 10 hours on LOW, 4 to 5 hours on HIGH
ATTENTION: Minimal

8 medium potatoes, peeled and cut in half lengthwise

1¹/₂ cups (340 g) frozen Seasoning Blend Vegetables (page 29), partially thawed

2 cups (500 g) pizza sauce

Salt and freshly ground black pepper

Put the potato halves in the slow cooker, cover them with the partially thawed vegetables, and pour the pizza sauce over the vegetables. Cover and cook on LOW for 8 to 10 hours or on HIGH for 4 to 5 hours, or until the potatoes are tender.

Before serving, season the mixture with salt and pepper to taste.

YIELD: 8 servings

NUTRITIONAL ANALYSIS: One serving of the basic recipe contains 161 calories; 2 g fat; 5 g protein; 33 g carbohydrate; and 3 g dietary fiber.

ADD IT IN! Add 8 ounces (225 g) sliced pepperoni to the pizza sauce.

TRY THIS! Top each serving of Pizza Potatoes with shredded mozzarella and serve with a crisp green salad packed with lots of veggies.

Fabulous Foil Potatoes

You may have made these in the oven before. But once you discover that the slow cooker works just as well and requires less attention, that may change. Experiment with seasonings and garnishes for variety.

COOKING TIME: 10 to 12 hours   **ATTENTION:** Minimal

4 medium potatoes, unpeeled, scrubbed, and thinly sliced

2 medium onions, very thinly sliced and separated into rings

Salt and freshly ground black pepper

12 tablespoons (1½ sticks, or 168 g) butter

Spray the inside of the slow cooker with cooking spray. Line the slow cooker with enough aluminum foil to enclose all the ingredients.

Put half of the potato slices in the slow cooker and spread them out evenly. Top the potato slices with half of the onion rings. Sprinkle the mixture with salt and pepper and dot it with half of the butter. Layer on the remaining potato slices and onion rings, season the mixture with more salt and pepper, and dot it with the rest of the butter. Crimp the edges of the aluminum foil to seal the contents. Cover and cook on LOW for 10 to 12 hours.

YIELD: 4 servings

NUTRITIONAL ANALYSIS: One serving of the basic recipe contains 422 calories; 35 g fat; 4 g protein; 27 g carbohydrate; and 3 g dietary fiber.

TRY THIS! For a restaurant-quality dish, experiment with a mandoline, a tool for cutting potatoes, cucumbers, carrots, and other produce into uniform, precise slices. Or, for the campfire look, just use a knife and your good judgment.

Saucy Cream-Cheese Potatoes

Creamy, tender potatoes with just a hint of garlic. Perfect as a side dish or as a lunchtime meal, especially with a scallion garnish.

COOKING TIME: 6 to 8 hours on LOW, 3 to 4 hours on HIGH
ATTENTION: Minimal

6 large potatoes, unpeeled, scrubbed, and thinly sliced

One 8-ounce (225-g) package cream cheese, cut into cubes

1 teaspoon (6 g) garlic salt

1/2 teaspoon freshly ground black pepper

Spray the inside of the slow cooker with cooking spray.

Put one-third of the potato slices in the slow cooker and spread them out evenly. Top them with half of the cream cheese and sprinkle them with half of the garlic salt and pepper. Layer on another third of the potato slices and the rest of the cream cheese, and sprinkle the mixture with the remainder of the garlic salt and pepper. Spread the rest of the potato slices over the top. Cover and cook on LOW for 6 to 8 hours or on HIGH for 3 to 4 hours, or until the potato slices are tender.

Before serving, stir the mixture well.

YIELD: 6 servings

NUTRITIONAL ANALYSIS: One serving of the basic recipe contains 230 calories; 13 g fat; 5 g protein; 23 g carbohydrate; and 2 g dietary fiber.

TRY THIS! For extra color, flavor, and protein, top this dish with shredded Swiss or white cheddar cheese and a sprinkling of paprika just before serving; serve bubbly hot as soon as the cheese melts.

Scalloped Potatoes with Bacon

This is great hearty fare on a cold winter's night. You can serve leftovers alongside fried eggs for breakfast.

PREP TIME: 30 minutes   **COOKING TIME:** 3–4 hours on HIGH, 7–8 hours on LOW

5 pounds (2275 g) potatoes

1/2 pound (230 g) cooked bacon

Salt and pepper to taste

1 cup (235 ml) chicken stock or broth

Peel the potatoes and cut them into 1/4-inch-thick (6-mm) rounds. Chop the bacon into small pieces. Put a layer of potatoes on the bottom of the slow cooker. Season with salt and pepper and scatter some of the bacon over the potatoes. Repeat layers with the remaining potatoes and bacon. Pour the stock over the potatoes. Cook for 3 to 4 hours on HIGH or 7 to 8 hours on LOW.

YIELD: 6 servings

NUTRITIONAL ANALYSIS: 520 calories; 19 g fat (32.7% calories from fat); 19 g protein; 68 g carbohydrate; 6 g dietary fiber; 32 mg cholesterol; 984 mg sodium.

ADD IT IN! Sprinkle some crumbled dried rosemary among the layers.

Cheesy Scalloped Potatoes

Potatoes win, hands down, as just about everyone's favorite food. They're easy to cook, nutritious, and, best of all, tasty!

COOKING TIME: 6 to 8 hours on LOW, 3 to 4 hours on HIGH
ATTENTION: Minimal

5 large potatoes, peeled and cut into 1/2-inch (6-mm) slices

1 large onion, cut into 1/2-inch (13-mm) rings

Salt and freshly ground black pepper

Two 10³/₄-ounce (305-g) cans condensed cheddar cheese soup

Spray the inside of the slow cooker with cooking spray.

Place one-third of the potato slices in the slow cooker and spread them out evenly. Top the potato slices with half of the onion rings and sprinkle the onion rings with salt and pepper to taste. Layer on another third of the potato slices and the remainder of the onion rings, and season the mixture with more salt and pepper. Add the rest of the potato slices, then pour the condensed soup over everything. Cover and cook on LOW for 6 to 8 hours or on HIGH for 3 to 4 hours, or until the potato slices are tender.

Before serving, stir the mixture and season it with additional salt and pepper to taste.

YIELD: 6 servings

NUTRITIONAL ANALYSIS: One serving of the basic recipe contains 191 calories; 7 g fat; 6 g protein; 27 g carbohydrate; and 3 g dietary fiber.

IT'S GOOD FOR YOU: Potatoes may be the latest health foods! Scientists recently discovered that chemicals in potatoes called kukoamines lowered blood pressure.

Cheesy Mashed Potatoes

This is an easy way to make great mashed potatoes.

PREP TIME: 30 minutes   **COOKING TIME:** 2¹/₂ hours on HIGH
ADDITIONAL STEPS: Mash the potatoes after cooking; add the milk and cheese

3 pounds (1365 g) potatoes

Salt and pepper to taste

1 cup (235 ml) milk

1 cup (115 g) shredded cheddar cheese

2 tablespoons (28 g) unsalted butter

Wash and peel the potatoes and cut them into 1-inch (2.5-cm) cubes. Put the potatoes into the slow cooker and season with salt and pepper to taste. Add 2 cups (470 ml) water and cook on HIGH for 2¹/₂ hours. Drain off most of the water and mash the potatoes in the slow cooker with a potato masher. Stir in the milk. Stir in the cheese and butter until melted.

YIELD: 6 servings

NUTRITIONAL ANALYSIS: 280 calories; 8 g fat (24.7% calories from fat); 11 g protein; 43 g carbohydrate; 4 g dietary fiber; 25 mg cholesterol; 150 mg sodium.

Cheesy Hash Browns

Nothing beats a cheesy hash-brown casserole as comfort food. The flavors meld, and the result is nothing short of magic.

COOKING TIME: 4$\frac{1}{2}$ to 6$\frac{1}{2}$ hours
ATTENTION: Add another ingredient during final 30 minutes

One 32-ounce (905-g) bag frozen hash brown potatoes, partially thawed

1 teaspoon (6 g) salt

$\frac{1}{2}$ teaspoon freshly ground black pepper

Two 10$\frac{3}{4}$-ounce (305-g) cans condensed cheddar cheese soup

1 cup (230 g) sour cream

Spray the slow cooker with cooking spray.

Put the partially thawed hash browns in the slow cooker and spread them out evenly. Sprinkle them with the salt and pepper, then top them with the condensed soup. Cover and cook on LOW for 4 to 6 hours, stirring occasionally.

A half hour before the dish is done, add the sour cream and stir to combine. Cook for an additional 30 minutes, or until the mixture is thoroughly heated.

YIELD: 10 servings

NUTRITIONAL ANALYSIS: One serving of the basic recipe contains 186 calories; 10 g fat; 5 g protein; 21 g carbohydrate; and 2 g dietary fiber.

ADD IT IN! For a richer casserole, add $\frac{1}{2}$ cup (25 g) sliced scallions and 3 tablespoons (42 g) butter, melted, to the soup. Add 1 cup (130 g) frozen peas to the mixture an hour before serving it, and garnish the finished dish with $\frac{1}{2}$ cup (56 g) shredded cheddar cheese.

TRY THIS! This dish is perfect for a homestyle supper with fried chicken, green beans, and good old-fashioned Jell-O for dessert. Or take it to your next potluck or church supper!

Easy Cheesy Potato Casserole

Home-style good! The creamy potato flavor and tasty hash browns are enhanced by the melted cheddar.

COOKING TIME: $6^1/_2$ to $8^1/_2$ hours on LOW, $3^1/_2$ to $4^1/_2$ hours on HIGH
ATTENTION: Add more ingredients during final 15 to 30 minutes

One 24-ounce (680-g) bag frozen Southern-style chunky hash brown potatoes, partially thawed

One $10^3/_4$-ounce (305-g) can condensed cream of potato soup

Salt and freshly ground black pepper

1 cup (113 g) grated cheddar cheese

Put the partially thawed hash browns and condensed soup in the slow cooker and stir to combine. Cover and cook on LOW for 6 to 8 hours or on HIGH for 3 to 4 hours.

Stir the mixture, season it with salt and pepper to taste, and sprinkle it with the grated cheese. Cover and cook for another 15 to 30 minutes, or until the cheese has melted.

YIELD: 10 servings

NUTRITIONAL ANALYSIS: One serving of the basic recipe contains 116 calories; 5 g fat; 5 g protein; 15 g carbohydrate; and 1 g dietary fiber.

ADD IT IN! Stir 1 pound (455 g) ham or sausage, chopped, and 1 cup (150 g) frozen peas, thawed, into the hash-brown mixture.

TRY THIS! Crank up the heat by using grated pepper jack cheese instead of the cheddar, and adding a few drops of hot sauce (red or the milder jalapeño green) to taste.

Au Gratin Potatoes

Another successful pairing of hash browns and cheesy goodness. Enjoy with breakfast, lunch, or dinner.

COOKING TIME: 7 to 9 hours on LOW, 3½ to 4½ hours on HIGH
ATTENTION: Minimal

Two 10¾-ounce (305-g) cans condensed cheddar cheese soup

One 13-ounce (390-ml) can evaporated milk

One 32-ounce (905-g) bag frozen hash brown potatoes, partially thawed

Salt and freshly ground black pepper

Spray the inside of the slow cooker with cooking spray.

Put the condensed soup and evaporated milk in the slow cooker and stir to combine. Add the partially thawed hash browns and stir again. Cover and cook on LOW for 7 to 9 hours or on HIGH for 3½ to 4½ hours.

Before serving, stir the mixture and season it with salt and pepper to taste.

YIELD: 10 servings

NUTRITIONAL ANALYSIS: One serving of the basic recipe contains 186 calories; 8 g fat; 7 g protein; 24 g carbohydrate; and 2 g dietary fiber.

ADD IT IN! Garnish the dish with canned french-fried onion rings just before serving it.

TRY THIS! You can substitute 10 thinly sliced or cubed baking potatoes for the hash browns in this recipe if you wish.

Creamed Potato and Celery Root

Celery root, also known as celeriac, is one of the more unprepossessing vegetables out there, but this gnarly lump of a vegetable has a delicate and distinctive flavor that we love. You won't be sorry that you've added this to your cuisine—it's perfectly matched with poultry or veal.

PREP TIME: 30 minutes   **COOKING TIME:** 3 hours on HIGH, 6–7 hours on LOW

2 pounds (910 g) celery root

3 pounds (1365 g) potatoes

Salt and pepper to taste

1 cup (235 ml) light cream

Thoroughly wash the celery root and potatoes. Peel them (with celery root, you will most easily accomplish this task with a knife) and cut them both into ¹/₂-inch (1-cm) cubes. Put the potatoes and celery root into the slow cooker. Season with salt and pepper to taste. Pour the cream over them and cook for 3 hours on HIGH or 6 to 7 hours on LOW. Stir to redistribute the cream and serve.

YIELD: 6 to 8 servings

NUTRITIONAL ANALYSIS: 211 calories; 6 g fat (25.1 % calories from fat); 5 g protein; 36 g carbohydrate; 5 g dietary fiber; 20 mg cholesterol; 121 mg sodium.

Mashed Potatoes with Scallions

The mild taste of scallions are a perfect complement to the potatoes' creamy texture.

PREP TIME: 30 minutes   **COOKING TIME:** 2¹/₂ hours on HIGH
ADDITIONAL STEPS: Mash the potatoes after cooking, adding the milk and scallions

3 pounds (1365 g) potatoes

Salt and pepper to taste

1 cup (235 ml) milk

1 cup (100 g) chopped scallions

2 tablespoons (28 g) unsalted butter

Wash and peel the potatoes. Cut them into 1-inch (2.5-cm) cubes. Put the potatoes into the slow cooker and season with salt and pepper to taste. Add 2 cups (470 ml) water. Cook on HIGH for 2¹/₂ hours, until the potatoes are tender. Drain off most of the water. Mash the potatoes in the slow cooker with a potato masher. Stir in the milk, scallions, and butter.

YIELD: 6 servings

NUTRITIONAL ANALYSIS: 209 calories; 2 g fat (6.7% calories from fat); 6 g protein; 44 g carbohydrate; 4 g dietary fiber; 6 mg cholesterol; 36 mg sodium.

Rustic Mashed Potatoes

An elegant pairing with any entrée. You can't fail to enjoy the rich flavor of slow-cooked, mashed potatoes.

COOKING TIME: 6 to 8 hours on LOW, 3 to 4 hours on HIGH
ATTENTION: Minimal

8 baking potatoes, cut into $1/2$-inch (1.3-cm) cubes

$1/4$ cup (60 ml) water

2 tablespoons (28 g) butter, cut into small pieces

$1^1/4$ (8 g) teaspoons salt

$1/4$ teaspoon freshly ground black pepper

$3/4$ to 1 cup (175 to 235 ml) milk

Put the potato cubes, water, butter, salt, and pepper in the slow cooker and mix well. Cover and cook on LOW for 6 to 8 hours or on HIGH for 3 to 4 hours, or until the potatoes are tender.

Add the milk to the slow cooker and mash the potato mixture with a potato masher or electric mixer until it is smooth.

YIELD: 8 servings

NUTRITIONAL ANALYSIS: One serving of the basic recipe (made with 1 cup milk) contains 190 calories; 4 g fat; 5 g protein; 35 g carbohydrate; and 3 g dietary fiber.

ADD IT IN! Add 2 cloves garlic, minced.

TRY THIS! Use sweet potatoes in place of baking potatoes in this dish for a delicious change of pace. Perfect with ham, roast pork, fried chicken or fish!

Smashed Garlic Potatoes

Tender, garlicky—delicious! These potatoes make a stylish appearance next to green vegetables and a steak, be it beef or salmon.

COOKING TIME: 7 to 9 hours on LOW, $3^1/2$ to $4^1/2$ hours on HIGH
ATTENTION: Minimal

3 pounds (1.4 kg) white potatoes, cut into cubes of uniform size

$1/2$ cup (120 ml) water

2 tablespoons plus 1 teaspoon (28 g) minced garlic in olive oil, undrained

1 teaspoon (6 g) salt

¼ to ½ cup (60 to 120 ml) milk

Put the potato cubes, water, garlic with olive oil, and salt in the slow cooker and mix well. Cover and cook on LOW for 7 to 9 hours or on HIGH for 3½ to 4½ hours, or until the potatoes are tender.

Add ½ cup of the milk and mash the potatoes coarsely. Continue mashing the potatoes and adding milk until the desired consistency is achieved.

Serve the potatoes immediately or keep them warm in the slow cooker for up to 2 hours.

YIELD: 10 servings

NUTRITIONAL ANALYSIS: One serving of the basic recipe (made with ½ cup milk) contains 122 calories; 1 g fat; 3 g protein; 26 g carbohydrate; and 2 g dietary fiber.

ADD IT IN! Add 4 ounces (115 g) cream cheese with onion and chives just before adding the milk.

New Potatoes with Dill

Adding the dill at the last minute keeps it nice and green, and lends a flavor explosion.

PREP TIME: 10 minutes   **COOKING TIME:** 2 hours on HIGH, 3–4 hours on LOW
ADDITIONAL STEPS: Add the chopped dill at the end

3 pounds (1365 g) baby new potatoes

Salt and pepper to taste

2 tablespoons (28 g) unsalted butter

2 tablespoons (8 g) chopped fresh dill

Wash the potatoes and put them into the slow cooker. Season with salt and pepper to taste. Add 2 cups (470 ml) water and the butter. Cook on HIGH for 2 hours or on LOW for 3 to 4 hours. Remove the potatoes from the cooker with a slotted spoon and put them into a bowl.

Stir the dill into the potatoes and serve.

NUTRITIONAL ANALYSIS: 213 calories; 4 g fat (16.7% calories from fat); 5 g protein; 41 g carbohydrate; 4 g dietary fiber; 10 mg cholesterol; 53 mg sodium.

New Potatoes with Garlic and Parsley

Slow-cooked garlic and fresh parsley add a nice kick to everybody's favorite starch.

PREP TIME: 10 minutes   COOKING TIME: 2 hours on HIGH, 3–4 hours on LOW
ADDITIONAL STEPS: Add the chopped parsley at the end

3 pounds (1365 g) baby new potatoes

Salt and pepper to taste

6 to 8 cloves garlic, peeled

2 tablespoons (30 ml) extra-virgin olive oil

2 tablespoons (8 g) chopped fresh parsley

Wash the potatoes and put them into the slow cooker. Season with salt and pepper to taste. Add 2 cups (470 ml) water, the garlic, and the olive oil. Cook on HIGH for 2 hours or on LOW for 3 to 4 hours. Remove the potatoes from the cooker with a slotted spoon and put them into a bowl.

Stir the parsley into the potatoes.

YIELD: 4 to 6 servings

NUTRITIONAL ANALYSIS: 226 calories; 5 g fat (18.5% calories from fat); 5 g protein; 42 g carbohydrate; 4 g dietary fiber; 0 mg cholesterol; 15 mg sodium.

Potato and Sauerkraut Bake

If you can find it, use the fresh-pack sauerkraut found in the refrigerated section (usually near the hot dogs)—it's got much more flavor than the canned variety. This is really nice with brats at a summer cookout.

PREP TIME: 30 minutes   COOKING TIME: 3 hours on HIGH, 5–6 hours on LOW
ADDITIONAL STEPS: Rinse the sauerkraut

1 pound (455 g) sauerkraut

3 pounds (1365 g) potatoes

Pepper to taste

1 cup (230 g) sour cream

Put the sauerkraut into a colander and rinse well under cold water. Peel the potatoes and slice into 1/4-inch-thick (6-mm) rounds.

Put a layer of sauerkraut on the bottom of the slow cooker and top with a layer of potatoes. Season with pepper to taste (the kraut is already salty). Repeat with the remaining sauerkraut and potatoes. Cook for 3 hours on HIGH or 5 to 6 hours on LOW. Serve with a dollop of sour cream on top.

YIELD: 6 servings

NUTRITIONAL ANALYSIS: 276 calories; 8 g fat (26.5% calories from fat); 7 g protein; 46 g carbohydrate; 6 g dietary fiber; 17 mg cholesterol; 534 mg sodium.

ADD IT IN! Sprinkle the top with caraway seeds for extra flavor.

Potatoes with Peppers and Onions

This is a great recipe for a summer cookout, especially if you're sick of over-mayonnaised macaroni or potato salad. Try serving this with grilled fish or chicken. Use different-colored peppers to pack a visual punch.

PREP TIME: 30 minutes   **COOKING TIME:** 3 hours on HIGH, 5–6 hours on LOW

4 pounds (1820 g) potatoes

2 medium-size onions (about 1 pound or 455 g)

2 medium-size bell peppers, any colors (about 1 pound or 455 g)

Salt and pepper to taste

2 to 3 tablespoons (30 to 45 ml) extra-virgin olive oil

Wash and peel the potatoes and slice them into 1/4-inch-thick (6-mm) rounds. Peel the onions and slice them 1/4 inch (6 mm) thick. Core the peppers and cut them into rings.

Layer some of the potatoes in the slow cooker and season with salt and pepper. Add a layer of some of the onions and peppers. Repeat layers with the remaining ingredients. Pour the olive oil and $^1/_2$ cup (120 ml) of water over all and cook for 3 hours on HIGH or 5 to 6 hours on LOW.

YIELD: 6 servings

NUTRITIONAL ANALYSIS: 323 calories; 7 g fat (19.4% calories from fat); 7 g protein; 60 g carbohydrate; 6 g dietary fiber; 0 mg cholesterol; 20 mg sodium.

Baked Sweet Potatoes

Sweet potatoes are fabulously nutritious and have no added calories or fats when baked. Enjoy straight from the slow cooker, add a dollop of whipped butter, or slather on the brown sugar and honey.

COOKING TIME: 4 to 6 hours   **ATTENTION:** Minimal

5 medium sweet potatoes, unpeeled, scrubbed well but not dried

Put the damp sweet potatoes in the slow cooker. Cover and cook on LOW for 4 to 6 hours. The baking time will depend on the sizes of the sweet potatoes. Sweet potatoes of uniform size will be done at the same time.

YIELD: 5 servings

NUTRITIONAL ANALYSIS: One serving of the basic recipe contains 137 calories; .4 g fat; 2 g protein; 32 g carbohydrate; and 4 g dietary fiber.

DID YOU KNOW? Many people call sweet potatoes—especially the orange-fleshed kinds—yams, but a yam is really a tropical root, while a sweet potato is actually an enlarged underground stem called a rhizome. That's why when you put a sweet potato into a glass of water, leaves sprout from the top and roots grow down into the water.

⬬ Maple-Apple Sweet Potatoes

Tender potatoes drip with the sweetness of a maple-apple glaze. Suitable to sit alongside any main course. Serve with the maple-apple syrup spooned over the potatoes.

COOKING TIME: 6 to 8 hours on LOW, 3 to 4 hours on HIGH
ATTENTION: Minimal

¼ cup (81 g) pure maple syrup
¼ cup (60 ml) apple juice
4 small sweet potatoes, peeled and quartered
Salt

Put the maple syrup and apple juice in the slow cooker and mix well. Add the quartered sweet potatoes and stir to coat them. Cover and cook on LOW for 6 to 8 hours or on HIGH for 3 to 4 hours, or until the potatoes are fork-tender.

Before serving, stir the mixture and season it with salt to taste.

YIELD: 4 servings

NUTRITIONAL ANALYSIS: One serving of the basic recipe contains 195 calories; .5 g fat; 2 g protein; 47 g carbohydrate; and 4 g dietary fiber.

ADD IT IN! Stir in 1 tablespoon (14 g) butter just before seasoning the potatoes with the salt.

IT'S GOOD FOR YOU: Sweet potatoes are excellent sources of vitamin A (as beta-carotene) and are good sources of vitamin C and manganese. They're rich in antioxidants, and have recently been classified as an "antidiabetic" food because they help stabilize blood sugar and lower insulin resistance.

Candied Sweet Potatoes

Candied Sweet Potatoes and the slow cooker are a fabulous combination, as you can cook, warm, and serve in the same dish. That's key when trying to manage your holiday kitchen.

COOKING TIME: 6 to 8 hours on LOW, 3 to 4 hours on HIGH
ATTENTION: Minimal

Two 15-ounce (417-g) cans cut sweet potatoes in light syrup, undrained

$1/4$ cup (56 g) brown sugar, packed

4 tablespoons (55 g) butter, melted

1 teaspoon (6 g) salt

$1/8$ teaspoon freshly ground black pepper

Put the sweet potatoes in the slow cooker and mash them with a potato masher. Combine the brown sugar, melted butter, salt, and pepper in a small bowl and pour the mixture over the mashed sweet potatoes. Cover and cook on LOW for 6 to 8 hours or on HIGH for 3 to 4 hours.

YIELD: 8 servings

NUTRITIONAL ANALYSIS: One serving of the basic recipe contains 192 calories; 49 g fat; 1 g protein; 34 g carbohydrate; and 3 g dietary fiber.

TRY THIS! Your Candied Sweet Potatoes will pack a holiday punch if you add a splash of brandy or bourbon along with the brown sugar, melted butter, and seasonings. Garnish the dish with chopped nuts or marshmallows.

Peachy Sweet Potatoes

A refreshing change from brown sugar and butter. Even people who don't particularly care for sweet potatoes love these.

COOKING TIME: 5 to 7 hours on LOW, $2^1/2$ to $3^1/2$ hours on HIGH
ATTENTION: Minimal

6 sweet potatoes, peeled and cut into $1/2$-inch (1.3-cm) chunks

1 cup (262 g) peach pie filling

1 teaspoon finely minced fresh ginger

¹/₄ teaspoon salt

¹/₄ teaspoon freshly ground black pepper

Spray the inside of the slow cooker with cooking spray.

Put the sweet potato chunks, pie filling, minced ginger, salt, and pepper in the slow cooker and mix well. Cover and cook on LOW for 5 to 7 hours or on HIGH for 2¹/₂ to 3¹/₂ hours, or until the sweet potatoes are fork-tender.

YIELD: 6 servings

NUTRITIONAL ANALYSIS: One serving of the basic recipe contains 137 calories; .3 g fat; 2 g protein; 32 g carbohydrate; and 4 g dietary fiber.

ADD IT IN! Garnish the dish with ¹/₂ cup (55 g) chopped pecans or walnuts.

TRY THIS! Enjoy these with apple pie filling and a teaspoon of ground cinnamon instead of the peach pie filling and grated ginger.

Orange Sweet Potatoes

Here's another change-of-pace recipe for sweet potatoes. Orange juice makes it zesty.

COOKING TIME: 6 to 8 hours on LOW, 3 to 4 hours on HIGH
ATTENTION: Minimal

Two 15-ounce (417-g) cans cut sweet potatoes in light syrup, drained

1 cup (284 g) frozen orange juice concentrate

³/₄ cup (169 g) brown sugar, packed

Salt and freshly ground black pepper

Spray the inside of the slow cooker with cooking spray.

Put the drained sweet potato pieces in the slow cooker.

In a large saucepan over medium-low heat, cook the frozen orange juice concentrate and brown sugar until thickened. Pour the sauce over the sweet potatoes. Cover and cook on LOW for 6 to 8 hours or on HIGH for 3 to 4 hours.

Before serving, stir the mixture and season it with salt and pepper to taste.

YIELD: 8 servings

NUTRITIONAL ANALYSIS: One serving of the basic recipe contains 249 calories; .4 g fat; 2 g protein; 61 g carbohydrate; and 4 g dietary fiber.

ADD IT IN! Add $1/2$ teaspoon ground nutmeg along with the salt and pepper, and garnish the dish with $1/2$ cup (55 g) chopped pecans.

TRY THIS! For a classic sweet potato casserole, skip the salt and pepper and cover the top of the dish with mini-marshmallows when you're ready to serve it. Serve as soon as the marshmallows melt.

Mashed Turnips

Poor turnips have an undeserved reputation among the Young and Judgmental of being dull and gag-inducing, but these root veggies have a sweet, sharp taste that's really delightful. Here, we use cider to balance the sharp tang with more sweetness.

PREP TIME: 30 minutes   **COOKING TIME:** 2 hours on HIGH, 4–5 hours on LOW
ADDITIONAL STEPS: Mash the turnips after cooking

2 pounds (910 g) turnips

$1/2$ cup (120 ml) apple cider

1 teaspoon (2.3 g) ground coriander

Salt and pepper to taste

2 tablespoons (28 g) unsalted butter

Peel the turnips and cut them into 1-inch (2.5-cm) cubes. Put the turnips into the slow cooker and add the cider and coriander, along with salt and pepper to taste. Cook for 2 hours on HIGH or 4 to 5 hours on LOW. Add the butter and mash the turnips with a potato masher.

YIELD: 6 to 8 servings

NUTRITIONAL ANALYSIS: 58 calories; 3 g fat (44.3% calories from fat); 1 g protein; 8 g carbohydrate; 2 g dietary fiber; 8 mg cholesterol; 91 mg sodium.

Creamed Jerusalem Artichokes

Also known as sunchokes, these tubers are the root of a sunflower plant and have a rich, mild flavor. This dish is perfect for when you want something a little different.

PREP TIME: 30 minutes   **COOKING TIME:** 2 hours on HIGH, 5–6 hours on LOW

1 pound (455 g) Jerusalem artichokes

1 cup (245 g) Alfredo sauce

Salt and pepper to taste

¹/₂ cup (40 g) shredded Parmesan cheese

Peel the Jerusalem artichokes and cut into 1-inch (2.5-cm) pieces. Put them into the slow cooker and add the Alfredo sauce along with salt and pepper to taste. Stir, then top with the Parmesan. Cook for 2 hours on HIGH or 5 to 6 hours on LOW, until the chokes are tender.

YIELD: 4 servings

NUTRITIONAL ANALYSIS: 248 calories; 14 g fat (49.0% calories from fat); 9 g protein; 23 g carbohydrate; 2 g dietary fiber; 42 mg cholesterol; 504 mg sodium.

ADD IT IN! Try stirring some chopped fresh tarragon into this dish before cooking.

Butternut Squash Puree

It doesn't get any easier than this slow-cooker method to make this fall classic. To make this dish even easier, buy the squash already peeled. (We always feel guilty doing that, but then again, we frequently mangle our fingers peeling those suckers.)

PREP TIME: 30 minutes   **COOKING TIME:** 2 hours on HIGH, 4–5 hours on LOW
ADDITIONAL STEPS: Add the butter and mash the squash after cooking

1 butternut squash (about 3 pounds or 1365 g)

Salt and pepper to taste

¹/₂ cup (115 g) light brown sugar

1 teaspoon (2.3 g) ground cinnamon

3 tablespoons (42 g) unsalted butter

Peel the squash and cut it in half lengthwise. Scoop out and discard the seeds and any pulp in the seed cavity. Cut the squash into 2- or 3-inch (5- or 7.5-cm)

chunks and put into the slow cooker. Add salt and pepper to taste, $^1/_2$ cup (120 ml) water, the brown sugar, and the cinnamon. Cook on HIGH for 2 hours or on LOW for 4 to 5 hours, until the squash is quite soft. Add the butter and mash with a potato masher.

YIELD: 6 to 8 servings

NUTRITIONAL ANALYSIS: 137 calories; 4 g fat (26.9% calories from fat); 1 g protein; 26 g carbohydrate; 3 g dietary fiber; 12 mg cholesterol; 53 mg sodium.

Simple White Rice

No peeking allowed! This rice cooks itself to perfection, as long as you don't lift the lid.

COOKING TIME: 6 to 8 hours   **ATTENTION:** Minimal

2$^1/_4$ cups (529 ml) water

1 cup (185 g) raw long-grain converted rice

3 tablespoons (42 g) margarine

$^1/_2$ to 1 tablespoon (2 to 4 g) dried or minced fresh parsley

1 teaspoon salt

Spray the inside of the slow cooker with cooking spray.

Put the water, raw rice, margarine, parsley, and salt in the slow cooker and stir to combine. Cover and cook on LOW for 6 to 8 hours, or just until the rice is tender.

YIELD: 6 servings

NUTRITIONAL ANALYSIS: One serving of the basic recipe contains 163 calories; 6 g fat; 2 g protein; 25 g carbohydrate; and .3 g dietary fiber.

ADD IT IN! Add $^1/_4$ teaspoon freshly ground black pepper.

TRY THIS! Substitute chopped fresh chives or mint for the parsley for a refreshingly different taste.

Yellow Rice

You can't beat Yellow Rice with black beans or roast pork. Add fried plantains and café con leche for a virtual trip to Cuba.

COOKING TIME: 6 to 8 hours   **ATTENTION:** Minimal

2¼ cups (529 ml) water

1 cup (185 g) raw long-grain converted rice

2½ tablespoons (35 ml) olive oil

½ teaspoon saffron threads

1 teaspoon salt

¼ teaspoon freshly ground black pepper

Spray the inside of the slow cooker with cooking spray.

Put the water, raw rice, olive oil, saffron threads, salt, and pepper in the slow cooker and stir well. Cover and cook on LOW for 6 to 8 hours, or just until the rice is tender. Resist the urge to lift the lid while the rice is cooking!

YIELD: 6 servings

NUTRITIONAL ANALYSIS: One serving of the basic recipe contains 163 calories; 6 g fat; 2 g protein; 25 g carbohydrate; and .5 g dietary fiber.

TRY THIS! To turn your Cuban Yellow Rice into Indian Golden Rice, use canola oil, ground turmeric, and black mustard seeds instead of the olive oil, saffron, and black pepper. Add a teaspoon of whole cumin or ½ teaspoon of ground cumin and ½ teaspoon of ground fenugreek with the other spices, and enjoy your trip to the Far Pavilions!

Almond Rice

The almonds in this dish add a subtle crunch. You'll find that converted rice works well in a slow cooker if you like the grains separate.

PREP TIME: 20 minutes   **COOKING TIME:** 3 hours on HIGH, 5–6 hours on LOW
ADDITIONAL STEPS: Toast the almonds

1 cup (92 g) sliced blanched almonds

3 cups (585 g) converted rice

3 cups (705 g) chicken stock or broth

Salt and pepper to taste

Preheat the oven to 350°F (180°C or gas mark 4). Spread the almonds on a cookie sheet and bake for 10 to 12 minutes, until golden brown. Put the rice into the slow cooker. Stir in the almonds. Add the stock and 3 cups (705 ml) water. Season with salt and pepper to taste. Cook for 3 hours on HIGH or 5 to 6 hours on LOW, until the liquid is absorbed and the rice is tender.

YIELD: 8 to 10 servings

NUTRITIONAL ANALYSIS: 296 calories; 8 g fat (23.4% calories from fat); 8 g protein; 49 g carbohydrate; 1 g dietary fiber; 0 mg cholesterol; 646 mg sodium. Exchanges: 3 Grain(Starch); $^{1}/_{2}$ Lean Meat; $1^{1}/_{2}$ Fat.

Coconut Rice

A favorite accompaniment in island cuisines, this dish has a distinctive flavor that makes it a terrific match for many kinds of grilled fish. Add a fruit salsa and enjoy!

PREP TIME: 10 minutes   **COOKING TIME:** 3 hours on HIGH, 5–6 hours on LOW
ADDITIONAL STEPS: Stir in the chives just before serving

---

3 cups (585 g) converted rice

1 (12-ounce or 355-ml) can coconut milk

Salt and pepper to taste

$^{1}/_{4}$ cup (12 g) chopped fresh chives

Put the rice into the slow cooker. Stir in the coconut milk. Add 4 cups (940 ml) water. Season with salt and pepper to taste. Cook for 3 hours on HIGH or 5 to 6 hours on LOW, until the liquid is absorbed and the rice is tender. Stir in the chives.

YIELD: 8 to 10 servings

NUTRITIONAL ANALYSIS: 283 calories; 8 g fat (25.6% calories from fat); 6 g protein; 48 g carbohydrate; 1 g dietary fiber; 0 mg cholesterol; 5 mg sodium.

🥔 Curried Rice

This kicky rice dish is a diverting summer side with grilled chicken and vegetable kabobs.

PREP TIME: 10 minutes   **COOKING TIME:** 3 hours on HIGH, 5–6 hours on LOW

3 cups (585 g) converted rice

1 cup (165 g) golden raisins

2 tablespoons (15 g) curry powder

Salt and pepper to taste

Put the rice into the slow cooker. Stir in the raisins and curry powder. Add 5 cups (1200 ml) water. Season with salt and pepper to taste. Cook for 3 hours on HIGH or 5 to 6 hours on LOW, until the liquid is absorbed and the rice is tender.

YIELD: 8 to 10 servings

NUTRITIONAL ANALYSIS: 252 calories; trace fat (0.8% calories from fat); 5 g protein; 58 g carbohydrate; 1 g dietary fiber; 0 mg cholesterol; 2 mg sodium.

🥔 Easy Risotto

This no-muss, no-fuss version of risotto does away with the tedious stirring and adding of liquid that's necessary with stovetop risottos. The result is a nice, creamy risotto.

PREP TIME: 10 minutes   **COOKING TIME:** 1 hour

2 cups (390 g) Arborio rice

1/4 cup (60 ml) extra-virgin olive oil

1 cup (235 ml) light cream

Salt and pepper to taste

Put the rice into the slow cooker with the olive oil. Turn on the cooker to HIGH and cook the rice, stirring occasionally, for 15 to 20 minutes, until the rice is a little translucent around the edges. Add the cream and 2 1/2 cups (590 ml) water. Season with salt and pepper to taste. Reduce the heat to LOW and cook for 30 to 40 minutes, until the liquid is almost absorbed and the rice is tender on the outside and just slightly chewy on the inside (al dente).

NUTRITIONAL ANALYSIS: 228 calories; 10 g fat (40.3% calories from fat); 3 g protein; 30 g carbohydrate; 0 g dietary fiber; 16 mg cholesterol; 16 mg sodium.

ADD IT IN! You can substitute white wine and/or chicken stock for the water. As with any risotto, this basic recipe can be used as a base for many additions, such as mushrooms, peas, shellfish, saffron—the list goes on. For extra flavor buy fresh Parmesan and grate it over the risotto when finished.

Easy Spanish Rice

A nice side dish or burrito filling, this is a good way to spice up the daily starch.

PREP TIME: 20 minutes **COOKING TIME:** 3 hours on HIGH, 5–6 hours on LOW

3 cups (585 g) converted rice

1 (12-ounce or 395-g) can diced tomatoes with peppers and onions

2 tablespoons (15 g) chili powder

Salt and pepper to taste

Put the rice into the slow cooker. Add the tomatoes and 4 cups (940 ml) water. Stir in the chili powder. Season with salt and pepper to taste. Cook for 3 hours on HIGH or 5 to 6 hours on LOW, until the liquid is absorbed and the rice is tender.

YIELD: 8 to 10 servings

NUTRITIONAL ANALYSIS: 216 calories; trace fat (1.5% calories from fat); 5 g protein; 48 g carbohydrate; 1 g dietary fiber; 0 mg cholesterol; 18 mg sodium.

ADD IT IN! You can spice up this dish with whatever kind of hot chile or hot sauce appeals most to you.

Mushroom Rice

The rich, earthy flavor of the mushrooms and the deep flavor of the beef broth make this a side dish you will use often. It's great with lamb chops or steak.

PREP TIME: 10 minutes **COOKING TIME:** 3 hours on HIGH, 5–6 hours on LOW
ADDITIONAL STEPS: Sauté the mushrooms before adding to the slow cooker

1 tablespoon (15 ml) cooking oil

2 cups (140 g) sliced mushrooms

3 cups (585 g) converted rice

3 cups (705 ml) beef stock or broth

Salt and pepper to taste

Heat a sauté pan over medium-high heat. Add the oil and sauté the mushrooms until they release their liquid.

Put the rice into the slow cooker. Stir in the mushrooms. Add the stock and 2 cups (470 ml) water. Season with salt and pepper to taste. Cook for 3 hours on HIGH or 5 to 6 hours on LOW, until the liquid is absorbed and the rice is tender.

YIELD: 6 to 8 servings

NUTRITIONAL ANALYSIS: 226 calories; 1 g fat (6.0% calories from fat); 5 g protein; 46 g carbohydrate; trace dietary fiber; 0 mg cholesterol; 638 mg sodium.

Lemon Ginger Rice

This sophisticated dish has a clean, crisp flavor that goes well with fish, chicken, or pork.

PREP TIME: 20 minutes **COOKING TIME:** 3 hours on HIGH, 5–6 hours on LOW
ADDITIONAL STEPS: Grate the lemon zest; juice the lemons; peel and mince the ginger

2 lemons

1 tablespoon (6 g) minced fresh ginger root

3 cups (585 g) converted rice

Salt and pepper to taste

Grate the lemon zest, and then juice the lemons. Peel and mince the ginger.

Put the rice into the slow cooker. Stir in the lemon zest and juice. Stir in the ginger. Add 5 cups (1175 ml) water. Season with salt and pepper to taste. Cook for 3 hours on HIGH or 5 to 6 hours on LOW, until the liquid is absorbed and the rice is tender.

YIELD: 8 to 10 servings

NUTRITIONAL ANALYSIS: 207 calories; trace fat (0.2% calories from fat); 5 g protein; 47 g carbohydrate; trace dietary fiber; 0 mg cholesterol; trace sodium.

Pecan Wild Rice Pilaf

This dish is so good with roast chicken or turkey, and it's not bad with ham either!

PREP TIME: 10 minutes (40 mintues if rice isn't already par-cooked)
COOKING TIME: 3 hours on HIGH, 5–6 hours on LOW
ADDITIONAL STEPS: Par-cook the wild rice

1 cup (165 g) par-cooked wild rice (see note below)

2 cups (390 g) converted rice

Salt and pepper to taste

1 cup (100 g) chopped pecans

Put the par-cooked wild rice and the converted rice into the slow cooker. Add 6 cups (1410 ml) water and season with salt and pepper. Stir in the pecans. Cook for 3 hours on HIGH or 5 to 6 hours on LOW, until the water is absorbed and the rice is tender.

YIELD: 8 to 10 servings

NUTRITIONAL ANALYSIS: 232 calories; 8 g fat (30.9% calories from fat); 5 g protein; 36 g carbohydrate; 1 g dietary fiber; 0 mg cholesterol; 1 mg sodium.

ADD IT IN: Stir in 2 tablespoons (28 g) unsalted butter and 1 tablespoon (5 g) chopped fresh sage just before serving.

NOTE: To par-cook wild rice, place the wild rice in a saucepan and add enough water to cover the rice by 3 to 4 inches. Bring to a boil over medium-high heat and then reduce the heat to medium-low. Cook at a low boil for 30 minutes. Drain the rice and proceed with the recipe. You can also purchase wild rice already par-cooked.

Rice Pilaf

This is the classic rice pilaf with toasted orzo pasta. It's easy and elegant in the slow cooker.

PREP TIME: 30 minutes   **COOKING TIME:** 2 hours on HIGH, 4–5 hours on LOW
ADDITIONAL STEPS: Toast the orzo before adding to the slow cooker

2 tablespoons (30 ml) cooking oil

1 cup (185 g) orzo

2 cups (390 g) converted rice

1 medium-size onion

Salt and pepper to taste

Heat a sauté pan over medium heat. Add the oil and then add the orzo. Cook, stirring often, until the orzo is golden brown.

Put the orzo into the slow cooker and add the rice. Chop the onion into small dice and add to the slow cooker. Season with salt and pepper to taste. Add 5 cups (1175 ml) water and stir. Cook for 2 hours on HIGH or 4 to 5 hours on LOW, until the water is absorbed and the rice is tender.

YIELD: 8 to 10 servings

NUTRITIONAL ANALYSIS: 283 calories; 4 g fat (12.1% calories from fat); 7 g protein; 55 g carbohydrate; 1 g dietary fiber; 0 mg cholesterol; 2 mg sodium.

ADD IT IN! Our mom is very fond of serving rice pilaf at big family gatherings, and she always puts chopped celery in. We concur—why not try it here?

Saffron Rice with Dried Cranberries

Saffron is one of our favorite spices, just because of what it is: Who the heck ever thought that plucking the yellow stigmas from crocuses would add a taste sensation to his or her cooking? It undoubtedly does, however, so we applaud such creativity. Some cooks like to toast their saffron lightly in a sauté pan before adding it to the rice.

PREP TIME: 10 minutes **COOKING TIME:** 2 hours on HIGH, 5–6 hours on LOW

3 cups (585 g) converted rice

½ teaspoon saffron

1 cup (120 g) dried cranberries

Salt and pepper to taste

Put the rice into the slow cooker. Stir in the saffron and cranberries. Add 5 cups (1175 ml) water. Season with salt and pepper to taste. Cook for 2 hours on HIGH or 5 to 6 hours on LOW, until the liquid is absorbed and the rice is tender.

YIELD: 8 to 10 servings

NUTRITIONAL ANALYSIS: 205 calories; trace fat (0.0% calories from fat); 5 g protein; 46 g carbohydrate; trace dietary fiber; 0 mg cholesterol; trace sodium.

CHAPTER 16

DESSERTS

Who doesn't look forward to dessert? It can be the highlight of the meal or a delicious complement to coffee or tea. Although desserts are not traditionally thought of as slow-cooker fare, many lend themselves well to being cooked, and even served, from the slow cooker. Try our Cherry Cobbler (page 317), Chunky Applesauce (page 331), or Golden Fruit Compote (page 332). Super easy and sinfully delicious. Try a new dessert every night!

Vanilla Upside-Down Cake

Oopsie daisy! We got turned upside down—upside down about everything except the yummy quotient of this cake, served with ice cream or a drizzle of chocolate syrup. Check it out!

COOKING TIME: 2 to 3 hours   **ATTENTION:** Minimal

1 cup (120 g) all-purpose baking mix

1 cup (200 g) Vanilla Sugar (page 28)

1/2 cup (120 ml) milk

1²/₃ cups (392 ml) hot water

Spray the inside of the slow cooker with cooking spray.

Put the baking mix, ¹/₂ cup (100 g) of the Vanilla Sugar, and the milk in a medium-size bowl and mix well. Spoon the batter evenly into the slow cooker. Mix the remaining ¹/₂ cup (100 g) of the Vanilla Sugar and the hot water in a separate bowl and pour the mixture over the batter in the slow cooker. Cover and cook on HIGH for 2 to 3 hours, or until the center of the cake springs back when pressed.

Scoop the cake out of the slow cooker and serve it with whipped cream, chocolate sauce, or ice cream.

YIELD: 8 servings

NUTRITIONAL ANALYSIS: One serving of the basic recipe contains 166 calories; 3 g fat; 2 g protein; 35 g carbohydrate; and .4 g dietary fiber.

TRY THIS! To make a Chocolate Upside-Down Cake, mix 3 tablespoons (15 g) unsweetened cocoa into the baking mix and 1/3 cup (27 g) cocoa into the Vanilla Sugar-hot water mixture.

Cherry Cobbler

This cobbler is super simple, so you may find yourself preparing it frequently. Or will that be because it's simply delicious?

COOKING TIME: 3 to 4 hours on LOW, 1^1/$_2$ to 2 hours on HIGH
ATTENTION: Minimal

One 21-ounce (595-g) can cherry pie filling

One 18^1/$_2$-ounce (511-g) box yellow cake mix

4 tablespoons (55 g) butter, melted

Put the pie filling in the slow cooker and spread it out evenly. In a medium-size bowl, stir the cake mix and melted butter until a crumbly mixture forms, then sprinkle the mixture over the pie filling. Cover and cook on LOW for 3 to 4 hours or on HIGH for 1^1/$_2$ to 2 hours.

YIELD: 8 servings

NUTRITIONAL ANALYSIS: One serving of the basic recipe contains 416 calories; 13 g fat; 3 g protein; 72 g carbohydrate; and 1 g dietary fiber.

ADD IT IN: Sprinkle ^{1}/$_2$ cup (55 g) chopped pecans over the crumb mixture before cooking the cake.

Peach Cobbler

This is a fabulous way to use up leftover biscuits. It's so yummy, you can serve it warm or cold, with or without ice cream. Any way you please, it's a real crowd-pleaser.

COOKING TIME: 1 1/2 to 2 hours
ATTENTION: Remove cover during final 30 minutes

5 biscuits, each broken into 4 to 6 pieces

One 21-ounce (595-g) can peach pie filling

3/4 cup (63 g) crushed cinnamon graham crackers

Spray the inside of the slow cooker with cooking spray.

Place half of the biscuit pieces in the slow cooker and spread them out evenly. Spread half of the pie filling over the biscuits and pour half of the crushed graham crackers over the pie filling. Layer on the remaining biscuit pieces, pie filling, and crushed graham crackers. Cover and cook on HIGH for 1 1/2 to 2 hours.

A half hour before the cobbler is done, remove the lid of the slow cooker. Serve the cobbler warm or cold.

YIELD: 6 servings

NUTRITIONAL ANALYSIS: One serving of the basic recipe contains 204 calories; 7 g fat; 4 g protein; 31 g carbohydrate; and 1 g dietary fiber.

TRY THIS! Substitute cinnamon crumb topping for the crushed cinnamon graham crackers. Make your own crumb topping by combining 1/4 cup (56 g) brown sugar, packed; 1/2 teaspoon apple pie spice; and 8 tablespoons (1 stick, or 112 g) butter, softened.

Blueberry Cobbler

Hot blueberry cobbler—yum! We specify yellow cake mix, but you can use spice cake, if you prefer.

PREP TIME: 15 minutes **COOKING TIME:** 2 hours on HIGH, 4–5 hours on LOW

2 pints (580 g) fresh or frozen blueberries

1 package (4 cups or 500 g) yellow cake mix, divided

1 egg

$^1/_2$ cup (120 ml) vegetable oil

Put the blueberries into the slow cooker. Add $^3/_4$ cup (95 g) cake mix and stir. In a mixing bowl, combine the remaining $3^1/_4$ cups (405 g) cake mix, the egg, the oil, and 1 cup (235 ml) water. Stir to make a smooth batter and pour it over the blueberries. Cook for 2 hours on HIGH or 4 to 5 hours on LOW, until the cake is cooked through and the blueberries are bubbling.

YIELD: 6 to 8 servings

NUTRITIONAL ANALYSIS: 576 calories; 25 g fat (39.0% calories from fat); 5 g protein; 84 g carbohydrate; 3 g dietary fiber; 25 mg cholesterol; 629 mg sodium.

ADD IT IN! Top with whipped cream or vanilla ice cream.

Cinnamon Swirl-Cherry Delight

Cherry and cinnamon are delightful together. A wonderful change-of-pace dessert that's served best in a bowl, with vanilla ice cream.

COOKING TIME: 2 to 3 hours	**ATTENTION:** Minimal

One 21-ounce (595-g) can cherry pie filling

Half of a 21-ounce (595-g) box cinnamon swirl cake mix

4 tablespoons (55 g) butter, melted

Spray the inside of the slow cooker with cooking spray.

Put the pie filling in the slow cooker and spread it out evenly. In a medium-size bowl, stir the cake mix and melted butter until a crumbly mixture forms, then sprinkle the mixture over the pie filling. Cover and cook on LOW for 2 to 3 hours.

Serve the cake at room temperature.

YIELD: 5 servings

NUTRITIONAL ANALYSIS: One serving of the basic recipe contains 371 calories; 13 g fat; 2 g protein; 63 g carbohydrate; and 1 g dietary fiber.

ADD IT IN! Sprinkle ¼ cup (31 g) slivered almonds over the crumb mixture before cooking the cake.

Strawberry-Chocolate Crumble

Who doesn't go straight for the strawberry and chocolate on the dessert tray? This scrumptious dessert satisfies both cravings, particularly when served with Neapolitan ice cream.

COOKING TIME: 3 to 4 hours on LOW, 1½ to 2 hours on HIGH
ATTENTION: Minimal

One 18-ounce (510-g) can strawberry pie filling

One 21-ounce (595-g) box chocolate cake mix

8 tablespoons (1 stick, or 112 g) butter, melted

Spray the inside of the slow cooker with cooking spray.

Put the pie filling in the slow cooker and spread it out evenly. In a medium-size bowl, stir the cake mix and melted butter until a crumbly mixture forms, then sprinkle the mixture over the pie filling. Cover and cook on LOW for 3 to 4 hours or on HIGH for 1 1/2 to 2 hours.

Serve the cake at room temperature.

YIELD: 8 servings

NUTRITIONAL ANALYSIS: One serving of the basic recipe contains 293 calories; 19 g fat; 3 g protein; 33 g carbohydrate; and 1 g dietary fiber.

ADD IT IN! Garnish the cake with chocolate curls.

Cinnamon Eggnog Bread Pudding

Smooth, creamy, and soothing, a good bread pudding is a fine ending to any meal. You can serve this one hot or cold.

PREP TIME: 15 minutes　　　　　**COOKING TIME:** 4–5 hours on LOW

1 (1-pound or 455-g) loaf cinnamon swirl bread

3 cups (705 ml) eggnog

3 eggs

Cut the bread into 2-inch (5-cm) cubes and put them into the slow cooker, pushing them in lightly to flatten. In a bowl, whisk together the eggnog and the eggs, then pour the mixture over the bread. Press the bread down with a spoon so that it is all soaked in the egg mixture. Cook for 4 to 5 hours on LOW.

Serve hot or cold.

YIELD: 4 to 6 servings

NUTRITIONAL ANALYSIS: 477 calories; 22 g fat (40.6% calories from fat); 12 g protein; 60 g carbohydrate; 0 g dietary fiber; 168 mg cholesterol; 733 mg sodium.

Banana Bread

Banana Bread is a delicious side for breakfast, lunch, or dinner. A toasted slice of Banana Bread with butter is fabulous.

COOKING TIME: 4 to 6 hours   **ATTENTION:** Minimal

One 8-ounce (225-g) box banana bread mix

½ cup (55 g) coarsely chopped pecans

Coat the interior of the slow cooker's baking unit with cooking spray, and position the slow cooker's rack on the floor of the machine. If your slow cooker did not come with this equipment, use any baking pan and rack that fit inside the machine.

Prepare the banana bread according to the package directions, stir in pecans, and pour the batter into the pan. Cover the pan and place it on the rack in the slow cooker. Partially cover the slow cooker, propping the lid open with a twist of foil or a wooden skewer to allow the steam to escape, and cook on HIGH for 4 to 6 hours.

Turn the heat OFF and allow the slow cooker to cool for 20 minutes, or until you can remove the pan without burning yourself. Serve the bread warm or at room temperature.

YIELD: 5 servings

NUTRITIONAL ANALYSIS: One serving of the basic recipe contains 251 calories; 12 g fat; 3 g protein; 35 g carbohydrate; and 1 g dietary fiber.

Crust-Free Cheesecake

This cheesecake has no crust to compete with its delicious flavor. Whether you introduce whipped cream or fruit glaze to the debate is up to you.

COOKING TIME: 3 to 5 hours　　　　　　**ATTENTION:** Minimal

12 ounces (340 g) cream cheese, softened

½ cup (50 g) Vanilla Sugar (page 28)

1 whole egg plus 1 egg white

Coat the interior of the slow cooker's baking unit with cooking spray, and position the slow cooker's rack on the floor of the machine. If your slow cooker did not come with this equipment, use any baking pan and rack that fit inside the machine.

Put the softened cream cheese, Vanilla Sugar, whole egg, and egg white in a large bowl and beat with a mixer until well blended; do not overbeat the batter. Pour the batter into the pan and place the pan on the rack in the slow cooker. Cover and cook on HIGH for 3 to 5 hours, or until the sides of the cheesecake look dry and just a little cracked, and its center is firm but still jiggles a bit when shaken.

Turn the heat OFF and allow the slow cooker to cool for 20 minutes, or until you can remove the pan without burning yourself. Run a knife around the edges of the pan to release the cake and to prevent cracks from forming. Allow it to cool completely, then cover it and place it in the refrigerator for at least 3 hours.

To serve the cheesecake, cover the pan with a plate, then carefully invert the pan and let the cheesecake release onto the plate. Place another plate over the cheesecake and invert the cake again, so that the cheesecake is right side up. Garnish the cake with fruit, glaze, or whipped topping, or just slice, serve, and enjoy it.

YIELD: 10 servings

NUTRITIONAL ANALYSIS: One serving of the basic recipe contains 167 calories; 12 g fat; 4 g protein; 11 g carbohydrate; and 0 g dietary fiber.

TRY THIS! Pour the batter into a graham cracker pie shell in a pie pan, and bake it as directed above.

Layered Crêpe Dessert

This rich dessert features the classic flavor combination of raspberries and chocolate.

PREP TIME: 15 minutes	COOKING TIME: 4–5 hours

20 premade dessert crêpes

4 cups (700 g) good-quality semisweet chocolate chips

4 cups (440 g) red raspberries

Spray the crock with nonstick cooking spray. Arrange 4 crêpes to cover the bottom of the cooker and top with 1 cup (175 g) chocolate and 1 cup (110 g) raspberries. Repeat the layers, ending with crêpes. Cook for 4 to 5 hours on LOW, then turn off the slow cooker and allow the dessert to sit for 30 minutes. Cut into wedges.

YIELD: 6 to 8 servings

NUTRITIONAL ANALYSIS: 559 calories; 32 g fat (46.8% calories from fat); 8 g protein; 74 g carbohydrate; 10 g dietary fiber; 62 mg cholesterol; 79 mg sodium.

ADD IT IN: A whipped cream topping would be perfect, or add a dollop of crème fraîche if you want to gussy it up a little.

Peaches with Dumplings

This is a great dessert on those summer days when the peaches are at their ripest.

PREP TIME: 30 minutes	COOKING TIME: 2 hours

3 pounds (1365 g) peaches

1¾ cups (350 g) sugar, divided

2 cups (250 g) self-rising flour

¾ cup (170 g) shortening, such as Crisco

Bring a large pot of water to a boil and drop the peaches in for 30 seconds. Drain and run under cold water to cool. Peel the peaches and cut the flesh from the pits (stones) and into wedges. Put the peaches into the slow cooker and add 1 cup (200 g) sugar. Stir to combine.

In a mixing bowl, combine the flour and the remaining 3/4 cup (150 g) sugar. Stir. Add the shortening and cut it into the dry ingredients with a pastry cutter, two knives, or your fingers. Stir 1 cup (235 ml) water into the dry ingredients just enough to make a batter.

Drop the batter by spoonfuls onto the peaches in the slow cooker. Cook for 2 hours on HIGH, until the biscuit batter is cooked through and the peaches are bubbling.

YIELD: 4 to 6 servings

NUTRITIONAL ANALYSIS: 600 calories; 26 g fat (38.6% calories from fat); 4 g protein; 89 g carbohydrate; 1 g dietary fiber; 0 mg cholesterol; 530 mg sodium.

ADD IT IN: Adding 1 teaspoon (2.2 g) nutmeg or 2 teaspoons (4.6 g) cinnamon to the peaches makes a nice spice accent. Feel free to serve with ice cream or whipped cream.

Rice Pudding

Making Rice Pudding doesn't have to be a production. With three ingredients commonly found in the kitchen, you can have a warm and comforting dessert.

COOKING TIME: 4 to 6 hours   **ATTENTION:** Stir after first hour

2½ cups (413 g) cooked rice

One 14-ounce (398-g) can sweetened condensed milk

3 eggs, well beaten

Spray the inside of the slow cooker with cooking spray.

Put the cooked rice, condensed milk, and beaten eggs in the slow cooker and stir well. Cover and cook on LOW for 4 to 6 hours, stirring only once, after 1 hour.

Serve the pudding warm or cold.

YIELD: 6 servings

NUTRITIONAL ANALYSIS: One serving of the basic recipe contains 349 calories; 9 g fat; 11 g protein; 58 g carbohydrate; and .3 g dietary fiber.

TRY THIS! For a richer, more traditional pudding, add 3/4 cup (109 g) raisins; 2 tablespoons (28 g) butter, melted; 1 teaspoon vanilla extract (5 ml); and 1/8 teaspoon ground nutmeg.

Baked Apples with Raisins

Serve these apples warm or chilled, along with a selection of cheeses.

COOKING TIME: 3 to 5 hours	ATTENTION: Minimal

6 baking apples, cored

1/2 cup (73 g) raisins

1 cup (189 g) Cinnamon Sugar (page 27)

1 cup (235 ml) hot water

Place the cored apples upright in the slow cooker. Fill the center of each apple with one-sixth of the raisins. In a small bowl, combine the water and Cinnamon Sugar, then pour the mixture over the apples. Cover and cook on LOW for 3 to 5 hours.

YIELD: 6 servings

NUTRITIONAL ANALYSIS: One serving of the basic recipe contains 237 calories; .7 g fat; .7 g protein; 62 g carbohydrate; and 6 g dietary fiber.

ADD IT IN! Add 2 tablespoons (28 g) butter, melted, and 1/2 teaspoon apple pie spice to the Cinnamon Sugar-hot water mixture.

Homey Baked Apples

We like the tartness that dried cranberries bring to the mix, but you can substitute any of your favorite dried fruits here.

PREP TIME: 20 minutes	COOKING TIME: 3–5 hours

6 large cooking apples, such as Cortland

1 1/2 (180 g) cups dried cranberries

1 cup (340 g) maple syrup

Core the apples and put them upright in the slow cooker. Pour 1/2 cup (120 ml) water into the bottom of the cooker. Fill the center of each apple with the dried cranberries, and drizzle the maple syrup over the apples. Cook on LOW for 3 to 5 hours, until the apples are soft but not mushy.

YIELD: 6 servings

NUTRITIONAL ANALYSIS: 220 calories; 1 g fat (2.3% calories from fat); trace protein; 57 g carbohydrate; 4 g dietary fiber; 0 mg cholesterol; 5 mg sodium.

Granola Apple Crisp

Slow cookers are not known for their browning and crisping abilities, but by using granola as our topping, we can build that quality in, and the result is a great dessert. It is a bit more on the chewy side than an oven-baked crisp, but we love it anyway.

PREP TIME: 30 minutes   **COOKING TIME:** 2–3 hours on HIGH, 4–5 hours on LOW

3 pounds (1365 g) apples, such as Granny Smith

1 cup (200 g) sugar

2 cups (300 g) granola

Peel and core the apples. Cut the apples into wedges and put them into a large bowl. In a small bowl, stir together the sugar and cinnamon together and toss with the apples. Put the mixture into the slow cooker. Top with the granola and cook on HIGH for 2 to 3 hours or on LOW for 4 to 5 hours, until the apples are soft and bubbling.

YIELD: 6 to 8 servings

NUTRITIONAL ANALYSIS: 340 calories; 9 g fat (22.1% calories from fat); 4 g protein; 66 g carbohydrate; 8 g dietary fiber; 0 mg cholesterol; 4 mg sodium.

ADD IT IN! We generally consider vanilla ice cream de rigueur as an accompaniment to any crisp.

Warm Applesauce

This homey favorite is terrific served over ice cream or pound cake.

PREP TIME: 20 minutes   **COOKING TIME:** 4–6 hours

6 large cooking apples, such as Cortland

¾ cup (150 g) sugar

1 tablespoon (7 g) apple pie spice, or more to taste

Peel and core the apples, then cut them into small chunks. Put the apples, sugar, and spice into the slow cooker and add ¼ cup (60 ml) water, stirring to combine. Cover and cook on LOW for 4 to 6 hours.

YIELD: 6 servings

NUTRITIONAL ANALYSIS: 181 calories; 1 g fat (2.4% calories from fat); trace protein; 47 g carbohydrate; 4 g dietary fiber; 0 mg cholesterol; 1 mg sodium.

Caramel Apples

An eternal favorite that evokes memories of fall carnivals and fairs. You can easily halve this recipe, but you'd end up with just half the fun.

COOKING TIME: 1 to 1½ hours   **ATTENTION:** Stir frequently

8 wooden sticks

8 medium apples, washed and dried

2 pounds (910 g) caramel candies

¼ cup (60 ml) water

Insert a stick into the stem end of each apple. Line the counter with enough waxed paper to hold all the apples.

Combine the caramels and water in the slow cooker. Cover and cook on HIGH for 1 to 1½ hours, stirring frequently.

Turn the heat to LOW. When the slow cooker has cooled enough to allow you to work without burning yourself, dip an apple into the hot caramel, turning the apple to coat it all the way around. Try to dip the apple up to the stick, but be careful not to burn yourself on the edge of the slow cooker. Let the excess caramel drip back into the slow cooker, then set the apple down to cool on the waxed paper. Repeat with the remaining apples.

YIELD: 8 servings

NUTRITIONAL ANALYSIS: One serving of the basic recipe contains 562 calories; 13 g fat; 5 g protein; 118 g carbohydrate; and 5 g dietary fiber.

Hot Spiced Pears

For centuries, people have enjoyed the spicy goodness of baked pears. This luscious dessert is flavorful enough to stand alone, but it's also fabulous served over waffles, pancakes, pound cake, or ice cream.

COOKING TIME: 8 to 10 hours	**ATTENTION:** Minimal

8 pears, peeled, cored, and sliced

One 8-ounce (225-g) can pineapple chunks, undrained

1 tablespoon (7 g) apple pie spice

Put the pear slices, pineapple chunks, pineapple juice, and apple pie spice in the slow cooker and stir to combine. Cover and cook on LOW for 8 to 10 hours.

Stir the mixture again and serve it warm or cold.

YIELD: 8 servings

NUTRITIONAL ANALYSIS: One serving of the basic recipe contains 117 calories; .8 g fat; .8 g protein; 30 g carbohydrate; and 5 g dietary fiber.

TRY THIS! Add ¼ cup (36 g) raisins, and substitute apples or peaches for half of the pears. Top with whipped cream or ice cream.

Poached Pears in Red Wine

This dish is simple and elegant as a stand-alone dessert, or you can use these pears in tarts or napoleons.

PREP TIME: 30 minutes   **COOKING TIME:** 4 hours

6 pears

2 cups (400 g) sugar

4 cups (940 ml) red wine

Peel the pears, leaving the stems intact. Put the pears into the slow cooker. In a small bowl, combine the sugar and wine. Add to the slow cooker. Cook on LOW for 4 hours, until the pears are soft but not mushy. Remove the pears from the poaching liquid. You may serve them warm or cold. The poaching liquid can be reduced to make a syrup to go with the pears; simply boil it over high heat until it thickens.

YIELD: 6 servings

NUTRITIONAL ANALYSIS: 475 calories; 1 g fat (1.7% calories from fat); 1 g protein; 96 g carbohydrate; 5 g dietary fiber; 0 mg cholesterol; 104 mg sodium.

ADD IT IN: Add 2 tablespoons (14 g) ground cinnamon to the sugar-wine mixture for added flavor.

Poached Pears

These raspberry-and-cinnamon-infused pears taste as good as they look. Enjoy them chilled, with gingerbread and whipped cream.

COOKING TIME: 3¹/₂ to 4 hours   **ATTENTION:** Minimal

1¹/₂ quarts (1.4 ml) cranberry-raspberry juice

¹/₄ cup (47 g) Cinnamon Sugar (page 27)

5 firm pears, peeled and cored but with the stem intact

Put the cranberry-raspberry juice and Cinnamon Sugar in the slow cooker and stir until the sugar has dissolved. Add the pears, submerging them in the juice mixture. Cover and cook on LOW for 3¹/₂ to 4 hours, or until the pears are tender.

Turn the heat OFF and allow the slow cooker to cool for 20 minutes, or until the pears are safe enough to handle. Remove the pears and syrup from the slow cooker and refrigerate them until they're very cold.

Serve the pears chilled, in shallow bowls, drizzled with the syrup.

YIELD: 5 servings

NUTRITIONAL ANALYSIS: One serving of the basic recipe contains 326 calories; .6 g fat; .6 g protein; 82 g carbohydrate; and 4 g dietary fiber.

TRY THIS! Substitute your favorite white, blush, or red wine for up to 2 cups (470 ml) of the juice. Garnish the dish with fresh raspberries.

Chunky Applesauce

It's fun and easy to make your own mouth-watering applesauce. Serve it warm, or chill it first.

COOKING TIME: 4 to 6 hours **ATTENTION:** Minimal

6 large cooking apples, peeled, cored, and cut into chunks of uniform size

$\frac{1}{2}$ to $\frac{3}{4}$ cup (95 to 142 g) Cinnamon Sugar (page 27)

$\frac{1}{2}$ teaspoon ground nutmeg

$\frac{1}{4}$ cup (60 ml) water

Put the apple chunks, Cinnamon Sugar, ground nutmeg, and water in the slow cooker and stir to combine. Cover and cook on LOW for 4 to 6 hours.

Before serving, stir the applesauce and add more Cinnamon Sugar to taste.

YIELD: 6 servings

NUTRITIONAL ANALYSIS: One serving of the basic recipe (made with $\frac{1}{2}$ cup Cinnamon Sugar) contains 142 calories; .7 g fat; .3 g protein; 37 g carbohydrate; and 4 g dietary fiber.

Golden Fruit Compote

This compote is as delightfully fruity as it is pretty when served cold with white cake, pound cake, or vanilla ice cream. It's also wonderful served warm as an alternative to cranberry sauce.

COOKING TIME: 8 to 10 hours
ATTENTION: Stir every 2 hours; add water as necessary

Two 20-ounce (570-g) cans pineapple chunks, undrained

One 15-ounce (417-g) package golden raisins or dried mixed apples, peaches, and apricots

1 cup (120 ml) water

½ teaspoon apple pie spice

Put the pineapple chunks, raisins, water, and apple pie spice in the slow cooker and stir to combine. Cover and cook on LOW for 8 to 10 hours, or until the flavors have melded and the mixture has become very thick, stirring every 2 hours and adding water as needed.

YIELD: 10 servings

NUTRITIONAL ANALYSIS: One serving of the basic recipe (made with golden raisins) contains 197 calories; .3 g fat; 2 g protein; 52 g carbohydrate; and 3 g dietary fiber.

ADD IT IN: Substitute apple juice for the water.

Chocolate-Nut Delights

Indulge your love affair with chocolate—create decadent delights using chocolate and your favorite nuts. Set the mood by serving them in petite, lacy baking cups on an embellished silver tray.

COOKING TIME: 45 to 75 minutes	**ATTENTION:** Stir every 15 minutes

1¹/₂ pounds (683 g) semisweet baking chocolate, coarsely chopped

1 pound (455 g) white chocolate squares, coarsely chopped

Two 10-ounce (280-g) cans deluxe mixed nuts or your favorite nuts

Spray the inside of the slow cooker with cooking spray. Line the counter with enough waxed paper to hold all the nut clusters while they harden.

Put the semisweet baking chocolate and white chocolate in the slow cooker. Cover and cook on LOW for 45 to 75 minutes, or until the chocolate melts, stirring every 15 minutes.

Add the nuts and mix well. Turn the heat OFF and allow the mixture to cool slightly, then use a tablespoon to drop it in 1¹/₂-inch (3.8-cm) mounds onto the waxed paper. Allow the nut clusters to cool and harden.

Store the nut clusters at room temperature in an airtight container.

YIELD: 36 nut clusters

NUTRITIONAL ANALYSIS: One serving of the basic recipe (made with mixed nuts) contains 251 calories; 19 g fat; 4 g protein; 23 g carbohydrate; and 2 g dietary fiber.

TIP: Make sure not to overheat the chocolate, which melts better and faster at lower temperatures. Be extremely careful not to allow even a drop of water into the slow cooker or the chocolate will seize and become grainy. A little vegetable oil will restore the chocolate, but it will also affect the flavor.

DID YOU KNOW? Chocolate is a multibillion-dollar industry in the United States, but it wasn't always that way. Chocolate started out as a beverage used by the indigenous peoples of South America, evolved into a fashionable drink favored by the elite of Europe, and was finally used, in the mid-1800s, to make the superbly edible confections enjoyed today.

Chocolate Bread Pudding

Chocolate bread pudding is both decadent and cozy—all in all, it's a mouthwatering dessert. You can serve this hot or cold.

PREP TIME: 15 minutes   **COOKING TIME:** 4–5 hours

---

5 or 6 chocolate muffins

3 cups (705 ml) light cream

3 eggs

Cut the muffins into 2-inch (5-cm) cubes and put them into the slow cooker, pushing them in lightly to flatten. In a bowl, whisk together the cream and the eggs, then pour the mixture over the muffins. Press the muffin cubes down with a spoon so that they are all soaked in the egg mixture. Cook for 4 to 5 hours on LOW.

Serve hot or cold.

YIELD: 4 to 6 servings

NUTRITIONAL ANALYSIS: 525 calories; 37 g fat (62.4% calories from fat); 11 g protein; 40 g carbohydrate; 3 g dietary fiber; 195 mg cholesterol; 343 mg sodium.

ADD IT IN! Top this yummy offering with whipped cream and a handful of fresh raspberries.

Chocolate Fondue

We have suggested angel food cake to dip into the fondue, but if you want to convince yourself that dessert is a healthy course, this is also delicious served with a variety of fruits, such as strawberries, kiwi, pineapple, and pears.

PREP TIME: 15 minutes   **COOKING TIME:** 2 hours

---

1 pound (455 g) good-quality semisweet chocolate (bar or chips)

1 cup (235 ml) half-and-half

1 store-bought angel food cake

If the chocolate is a solid piece, cut it into small pieces and put it into the slow cooker. If you use chips, just put them into the cooker. Pour the half-and-half over the chocolate and cook for 2 hours on LOW. Stir until the mixture is smooth. Cut the cake into cubes and dip it into the fondue.

YIELD: 6 to 8 servings

NUTRITIONAL ANALYSIS: 502 calories; 21 g fat (34.2% calories from fat); 8g protein; 81 g carbohydrate; trace dietary fiber; 11 mg cholesterol; 398 mg sodium.

NOTE: You can make this ahead and hold it on warm for an extended period while serving.

White Chocolate-Macadamia Nut Clusters

Pure decadence—macadamia nuts and white chocolate in a mantle of semisweet chocolate. Enjoy alone or with a splash of gourmet Hawaiian coffee.

COOKING TIME: 45 to 75 minutes | **ATTENTION:** Stir every 15 minutes

1½ pounds (683 g) semisweet chocolate candy melts

Two 6-ounce (168-g) cans whole macadamia nuts

¼ cup (43 g) white chocolate chips

Spray the inside of the slow cooker with cooking spray. Line the counter with enough waxed paper to hold all the nut clusters while they harden.

Put the candy melts in the slow cooker. Cover and cook on LOW for 45 to 75 minutes, or until the chocolate melts, stirring every 15 minutes.

Turn the heat OFF, add the macadamia nuts and white chocolate chips, and mix well. (The white chocolate chips should not melt.) Allow the mixture to cool slightly, then use a tablespoon to drop it in 1½-inch (3.8-cm) mounds onto the waxed paper. Allow it to cool completely and set.

Store the nut clusters at room temperature in an airtight container.

YIELD: 36 nut clusters

NUTRITIONAL ANALYSIS: One serving of the basic recipe contains 251 calories; 19 g fat; 4 g protein; 23 g carbohydrate; and 2 g dietary fiber.

DID YOU KNOW? Candy melts are easier to melt than baking chocolate because they're made using a special manufacturing process. They're a combination of cocoa, sugar, milk solids, vegetable oil, flavorings, and color.

INDEX

ABOUT THE AUTHORS

ROBERT HILDEBRAND is the executive chef at Three Stallions Inn, in Randolph, Vermont. His work has been featured in *Bon Appetit*, as well as several newspapers.

CAROL HILDEBRAND is an award-winning writer and editor. Her work has appeared in *Boston Magazine*, *The Old Farmer's Almanac*, *CIO*, *Darwin*, and many others.

SUZANNE BONET is a technical writer and a mother of two residing in the Gulf Coast region of Florida, in scenic Tampa Bay. Food and technical writing have long been entwined in her life. She learned the importance of well-crafted instructions to successful outcomes as a child who baked mounds of cookies, cakes, and pies. As an adult whose day job is writing instructions for using computer applications, her fondness for healthy home cooking and stress-free family dinners led her to depend heavily on her slow cooker—long before its return to "hot" appliance status. Empty nest syndrome inspired her to contemplate writing a slow-cooker cookbook for her girls to take with them to college. From those maternal stirrings evolved the three-ingredient slow-cooker recipe book you hold in your hands today.